728(09)

KU-875-289

NORTHAMPTON COLLEGE
R29432Y 0098

728 (09) JAC

THE ENGLISH COUNTRY HOUSE
A Grand Tour

THE ENGLISH COUNTRY HOUSE
A Grand Tour

Gervase Jackson-Stops and James Pipkin

THE NATIONAL TRUST
WEIDENFELD & NICOLSON

To Gill and Franny

THE LIBRARY
COLLEGE OF HIGHER EDUCATION
NORTHAMPTON

Frontispiece]
The Ante Room at Syon House, Middlesex,
designed by Robert Adam in 1762
for the 1st Duke of Northumberland.

Text copyright © Gervase Jackson-Stops 1985
Photographs copyright © James Pipkin 1985

All rights reserved. No part of this publication
may be reproduced, stored in a retrieval system, or
transmitted in any form or by any means, electronic,
mechanical, photocopying or otherwise, without the
prior permission of the copyright holders.

Designed by Trevor Vincent

George Weidenfeld & Nicolson Limited
91 Clapham High Street
London SW4

ISBN 0 297 78680 6

Filmset by Keyspools Ltd, Golborne, Lancashire
Colour separations by Newsele Litho Ltd.
Printed in Italy
Bound by L.E.G.O. Vicenza

CONTENTS

FOREWORD

English authors have long shown a marked preference for an empirical approach to their subjects. Working within his native tradition, Gervase Jackson-Stops has devised a new format that takes us room by room through the English country house: the result is the valuable book you hold in your hands. With its perceptive text and its splendid photographs by James Pipkin, *The English Country House: A Grand Tour* gives us a history of the essential components of these great dwellings, detailing such things as the evolution of the dining room, and the development of the long gallery from a mere place of exercise into a room for displaying pictures or sculptures, the ancestor of the modern museum gallery. Along the way we learn of the rituals and etiquette which contributed so significantly to the form and decoration of these rooms.

One of the most skilful things about this book is the way it frees us from restrictions which might derive from our twentieth-century perspective. Here the rhythms of life in earlier eras are keenly appreciated, and no doubt many readers will be surprised by the practical considerations that generated some of the features in these great houses. At Haddon, the wonderful Tudor house in Derbyshire which is one of my personal favourites, we find that a gate at the foot of the staircase was to keep the hungry dogs from joining the family upstairs after meals. We also learn that hanging tapestries in dining rooms were unheard of before the existence of reliable ventilation systems, for the simple reason that thick textiles retained the smell of food. Perhaps the greatest number of delights are to be found in the chapter devoted to bedrooms where we learn, among other things, that a state bed could be the costliest piece of furniture in a house, more valuable than the most important Old Master paintings.

The English Country House: A Grand Tour affords an excellent grasp of the fundamental form of these rural mansions, so different from most houses elsewhere in Europe. This has been of the keenest interest to us at the National Gallery of Art because of our special exhibition, *The Treasure Houses of Britain: Five Hundred Years of Private Patronage and Art Collecting*, for which Gervase Jackson-Stops has acted as guest curator. It takes no great leap of mental effort to imagine how, once built, these houses began to fill up with objects. Inhabited, frequently in unbroken family lines, by wealthy and privileged, but also well-read and well-travelled collectors, these houses have come to be great repositories of treasures of every description. Their collections, taken in conjunction with the architectural settings specially designed for them by masters such as Sir John Vanbrugh, William Kent and Robert Adam, give an extraordinary and enriching insight into the past. In a different way, they are as worthy of pilgrimage today as the great Gothic cathedrals of France, or the classical monuments of Greek and Roman antiquity. I hope that this book, and the exhibition which gave birth to it, will encourage a wider interest in the English country house and in its civilizing role, so central to our Western culture.

J. CARTER BROWN, *Director*
National Gallery of Art, Washington

The play of light on curving surfaces in the great hall at Castle Howard in Yorkshire, designed by Sir John Vanbrugh in 1699. The stone carving is by the Huguenot Jean Nadauld, and the wrought-iron balustrade by the Derbyshire smith John Gardom.

INTRODUCTION

This book on the architecture and interior decoration of the English country house was born almost literally in mid-Atlantic, as part of the preparations for a great exhibition mounted by the National Gallery of Art in Washington, entitled *The Treasure Houses of Britain: 500 Years of Private Patronage and Art Collecting*. It was natural that this show, one of the largest and most comprehensive ever staged by the Gallery, should be concerned primarily with objects – paintings and sculpture, furniture and textiles, metalwork, ceramics and books – drawn from over two hundred houses all over England, Scotland and Wales. At the same time, it was essential to show how these works of art were made or collected for specific settings; how country houses in the sixteenth and seventeenth centuries could be conceived as pantheons of family history and pride, and in the eighteenth as temples dedicated to different aspects of classical culture; how the different functions of rooms affected their form, contents and colouring; above all, how the marvellous unity of these interiors immeasurably enhances the appreciation and enjoyment of the objects they contain.

One way of doing this was to publish a book which would be a complement and companion to the catalogue, demonstrating the parallel development of the country house in terms of architecture and decoration rather than individual works of art. It was hoped that this would not only serve as a useful introduction for those intending to visit English country houses for the first time, but also offer new insights and a valuable record in visual terms for those already familiar with their treasures.

Since the invention of colour photography, there have been surprisingly few books which have done real justice to the country house interior – and none to equal the intensely evocative black-and-white illustrations of early *Country Life* volumes, such as Avray Tipping's folio series on *English Homes* produced in the 1920s, or the work of the late Edwin Smith published in the 1950s. A romantic and poetic eye is necessary to capture the extraordinary atmosphere of these 'precious relics of the past', as Henry James described them; an instinct for the telling detail as well as the great set piece and for the magical quality of English light. As an American, James Pipkin brings a fresh eye to bear on them, and his photographs convey the many facets of these remarkable buildings and their collections with a rare sensitivity. They pay tribute, as never before, to the skill of the architects, painters and sculptors, cabinet makers and tapestry weavers, goldsmiths and silversmiths, who made the English country house the envy of the rest of the world.

An attempt has been made to approach this theme in an equally new way in the text, which, after surveying the changing exterior of the country house over the centuries, and introducing the major architects and craftsmen concerned, is divided into chapters devoted to different types of room. We proceed (as we might in real life) from the hall to the staircase, saloon and gallery, dining room, withdrawing room, state bedchamber and dressing room, ending with the library and chapel. These rooms, chronologically arranged within each chapter, are drawn from houses all over England, from Castle Howard in Yorkshire to Cotehele in Cornwall, from Stourhead in the West Country to Houghton and Holkham on the north Norfolk coast – all of them regularly opened to the public. Our 'grand tour' shows how the uses of such rooms developed, and with them the decoration and furnishings that were thought suitable, using the currently fashionable vocabulary of ornament. We see why some have masculine and some feminine characteristics, why old traditions dying hard leave otherwise inexplicable traces of the past behind them, and how pagan and Christian symbolism is overtaken by the language of classical mythology – Mars presiding over the hall and Apollo the saloon, Bacchus over the dining room and Venus the bedchamber.

Every room illustrated in the book has been carefully chosen as an archetype – as little changed as possible since it was first conceived – and to that extent it is of course a simplification. The charm and character of so many houses lies in the layer on layer of different styles, and the contributions of several succeeding generations to the same room, for in matters of taste the English have never been purists like their Continental counterparts. On the other hand, the 'rooms of state' decorated with such lavish care in the seventeenth and eighteenth centuries, and often open to the public from the outset, tended not to change very greatly; they were made to last, with painted decoration, gilding and tapestries or wall-hangings of the highest quality; they were not subjected to the rigours of everyday use; and they were scrupulously protected by case-covers and curtains, leather tops made for marquetry tables, even chamois 'socks' for polished castors, for much of the year. Even when out of fashion, a 'state apartment' was often preserved by a family as a testimony to its ancient origins, or simply as an act of filial piety.

It is, therefore, with 'state apartments', known also in the eighteenth century as 'rooms of parade', that we are concerned, and no apology need be made for staying on the *piano nobile*, for in the private family rooms below in the 'rustic' or above on the attic floor so many more changes will generally have been made. We may lose some of the more lovable and eccentric interiors – theatres, like that at Chatsworth, and bath-houses, like that at Wimpole, gun rooms and smoking rooms, conservatories and bowers – as well as the fascinating self-contained world of the servants 'behind the green baize door'. But these have fared well in recent books on the country house and do not form part of the story of consistent development seen in the show rooms 'above stairs'.

The breakdown of divisions between state and private rooms in the early nineteenth century explains why this book does not go beyond the 1830s, though it is also true that by the Victorian period the golden age of the country house was drawing to a close, and it was public buildings – churches and town halls, colleges and museums – that were to occupy the centre of the architectural stage. Scottish houses and castles, with their own national characteristics, have also been purposely omitted for the sake of clarity.

Any book of this sort must be indebted to two pioneering works of recent years, John Cornforth and John Fowler's *English Decoration in the Eighteenth Century* (1974) and Mark Girouard's *Life in the English Country House* (1978), which remain essential reading for anyone seriously interested in the subject. A number of the quotations from contemporary sources, family papers and diaries, early guidebooks and inventories, were first published in their pages, where scholars will find the full bibliographical references. I am particularly grateful to John Cornforth whose encouragement and generous supply of information and ideas over a number of years have been invaluable.

Our thanks are also due to J. Carter Brown, the Director of the National Gallery of Art, Washington DC, to Gaillard F. Ravenel, the Gallery's Chief of Design and Installation, and to my colleagues in the National Trust, Angus Stirling and Martin Drury, for supporting the idea of this book from its inception; to the owners of all the houses illustrated in it for permission to photograph, and for the kindness and hospitality of owners and administrators alike – in particular the Duchess of Devonshire and Mr Michael Pearman at Chatsworth; Sybil, Marchioness of Cholmondeley at Houghton; Viscount Scarsdale and Mr Edward Paine at Kedleston; the late Lord Howard of Henderskelfe and the Hon. Simon Howard at Castle Howard; Lord Egremont and Mr Roger Webb at Petworth; Sir Francis Dashwood Bt, at West Wycombe; Mr Hugh Sackville-West and Mr Richard Wakeford at Knole; Mr John Strickson at Attingham; Mr Paul Duffy at Blenheim; Mr Merlin Waterson and Dr David Hopkinson at Blickling; Mr James Past at Bodiam; Major Edward Warrick at Boughton; Miss Elizabeth Proudfoot at Cotehele; Mr Anthony Mitchell and Mr Owen Justice at Dyrham; Mr Robert Walber at Felbrigg; Mr John Webster at Haddon; Mr Ian Hughes at Hardwick; Mr Frederick Jolly at Holkham; Mr Stanley Middlemiss at Little Moreton Hall; Mr Martin Knebel at Saltram; Mr Ashley Augier at Stourhead; Mrs Judith Rhodes at Sudbury; Mr John Saville at Syon; Mr John Eyre at Uppark; Mr Richard Fowler at The Vyne; Mrs Veronica Quarm at Wilton; and Miss Lavinia Wellicome at Woburn.

Frances Smyth, Chief of Publications at the National Gallery of Art, played a major role in organizing the publication of the book, as did the late Robin Wright of the National Trust, and we are also grateful to Michael O'Mara, Michael Dover and Martha Caute of Weidenfeld, Annie Chandos-Pole and Jonathan Marsden (who wrote most of the gazetteer entries), and not least to Maggie Grieve for turning scribble into typescript.

GERVASE JACKSON-STOPS

A NOTE ON THE PHOTOGRAPHS

The photographs in this book attempt to convey the feeling of an English country house in several complementary ways. Some of the photographs are general views that show how a house relates to its surroundings or that give an overall impression of a room's style, richness, scale or warmth. Other photographs focus on a detail and, by that focus, emphasize some aspect of the craftsmanship, artistry or taste reflected in the room. In a number of cases, two or more photographs are juxtaposed in an effort to show interrelationships or to point out the endless variety that occurred when decorative elements were created not in a mould or by a machine but through the individual efforts of a craftsman's hands.

In taking these photographs, natural light was used to the maximum extent possible. In part, this was done for the sake of historical accuracy: we wanted the photographs to replicate the atmosphere that existed when people lived in these rooms in previous centuries, and an important component of that atmosphere was the reliance on natural light. Even today there is nothing that equals the magical effect of late afternoon sunlight catching a section of cornice, a gilded rosette, a carved chimneypiece or an ornamental frieze. Indeed, my most exciting moments in these houses occurred while observing and attempting to capture on film some revealing but evanescent image involving the play of sunlight.

For me there have been many joys involved in producing this work. One was the opportunity to study some of the houses I fell in love with during my student days at Oxford. Another was the opportunity to meet many generous owners, administrators, curators and housemen who not only facilitated this venture but went far out of their way to contribute to the best possible result. Another was the satisfaction of seeing the work come together in this book and in the audio-visual programme that accompanies the exhibition. Finally, there was the chance to work with Gervase Jackson-Stops whose knowledge, boundless enthusiasm and hard work were constant sources of inspiration.

JAMES PIPKIN

1   Approaching the Country House

There may no longer be a lodge-keeper's wife in apron and mob cap to drop us a curtsey as we enter the gates of the country house, and our motor car may not be as romantic a conveyance as the phaeton or curricle of an earlier age, but in other ways our preparation for what is to come will equal and may even surpass the expectations aroused in our ancestors. The high park wall will be dappled with moss and lichens, and overhung with ivy; the woods inside it, grown to full maturity, will be alive with pheasants, partridges and woodcock; the clumps of ancient oaks and chestnuts, and the old lime avenues marching across the landscape, will have their lower branches trimmed by deer and cattle to a neat straight line, so that we can see through to an ice-house, a Gothick dog-kennel, or a glint of water in the valley below. Rounding a bend, we see the whole lake spread before us, duck and moorhen among the reeds, a balustraded bridge with a cascade below it, in the distance a column, an arch on the hill, or an Elizabethan hunting tower.

The road divides, one arm branching off to the stable block, as big as a country house in its own right, with central archway and clock-tower, while in the paddocks nearby groups of horses taking shade under the trees look like Stubbs's canvases brought to life. And then, finally, the great house itself comes into sight: sometimes a jumble of towers and gables, roofs and dormers, looking like a whole medieval village; sometimes a central block with giant portico and spreading wings like an Italian *palazzo* set down in the vivid green of English lawns; sometimes a towering mass of wall and window reflecting the sunlight from a thousand diamond panes, with gatehouses, garden walls and gazebos around it, like a great ship surrounded by tugs.

The infinite variety of these buildings, in stone and brick and timber of every hue, Gothic and Classical, Grecian, Egyptian and even Indian, is astonishing but bewildering. What can they have in common, these superhuman dwellings which seem not to have a standard plan like the monasteries and cathedrals which preceded them, but which look as if they have grown, organically, out of the English countryside? What were the motives that persuaded men and women to build on such a scale, without the prospect of saving their souls in the process? And how can these battlements and statues, mullions and sashes, domes and cupolas, tell a coherent story of taste and connoisseurship, when they seem as various as their creators, and as wayward as human nature itself?

The first chapter of this story is clear enough: the development from inward-looking castle to outward-looking house resulting from the gradual imposition of law and order which culminated in the accession of the Tudors. The symmetry of a medieval fortress like Bodiam Castle in East Sussex is like a perfectly wrought suit of armour, beautiful in its practicality – in fact so beautiful that it could be an illumination from a Flemish book of hours or the background to an equestrian portrait of an Italian *condottiere*. The castle was built between 1386 and 1388 by Sir Edward Dalyngrigge who received a licence from

Opposite] Bodiam Castle, built in 1386–8 by Sir Edward Dalyngrigge, reflected in the still waters of the moat. The Great Gatehouse with its rectangular towers guarding the entrance was an innovation, for earlier castles had isolated keeps like those at Rochester and Windsor. The gatehouse has three portcullises, arrow slits (*above*) and 'murder holes' through which boiling or caustic materials could be poured on unwelcome guests.

Overleaf] The north front of Oxburgh Hall, built about 1482 and moated like Bodiam, but outward-looking, decorative and fanciful compared to the strength and austerity of its predecessors. While it could withstand attack by a small band of marauders, Oxburgh was primarily a domestic rather than a military establishment.

Richard II 'to strengthen and crenellate his manor house of Bodyham near the sea in the County of Sussex with a wall of stone and lime, and to construct and make thereof a castle in defence of the adjacent countryside'. At this point in the Hundred Years War, the French had gained complete control of the Channel, and ports like Winchelsea and Rye and the estuaries beyond them were constantly threatened by raids. What was unusual about Sir Edward's scheme was that instead of fortifying his old manor house higher up the slope, he determined to build a new moated castle down by the river Rother which would both defend the valley in the national interest and serve as his privately owned residence.

Massive circular bastions guard the four corners, with square towers in the centre of each side, doubled on the north to form a gatehouse of daunting size. This gatehouse, replacing the free-standing keep which was a feature of earlier castles, was provided with no less than three portcullises, numerous arrow slits, and the famous pierced machicolations through which boiling or corrosive materials could be poured on besiegers way below. But to go through the gate and into the central courtyard must have been to enter another world. Sir Edward's living quarters now lie in ruins, for although Bodiam was never put to the test by the French (the English having regained control of the Channel in 1387), it was plundered by Parliamentary forces in the course of the Civil War. However, it is easy to discern the usual medieval plan: the door opposite the gatehouse leading into the 'screen passages' of the great hall, with the family's apartments beyond it in the east range, and the servants' quarters and garrison beyond the kitchen in the west range. Large arched windows must have lit these rooms, in marked contrast with the sheer stone walls of the exterior reflected in the still waters of the moat.

Oxburgh Hall in Norfolk is almost exactly a hundred years later than Bodiam and their ground plans, apart from the lack of corner towers at Oxburgh, look remarkably alike. But there the similarity ends, for this enchanting red-brick manor house, built at the end of the Wars of the Roses and visited by Henry VII in 1487 soon after its completion, is unashamedly extrovert. As a fortified and moated dwelling it would command some respect from the marauding bands of soldiery which were still a danger in this remote part of East Anglia. But it could have offered little defence against a concerted attack. Its stepped gables and large mullion windows, its gatehouse turrets decorated with panels of moulded brick, give it the air of a toy fort rather than a real castle. The machicolation of the gatehouse is actually false – despite the overhang, there is no gap through which to hurl missiles or pour boiling oil – while even the moat is too shallow to be a serious obstacle and seems merely to have been dug so as to reflect the fantastic outline of turrets, chimneys and battlements, and to throw dappled sunlight up on to the ceilings of the rooms which overlook it.

Flemish influence was always very strong in the eastern counties of England through the trading links established by the wool merchants and can be seen clearly at Oxburgh, just as Bodiam on the south coast is predominantly French in style, like a Norman or Angevin fortress. Compared with these, Haddon Hall in Derbyshire – the very centre of England – seems little touched by the architectural fashions of the Continent. Nikolaus Pevsner, rarely given to poetic fantasy, called it 'the English castle *par excellence*, not the forbidding fortress on an unassailable crag, but the large, rambling, safe, grey, lovable house of knights and

The outer gatehouse at Haddon Hall in Derbyshire, rising above the river Wye. The north-west tower, 50 feet high, was built about 1530 by Sir George Vernon, and proudly displays his coat of arms above the highest window.

Opposite] The entrance archway at Cotehele in Cornwall, with its cobbles worn smooth by generations of Edgcumbes, their retainers and friends. It was here that, in 1483, Sir Richard Edgcumbe cut the throat of the guard posted here by Richard III's corrupt lieutenant, Sir Henry Trenowth, and fled down the steep ravine to the river Tamar hotly pursued by Trenowth's horsemen.

their ladies, the unreasonable dream-castle of those who think of the Middle Ages as a time of chivalry and valour and noble feelings'. The setting of Haddon in the gentle rolling landscape of the Pennine foothills contributes to its peaceable character, though the little river Wye, winding round it on three sides, and the steeply rising ground up which the building seems to march, were no doubt chosen for reasons of defence. Peverel's Tower guarded the original entrance on the highest ground at the north-east corner of the building, recalling in its name the founder of the house, an illegitimate son of William the Conqueror known to history as 'Peverel of the Peak'. Twelfth-century masonry can be found not only on this front but also on the outer south and west walls and in the chapel at the junction between them, proving that the Norman stronghold covered almost as much ground as the present house.

From an architectural point of view, the most important part is the cross-wing, built between the upper and lower courtyards by Sir Richard Vernon, about 1370, and containing the great hall, with the usual arrangement of pantry, buttery and kitchen to one side, and the parlour with a great chamber above it on the other. The screens passage, a corridor formed at the lower end of the hall behind a carved oak screen, was the vital means of communication between the two courtyards at the centre of the house. Nowhere at Haddon is there any attempt at symmetry, nor are there many right angles, yet the anonymous master-masons who built in almost every generation managed to achieve a balanced grouping of different elements that is wonderfully satisfying. Outside, the crenellated walls may seem forbidding and give little away, but inside, the courtyards, windows, doors and chimney-breasts clearly express the function of the rooms which look into them.

Life in a late medieval house was of course that of a whole feudal community, not just the members of one noble family, and it is interesting to find how closely the planning and form of such houses resemble those of Oxford and Cambridge colleges, where the governing body of dons took the place of the family and the scholars were cast in the role of retainers. Knole in Kent can vie with the grandest of scholastic foundations, with no less than seven quadrangles. Here the outer Green Court, added by Henry VIII to Archbishop Bourchier's original house, has an especially collegiate character with its large number of small windows and doorways, each with flowerpots grouped round the steps carefully tended by the wives of gardeners or gamekeepers, grooms or estate carpenters. But Cotehele in Cornwall, only a fraction of the size, also has the air of a tiny 'hall of residence' in one of the ancient universities: the arch under the square, embattled gate looks as if it should contain a porter's lodge arranged with keys and pigeon-holes; the two little courtyards might be 'quads', with open archways and doors leading straight up narrow staircases where the swirl of black gowns and the drone of a distant tutorial might well be heard, along with the clatter of knives and forks from behind the heraldic stained-glass windows of the hall and the sound of organ practice in the nearby chapel. Once again the building is of many different dates and there is no sense of shame on the part of one generation trying to disguise the less sophisticated contributions of its predecessors. Sir Richard Edgcumbe's gatehouse tower of 1485, with its even courses of cut granite blocks, sits perfectly happily on the rough rubble

Right] The south front of Cotehele with Sir Richard Edgcumbe's gatehouse, built of cut granite blocks, set into much older walls of rough rubble with small round-headed lancet windows either side. The perfect example of a late medieval manor house, Cotehele is also like a smaller version of an Oxford or Cambridge college in plan, grouped round a series of diminutive quadrangles, with the great hall – the meeting place of the whole feudal community – at its centre.

Left] Part of the Green Court at Knole in Kent, with, on the left, the inner gatehouse known as Bourchier's Tower, constructed in a silvery-grey local stone known as Kentish rag. This was the original west front of the mid-fifteenth-century house built by Thomas Bourchier, Archbishop of Canterbury, to which Henry VIII tacked on an outer courtyard in 1543–8, having seized the house from Bourchier's successor, Thomas Cranmer. The shaped gables crowned by obelisks and the Sackville leopard are further additions made by Thomas Sackville, 1st Earl of Dorset in 1603–8. With its seven quadrangles and its infinite number of towers, chimneys, battlements and pinnacles, the house looks from the park like a medieval village.

walls pierced by tiny lancet windows dating from the 1350s; and in the main courtyard the big hood-moulded windows of the parlour with the great chamber above it, contributed by his son Sir Piers about 1520, are pushed right up against the east window of the chapel 'as though the builder were in some fearful hurry'.

The defensive inward-looking character of Cotehele was largely due to the remoteness and instability of Cornwall even after the end of the Wars of the Roses – the 'robberies, despoyleries of marchaunts, strangers, merthers, as well by water as by land, entries by force and wrongful imprisonments', which the Cornish gentry complained of in a petition to Richard III in 1483. In other parts of the country, law and order were sufficiently well established to allow outward-looking houses, with courtyards open on one side or sometimes dispensed with altogether. In areas where stone was hard to obtain, but where the medieval forests gave a plentiful supply of wood, timber-framed manor houses came into fashion despite their liability to destruction by fire. In East Anglia, the wood was rarely treated and remained its natural colour, while the plaster panels between were often painted and were also sometimes 'pargetted' or given moulded decoration. In the north-west, the fashion was to protect the oak with pitch and leave the plaster white to contrast with it. Little Moreton Hall in Cheshire is perhaps the most famous of all such 'black-and-white' buildings. Originally it took the form of a simple H-shaped house consisting of two ranges either side of a great hall, like the cross-wing at Haddon. In 1559, William Moreton added two great bay windows – one an oriel for the hall, the other lighting the parlour below and great chamber above – actually meeting at first-floor level, and carved with the date and the name of the carpenter Richard Dale. Already at this period the rooms on the upper storeys

THE LIBRARY
COLLEGE OF FURTHER EDUCATION
NORTHAMPTON

were becoming more important for it was here that the family's own apartments lay, with servants and retainers largely occupying those below. Timber-framing could express this well by cantilevering out so as to form bigger windows and wider spaces above.

William's son John Moreton, who succeeded in 1563, completed the east range begun by his father, and then built the whole of the south wing with its projecting gatehouse and long gallery on the second floor, so that by about 1580 Little Moreton appeared much as it does today. It is interesting to compare the heavy timbering of the earlier hall range with the much lighter and more decorative effect of the later building. The former is almost entirely structural, with simple herring-bone patterns varied occasionally with Gothic quatrefoils, achieved by carving and indenting the ends of the oak beams; while the squares of the latter are filled with curving members forming circles, diamonds and other more complicated shapes. The passion for intricate geometrical designs which can be found in Elizabethan knot gardens and embroidery can also be found in the many different glazing patterns of the leaded lights at Little Moreton, displaying a remarkable variety even in the same window.

But perhaps the most remarkable feature of Little Moreton is the long gallery which occupies the whole top floor of the south range, and which dominates the rest of the house. Precariously set on top of the roofs below, this looks as if it must have been added as a rash after-thought when construction of the rest was already well advanced. Its continuous line of mullion windows down each side is reminiscent of the rows of cabin windows overhanging the aft of an Elizabethan man-o'-war – and indeed the techniques of house-building and ship-building were closely allied at this period.

Until the accession of Elizabeth I, country houses, like churches, were generally built in a vernacular style, with regional characteristics that counted for more than the ideals of theorists or the whims of individual designers. But the mid-sixteenth century saw not only the first published treatise on the subject in the English language, John Shute's *First and Chief Groundes of Architecture*, published in 1563, but the gradual emergence of a new professional class of master-masons who could for the first time be called architects in the modern sense. Men like Robert Smythson, the builder of Wollaton, Worksop and Hardwick, or Robert Lyminge, who designed Hatfield and Blickling, took the place of those teams of autonomous craftsmen, stone-cutters, carpenters, bricklayers and plumbers who would all have contributed to the haphazard development of a late medieval building. At the same time those landowners who had particularly benefited from the suppression of the monasteries, and increased their incomes by widespread enclosure, by coal, lead and tin-mining, or by wise investment in the voyages of the discoverers, were embarking on a wholly new scale of building – what Sir John Summerson has so aptly described as the 'prodigy house' – inspiring a mixture of wonder, awe and surprise that is as powerful today as it must have been to contemporaries. Such houses were built with a very specific purpose: to entertain the court on the long 'royal progresses' which Elizabeth favoured, partly for reasons of economy, partly to keep a check on her subjects at a time when Catholicism and extreme Puritanism still posed grave threats, and partly to inspire loyalty by showing herself, receiving petitions, administering justice and collecting revenues as she went. On the courtier's side, the entertainment of the royal household was a vital means of securing

The south range of Little Moreton Hall in Cheshire, built by John Moreton between 1563 and 1580. One of the most spectacular timber-framed buildings in England, it shows how, in areas where building stone was scarce, master-carpenters and joiners displayed a structural ingenuity that often outshone the achievements of contemporary stonemasons. The top floor is almost entirely filled by the long gallery, perhaps added as an afterthought when the construction of the range was reasonably far advanced; its long rows of continuous mullion windows are reminiscent of Elizabethan fighting ships at the time of the Armada.

favours and positions for sons and dependents, powerful marriage alliances and the profitable outcome of lawsuits. 'Nothing succeeds like success' is the old saying, and to impress a monarch with the scale and luxury of palace life was calculated not only to establish a family's dominance of a certain county, but as a compliment to the Queen whose arms and cypher were used to decorate the house – a secular shrine for a worldly virgin.

The first of the great 'prodigy houses', Longleat in Wiltshire, stemmed from the enlightened circle of Renaissance scholars and statesmen who had been patronized by Lord Protector Somerset during Edward VI's brief reign. Sir John Thynne, the builder, had been his steward while Somerset House in London was being built in the late 1540s, and Thynne's own pure Renaissance *palazzo*, begun in 1567, was based on the pattern-books of Sebastiano Serlio and Jacques du Cerceau, among the most popular authors of architectural treatises on

The towers of Hardwick Hall seen from the south-west. This gigantic house, designed for Bess of Hardwick by Robert Smythson, was not begun until 1591 when she was over seventy. Yet she lived to see it completed in 1597 and to enjoy it for another eleven years.

the Continent, though the classical orders depicted by Shute were used as well. William Cecil, Lord Burghley, the greatest English statesman of the century, was another of Somerset's protégés and employed many of the same craftsmen and artists at his splendid palace of Burghley on the Northamptonshire-Lincolnshire border. Though slightly later than Longleat, Burghley has some more old-fashioned features, including the turreted gatehouse leading across a great central courtyard to the great hall on the medieval plan. Yet its projecting bay windows, its spectacular skyline bristling with chimneystacks in the shape of tall paired columns, and its curious obelisk spire are more typical of the vigorous Elizabethan imagination than the purity of Longleat.

The young Robert Smythson first appears in the Longleat accounts in 1568, and in his later independent work he combined the monumental Italianate simplicity of Longleat with the fantasy of houses like Burghley which look back to the achievements of the Perpendicular church-builders. His masterpiece, Hardwick Hall in Derbyshire, remains the most splendid and least altered of all Elizabethan houses. It was built between 1591 and 1597 by one of the most colourful characters of her age, the redoubtable Bess of Hardwick, whose four marriages had made her progressively richer and more powerful. Separated from her last husband the Earl of Shrewsbury, Bess had decided in 1684 to move back to her own family house at Hardwick and in the next few years transformed the little manor there into a very large house. In 1590, before this was finished, Lord Shrewsbury died, leaving her an immensely wealthy widow. Although she was now over seventy, the indomitable old woman immediately started work on a colossal new building only a hundred yards away.

In its symmetry, the large proportion of window to wall, and the austerity of its decoration (apart from the cresting of the six towers which bear Bess's initials and coronet), the exterior of Hardwick is revolutionary in design. Some have even seen an extraordinary premonition of Mies van der Rohe in its noble austerity and rationalism. The compact 'H'-plan adopted by Smythson represents a notable advance on courtyard houses like Burghley, Longleat and Chatsworth – which Bess had built with her second husband Sir William Cavendish – although this may partly have been due to the continued existence of the Old Hall where many of her retainers and attendants were still to be housed. The forecourt walls and entrance arch are also by Smythson, and the only part of his design which appears not to have been executed was the continuation of the colonnade round all four corners of the house, which would have turned the ground plan into a simple rectangle.

One of the peculiarities of the exterior of Hardwick is the way in which the windows increase progressively in height from the ground upward, accurately reflecting the status of the rooms inside: hall, kitchen and servants' quarters on the ground floor, family apartments on the first, and state rooms on the second. The effect of this is a powerful vertical emphasis, increased by the six towers which contain 'banqueting houses' reached from the roof like the smaller turrets at Longleat – and which were ordered to be 'highed' still further as an afterthought in 1594. The way these towers seem to shift and regroup when viewed from different angles, always dominating the wooded valley below, is as magical as the way the setting sun lights up the thousand quarries of the great mullion windows till the whole house seems ablaze.

Overleaf] An improbable rose-pink vision in the green Norfolk landscape, Blickling Hall is one of the most romantic of all Jacobean houses. Once the property of Sir John Fastolf (the basis of Shakespeare's Falstaff) and of Sir Thomas Boleyn, the father of Henry VIII's Queen, it was remodelled between 1619 and 1625 by Sir Henry Hobart, James I's Lord Chief Justice. His architect Robert Lyminge gave it its wonderfully fanciful silhouette of pepperpots and weather-vanes, statues and cupolas, framed by long service wings with Dutch gables.

One of the great mullion windows at Hardwick set on fire by the last rays of the evening sunset. An old Derbyshire rhyme celebrates 'Hardwick Hall, more glass than wall'; with its huge grid-patterns of leaded lights, it is a remarkable precursor of twentieth-century architecture.

The example of Hardwick did not immediately put an end to the idea of courtyard houses, especially as so many continued to be adaptations of earlier fortified buildings. But those built from scratch like Montacute House in Somerset or Hatfield, the great house in Hertfordshire built by Lord Burghley's younger son Robert Cecil, 1st Earl of Salisbury, followed the new 'H'- or 'E'-shaped plans – the latter sometimes thought to have developed as a compliment to the Queen for whose entertainment they were intended. The architect of Hatfield, the master mason Robert Lyminge, was also called upon to rebuild the old house at Blickling in Norfolk acquired by James 1's Lord Chief Justice Sir Henry Hobart, in 1616. Restricted to the rectangular area within the moat, Lyminge could not dispense with courtyards altogether, but these were reduced to little more than light wells, while the most lavish decoration was reserved for the exterior façades. If Hardwick impresses by its scale and simplicity, Blickling Hall does so by its sheer fantasy and invention. The winding country lane from Aylsham gives no warning of what is to come; it passes the church and suddenly, across an expanse of lawn bordered by yew hedges of gigantic size, appears an improbable vision: gabled, pinnacled and pepperpotted, built of the mellowest red brick with white stone quoins and window dressings like some charming garden gazebo which the touch of a wand or an ingenious scene-change has turned into an enchanted palace. This was indeed the great age of plays and masques, and architects like Lyminge, who helped to design elaborate stage scenery and machinery, also brought a sense of theatre to their more permanent buildings.

On the whole, the classical language of architecture derived from the Italian Renaissance masters, like Bramante and Brunelleschi, Palladio and Scamozzi, filtered into England only through means of pattern-books and engravings, so that it usually took the form of applied ornament, two-dimensional in effect, and embellishing buildings that remained largely vernacular in character. Inigo Jones's first-hand experience of Italy was thus to have revolutionary consequences, and particularly his second journey of 1613–14 in the train of the young Earl of Arundel, destined to be one of the greatest of English patrons and collectors of art. Jones's work was largely confined to the immediate circle of Charles 1's court, and the Civil War interrupted the full-scale adoption of his new Palladian style for a further half-century. But buildings like the Queen's House at Greenwich, the Banqueting House in Whitehall and St Paul's Church in Covent Garden were to act like time-fuses, exploding into the world of country-house design in the early eighteenth century. Meanwhile Jones's influence, if not his actual hand, can be seen in a group of buildings of the 1630s and 40s, including Stoke Bruerne in Northamptonshire, the first house in England to be given quadrant colonnades and wings following Palladio's villa designs, and Wilton House near Salisbury, where Jones collaborated with Isaac de Caux on a new garden front in 1636, rebuilt by his pupil John Webb after a disastrous fire ten years later.

John Aubrey records that 'King Charles the first did love Wilton above all places, and came thither every summer. It was he that did put Philip [Herbert] ... Earle of Pembroke upon making this magnificent garden and grotto, and to new build that side of the house that fronts the garden, with two stately pavilions at each end, all *al Italiano*.' In fact these pedimented 'pavilions' were adaptations of the old Tudor towers with gabled windows

which already existed on the adjoining entrance front. Jones and de Caux's real innovation was to produce a façade of calmly classical character, which seems as if it can hardly belong to the same century as the robust naïvety of a house like Blickling. A drawing exists for a façade over twice as long with a huge central pediment supported by six giant Corinthian columns – and this must have been taken seriously for the formal garden was actually laid out to this scale. But, as in the case of the Banqueting House at Whitehall, the reduced version has a balance and completeness of its own: the *piano nobile* or main floor is set above a low basement with small attic windows above, the monumental Venetian window in the centre balances the weight of the pavilions, and the crisply carved stone window-surrounds throw knife-edged shadows on the warm grey local stone. Reflected in the still waters of the Avon, or framed by the arches of Roger Morris's Palladian bridge built exactly a hundred years later in 1737, the composition has a restraint and nobility that is hard to parallel in a period of such unrest and upheaval.

The cost of the Civil War and Cromwell's rule was heavy not only in financial but also in cultural terms. The great courtier families like the Cecils and Herberts who had been the first to experiment with foreign styles and express interest in collecting Italian pictures and sculpture were no longer in the ascendant, and it was the lesser gentry, acquiring new power through Parliament and constitutional monarchy, who were the main country-house builders of Charles II's reign. Many of these had suffered exile in Holland and France during the Commonwealth, and their compact 'double-pile' houses (so called because they consisted of two rows of rooms back to back, normally separated by a central corridor or staircases) had the hipped roofs and dormers, modillion cornices and central pedimented doorcases found on Dutch houses of the date. Uppark in Sussex, though probably built as late as 1690 by the Comptroller of the King's Work's, William Talman, is typical of a form first popularized by Hugh May at Eltham Lodge in Kent in the early 1660s, and by William Winde at Combe Abbey in Warwickshire and Belton in Lincolnshire in the 1680s. Winde was actually born at Bergen-op-Zoom, while May spent much of his youth in The Hague and Rotterdam in the household of the Duke of Buckingham.

Like other houses of its type, Uppark has the feeling of a giant doll's house, but what is unusual is its site high up on the South Downs offering an incomparable view in clear weather to the blue ribbon of the English Channel, with the Isle of Wight beyond. Such an exposed position struck contemporaries as 'horrid', and most preferred the more domesticated landscape of a fertile valley, or a plain where the long straight avenues then fashionable could stretch to infinity. Even in the early nineteenth century, when the Duke of Wellington inspected the house as a possible gift from the nation after Waterloo, he found the ascent from the village of Harting too steep for his horses. The elevations of the house are simplicity itself: seven evenly-spaced bays each side and nine on the main façade, more tightly grouped in the middle so as to give added prominence to the pedimented centrepiece. This pediment originally contained the Earl of Tankerville's arms, but these were replaced in the mid-eighteenth century by those of Sir Matthew Fetherstonhaugh, who also substituted a grander stone doorcase in the south front and rebuilt Talman's original pair of pavilions, containing kitchen and stables. Apart from these minor changes,

Opposite] The south front of Wilton House, near Salisbury, framed in the arch of the Palladian bridge built over the river Avon in 1737. One of the earliest surviving façades in England in a purely classical style, it was almost certainly designed by Charles I's architect Inigo Jones in collaboration with Isaac de Caux in 1636. Philip Herbert, 4th Earl of Pembroke, was an intimate friend of the King as well as being Lord Chamberlain; Shakespeare's First Folio was dedicated to him and his elder brother, the 3rd Earl, and in their day Wilton was a haven for scholars, writers and artists.

Uppark remains an archetype of the late Stuart house: astylar (that is to say eschewing the classical orders), and with both floors assuming equal importance; but balanced and symmetrical in plan as well as in elevation, with a hall and saloon on the central axis flanked by 'apartments' at the four corners of the house. It might almost have been designed specially to fulfill Sir Roger Pratt's 'Rules for the Guidance of Architects' and 'Notes on the Building of Country Houses', written in the 1670s, where gracefulness is identified with usefulness in what has been called 'an architecture that neither deceives nor declaims'.

True Baroque architecture is of course deceitful and declamatory by its very nature, and Talman's later career, which showed him to have no small measure of these traits in his own character, saw a gradual shift from Dutch to French prototypes, approaching a full-blown Louis Quatorze style in his remarkable designs for a Trianon at Hampton Court for William III. One of his finest achievements was the south front of Chatsworth in Derbyshire, rebuilt

The south front of Chatsworth, Derbyshire, with the Emperor Fountain playing high above the trees. Designed by William Talman for the 1st Duke of Devonshire in 1687, the façade is based on Bernini's unexecuted project for the Louvre, and skilfully conceals the Elizabethan building behind it, whose principal rooms lay on the top floor. The long canal pond was dug in 1703 and, with the Sea Horse Fountain beyond it, is one of the surviving features of the original formal garden laid out for the Duke by George London and Henry Wise.

for the 1st Duke of Devonshire and based on Bernini's unexecuted project for the Louvre: the very design that Wren (Talman's superior as Surveyor of the King's Works) had been shown by 'the old reserv'd Italian' on his visit to Paris in 1665, when he 'had only time to copy it in my Fancy and Memory'. There were numerous problems in this remodelling of the old Elizabethan house which had been begun by Bess of Hardwick and her second husband Sir William Cavendish in the 1550s: as at Hardwick, the most important rooms with the tallest windows were on the top floor; moreover with an even number of bays, twelve in all, it was impossible to provide a central feature for what was essentially a side elevation. But Talman contrived to make a virtue of necessity, and his giant Ionic pilasters creating 'pavilions' either end, his enormously heavy cornice and balustrade, concealing the roof and crowned by four different types of stone vase, and his window frames with massive triple keystones, give such an effect of composure and self-confidence that it is hard to believe they mask a sixteenth-century building. The sash windows here are some of the earliest recorded in England, and the bars are now gilded (as they originally were), giving an effect of great magnificence, while the traveller and diarist Celia Fiennes records that in 1697 the windows in the rusticated basement were 'made with Grates before them and are for birds an Averye and so looking glass behind'. The only major change since Talman's day has been the loss of his central 'horseshoe' staircase, with curving flights and ironwork by Jean Tijou 'painted blew and tipt with gold'. This was replaced by Wyatville's angular flights in the early nineteenth century.

Talman quarrelled with the Duke of Devonshire, as with almost all his private clients, and was dismissed in 1696 before the completion of the west front. However, this follows the south elevation so closely that it can safely be credited to him. The fluted pilasters turn into columns flanking the three central bays and supporting a wide pediment, and the immediate inspiration here seems to be Louis XIV's famous pavilion at Marly built by Jules Hardouin-Mansart in 1680.

French influence is just as apparent in Talman's work for William Blathwayt of Dyrham Park in Avon who had 'never pretended to any fortune' but by his industry became Secretary at War to William III. Blathwayt had already employed a little-known Huguenot, Samuel Hauduroy, to re-design the west front of the sixteenth-century manor which was his wife's inheritance – and this, completed in 1694, was remarkably like a Parisian town house of the period with low wings forming a *cour d'honneur* and lacking only a gate-screen. Talman's east front, designed in 1698, is a more grandiose affair showing the influence of Versailles in its bold rectangular outline and its channelled rustication in the style of Mansart, though there are also echoes of Rubens' *Palazzi di Genova*, a favourite source book for English Baroque architects. The orangery built on to one side of it, and the corresponding arcade disappearing into the hillside on the other, to give an impression of symmetry, are also clearly based on the *Orangerie* at Versailles. Few traces now remain of the great formal garden at Dyrham laid out by George London and Henry Wise, but, apart from the cascade aligned on the centre of the orangery, this was more Dutch than French in style with small compartments, canals and fish tanks rather than the vistas and *patte d'oie* (or splayed avenues) of Le Nôtre.

In spite of almost continuous war with France, French influence on English art and architecture reached a peak at the turn of the century. The great exodus of skilled Huguenot craftsmen to England and Holland after the Revocation of the Edict of Nantes in 1685 also brought a designer of international standing in the shape of Daniel Marot, who entered the service of William of Orange and worked in London, Amsterdam and The Hague. Marot's highly individual brand of the Louis Quatorze style can be seen in two important country houses – Petworth in Sussex and Boughton in Northamptonshire. Both have a marked lack of central emphasis, though Petworth originally had a squared dome above the central three bays, and separate roofs to the 'pavilions' at either end which would have given it a more varied outline. The keystones above the windows are carved with pairs of wings, the Duke of Somerset's crest, derived from the lures used in hawking. Like the stags' antlers at Chatsworth, such decoration may have been considered suitable for what were essentially hunting lodges on however grand a scale. The enormous length of the house stresses the importance of the enfilade in a Baroque house – the alignment of the state rooms on one straight axis as a setting for the processions and ceremonial that were so important at this period. No one can have been more obsessed with formality than the 'Proud Duke' of Somerset, as he was known to his contemporaries. One of them described him living at Petworth 'in a grand retirement peculiar and agreable only to himself'; he insisted on his children always standing in his presence, and is said to have disinherited one of his daughters when he fell asleep and woke to find her seated. The architecture of Petworth is as grandiloquent as its creator, yet its refined French detail – busts on tapering plinths above the windows of the end pavilions, channelled rustication and a bracketed frieze with military trophies in the centre section – gave it a sophistication that is rare in houses of its date.

The north front of Boughton House, built by Ralph Montagu, several times ambassador to Louis XIV, is sparer and less ornate but still more like a French château. Long and low, it has a central arcade disguising a much older building (and a main entrance way off-centre), with a service wing on one side leading to a stable block based on part of the *Grandes Ecuries* at Versailles. The squared dome over the central arch recalls that formerly at Petworth, and at Montagu House in London, on the site of the present British Museum. Marot is known to have worked for Ralph Montagu (created 1st Duke in 1705) at his London house and the north front of Boughton is very close to one of his engravings. Once again the enfilade of state rooms above the arcade, first occupied by William III in 1695, is obvious from the elevation, while the pavilions at either end were intended for separate *appartements*, each consisting of bedchamber, dressing room and closet. Those in the left-hand pavilion were never finished and it remains without floors, ceilings or walls, just as the day the workmen downed tools and left nearly three hundred years ago.

The restraint and sophistication of the French Régence made little appeal to one of the greatest and most original of English architects, Sir John Vanbrugh, though his early imprisonment when a soldier in France inspired a lasting admiration for the bastions and fortifications of Vauban. Vanbrugh first made his mark as a playwright, and quite how, in 1699, he came to draw up designs for Castle Howard, the great mansion which the Earl of Carlisle proposed to build on his Yorkshire estate, may never be known. It was certainly a surprise for contemporaries to find, in Jonathan Swift's words, how 'Van's genius, without thought or lecture, is hugely turn'd to architecture'. With the constant help of Nicholas Hawksmoor, who acted as draughtsman and clerk of the works, Vanbrugh soon supplanted Talman as the architect chiefly employed by the Whig aristocracy, even displacing him as Comptroller of the King's Works in 1702.

His training in the theatre and his sense of movement and drama made Vanbrugh one of the first classical architects to express admiration for the Gothic, and in the boldness of the outline and grouping of his houses, and the building up of various elements into a climax, there is perhaps a conscious backward look to the triumphs of English medieval architecture. One of the major innovations at Castle Howard was its alignment on a north-south axis, instead of the more usual east-west, to take advantage of the spectacular views over the Howardian Hills, and also so that the long enfilade of state rooms (like that at Petworth) should be filled with sunlight, while only the entrance faced north. The two sides of the house are treated in utterly different fashion, much to the disgust of later Palladian enthusiasts. The north has an austere Doric order, relatively few windows, and channelled rustication on a plain base to look like 'one solid rock of stone', as Hawksmoor described it. Like some of Vanbrugh's later houses – Kimbolton, Grimsthorpe and Seaton Delaval – it was intended to have a definite 'castle air' about it, fulfilling Lord Carlisle's intention to re-create the spirit of the old fortress of Henderskelfe which stood nearby. By contrast, the south front was to have a fluted Corinthian order, with a pedimented central section to the main block like Chatsworth, but with lower wings each side marching outwards to slightly projecting domed bays at each end. The immense length of this front, all in one plane with only shallow breaks and recessions, gives it a much more festive Italian *palazzo* character. But these conscious disparities between the two façades are to a great extent resolved by the great central lantern and dome, obviously inspired by Wren's at Greenwich and St Paul's but octagonal in profile and thus better suited to the rectangular block on which it sits. The extraordinary series of statues and busts, urns and vases, which line the parapets are almost equivalent to the pinnacles in a Gothic cathedral, articulating the bays and providing an unforgettably elaborate silhouette. The outbuildings, servants' quarters, kitchens and stables were a vital part of the overall scheme with their archways, courtyards and groups of towers, intended to prolong the north to a total of 667 feet. But in the event, Lord Carlisle was diverted by equally ambitious plans for garden buildings and landscaping a vast area of parkland, and only those on the east side of the house were completed. The west wing was finally built by his son to a different, Palladian design by Sir Thomas Robinson, while a stable block was built further away by Carr of York. In spite of this sad end to the story, Castle Howard remains one of the most thrilling experiences in English architecture, all the more remarkable for being Vanbrugh's very first work.

The 'castle air', first experienced at Castle Howard, and in the mock-medieval walls and bastions which still greet visitors approaching the house from the south, reached its fullest expression at Blenheim Palace in Oxfordshire, given to the 1st Duke of Marlborough by a grateful nation after his decisive victory over the French and Bavarians in 1704 in the War of the Spanish Succession. Vanbrugh saw this house from the outset 'much more as an intended

Overleaf left] 'I have seen gigantic palaces before', wrote Horace Walpole after a visit to Castle Howard, 'but never a sublime one.' Sir John Vanbrugh's first work in architecture, and one of his greatest, was undertaken for the 3rd Earl of Carlisle in 1699 to replace the old castle of Henderskelfe, in a magnificent position on the edge of the North Yorkshire moors. Even in rain, the silhouettes of its domes and cupolas, urns and statues, shrouded in mist, have a brooding nobility and drama worthy of one who effortlessly combined the professions of soldier, playwright and architect.

Overleaf right] The Temple of the Four Winds on the edge of Wray Wood at Castle Howard. Built in 1726–8 and one of Vanbrugh's last works, it shows the influence of Palladio's Villa Rotonda, but so freely interpreted that it remains as individual and imaginative as any of his larger-scale masterpieces. As the century progressed, garden buildings of this kind became just as ambitious – and sometimes even more elaborate – than the façades of the houses to which they belonged.

monument of the Queen's glory than a private Habitation for the Duke'. Built in the park of the old royal manor of Woodstock, it was to be a combination of castle, citadel and monument, like the battle scene from a Handel oratorio, complete with fanfares of trumpets and drums. Here the architect's imaginative powers were given full reign and his gift for bringing movement and drama to inanimate stone and mortar were triumphantly affirmed. Unlike Castle Howard, which was conceived in terms of two long façades with no side elevations, Blenheim is more fully developed, with a four-square main block, anchored by corner towers – all built in golden-brown Oxfordshire stone brought by an army of workmen from the quarries at Taynton and Barrington. The towers have Vanbrugh's favourite round-headed windows and channelled rustication, and support gigantic arched gazebos (each concealing a number of chimneystacks) rather like the lower stage of a Wren church spire but far more massive and threatening in effect. The 'grenades' which crown them are capped with ducal coronets on reversed fleur-de-lis, and there are other references to Marlborough's victories in the lions savaging French cockerels above the arches leading into the Great Court, and the thirty-ton bust of Louis XIV captured at Tournai, above the central portico of the south front, 'hoisted upon the parapet like a head upon a pike'.

Left] Vanbrugh's gift for imparting 'movement' to architecture was never more brilliantly expressed than in the entrance front of Blenheim Palace, the great country house given by Queen Anne to the Duke of Marlborough as a thanks-offering on behalf of the nation after his famous victory over the French in 1704. The straight and curving colonnades, projecting and receding masses, and shifting perspectives, recall the manœuvres of a great military parade, with fanfares of trumpets and drums finding their equivalent in Grinling Gibbons's carved stone grenades, vases, statues and (over the gates to the two flanking courtyards) English lions savaging the French cockerel.

Overleaf] The long south front of Holkham Hall, with the column to Coke of Norfolk, the great agricultural reformer, beyond. Holkham was built by his predecessor, Thomas Coke, 1st Earl of Leicester, between 1734 and 1761, and is one of the most ambitious of all Palladian country houses. The main block was intended to contain the outstanding classical sculpture and Italian pictures acquired by Lord Leicester on the Grand Tour, while the four pavilions housed the chapel and kitchen, and family and guests' quarters respectively. Lord Leicester, his friend Lord Burlington, and the latter's protégé William Kent, all played a part in the design, which was executed by Matthew Brettingham.

Echoes of Bernini can be found in the colonnades flanking the forecourt; of Borromini in the riot of canted corners and broken pediments, and the interplay of squares, octagons and circles; and of Vauban in the colossal East Gate, carrying the great cistern which supplied the palace with water. But the idea of a central clerestoried hall seems to be derived from Elizabethan houses like Wollaton in Nottinghamshire, which Vanbrugh may have visited on a summer tour in 1695 when he told a correspondent that he had 'seen most of the great houses in the north'. The story of the architect's clashes with the autocratic, parsimonious, and ultimately philistine Duchess of Marlborough has often been told – one of their particular points of difference being the triumphal bridge spanning the valley on the main axis. This enormous structure, with windows in the piers inspired by Michelangelo's attic story of St Peter's, is now half drowned by the high water-level of Capability Brown's lake. According to the Duchess it contained thirty-three rooms, 'but that which makes it so much prettier than London Bridge', she wrote acidly, 'is that you may sit in six rooms and look out at window into the high arch while the coaches are driving over your head'. Their quarrel eventually led to Vanbrugh's dismissal in 1716, though Hawksmoor later returned to complete much of the work.

In the years that followed the Hanoverian succession, Vanbrugh was to find a still more serious adversary in the shape of Richard Boyle, 3rd Earl of Burlington, who was to lead a revolution in English architectural taste, returning for inspiration to the work of Inigo Jones and Andrea Palladio. Just as the Grand Tour was now considered an essential part of a nobleman's education, so Italy was recognized by Burlington's contemporaries as the fountain-head of artistic endeavour. But the Baroque architecture of Rome and Naples, too strongly associated with absolutism and the Papacy, appealed only to a minority – mostly made up of Tories, often with Catholic leanings – who employed architects like James Gibbs and Thomas Archer. The Whigs, who were to dominate English politics for the rest of the century, preferred the rationalism of the Italian Renaissance and its rediscovery of antiquity, seeing themselves as heirs of the Greek and Roman senators, just as the Venetians and Florentines had done in the sixteenth century. Palladio's country villas of the 1540s and 50s, based on the writings of the classical theorist Vitruvius and on a rudimentary knowledge of the classical monuments that had been excavated before his time, thus became the model for hundreds of eighteenth-century English country houses built by Lord Burlington's disciples, among them Colen Campbell, William Kent, Henry Flitcroft and Isaac Ware.

Burlington's own villa at Chiswick, begun about 1723, was the first of a series which was to make the Thames valley into a second Brenta. As a separate pavilion joined to an earlier house, it was of a comparatively modest size like its prototype, Palladio's Villa Rotonda near Vicenza. The same is true of Colen Campbell's Stourhead in Wiltshire, built at the same time for the banker Henry Hoare and based on the Villa Emo at Fanzolo. But Campbell's greatest achievement was to enlarge these simple farmhouses and barns of the Venetian mainland into palaces which could vie with Blenheim and Castle Howard in magnificence. Wanstead House in Essex, started as early as 1714, was the first of these, but the most important to survive is Houghton Hall in Norfolk, commissioned by Sir Robert Walpole, the first Englishman to assume the title of Prime Minister, in 1722.

In architectural terms, Houghton is as reserved and static in character as Blenheim is brash and *mouvementé*, and the difference would have been still more marked had it been built with pedimented towers like those at Wilton, as Campbell originally proposed. The present domes and cupolas were added by his successor Thomas Ripley, after his death in 1729. The plan of the main block is not so very different from late-seventeenth-century houses by Hooke and Talman, except for the greater emphasis on the *piano nobile* which contained the state or show rooms. Faced in smooth ashlar, this is placed above the 'rustic', so-called because of its rusticated stonework on the exterior, where the everyday family apartments lay – as they still do. The family's and guests' bedchambers were to be found on the 'attic floor' above the *piano nobile*, and what we today would call the attics were given over to servants' rooms, largely concealed behind the balustrade. Campbell's architecture is strictly based on Palladio's rules of 'harmonic proportions' – multiples of threes and fours, and an emphasis on cubes, which were held to be like the intervals of chords in musical notation. The *piano nobile* is, for instance, 18 feet high, while the rustic and attic floors are 12 feet. In contrast with Vanbrugh's houses where the greatest display was reserved for the entrance front, it is the garden façade at Houghton that is framed by curving quadrant colonnades leading to the kitchen and laundry courts. The position of the two-storey saloon, on the main axis of the house with the hall behind it, is marked by the central portico of engaged Ionic columns and pediment, crowned by three classical statues, while the 'pavilions' at the corners containing the two principal bedchambers are distinguished by Venetian windows of a type that were to recur again and again in English Palladian architecture.

The internal decoration of Houghton was left to another of Lord Burlington's particular protégés, the young William Kent, who was to emerge after Colen Campbell's premature death as the most gifted architect and garden designer of his generation. But the greatest monument to Kent's mature genius lies only a few miles away at Holkham Hall, the splendid mansion begun in 1734 by Walpole's political ally and Burlington's intimate friend, Thomas Coke, 1st Earl of Leicester. The genesis of the design of Holkham is complicated and it is likely that Burlington, Leicester and the executant architect Matthew Brettingham all played a part, though the external elevations are close to Kent's original drawings. The prototype here was Palladio's Villa Mocenigo, with its central block joined to pavilions at the four corners which contained modest stables, barns and servants' quarters. At Holkham, by contrast, one pavilion was a family wing, another was for guests, and the third and fourth contained a chapel and kitchen respectively. The removal of the family apartments out of the main block allowed a *piano nobile* of truly monumental proportions, where Lord Leicester's famous collections of Italian pictures and Greek and Roman sculpture could be displayed to their best advantage, and could be seen by visitors without invading the family's privacy.

The squat corner towers, and Venetian windows, like those of Kent's Horse Guards building in London, look back to Inigo Jones's Wilton, and the massive Corinthian portico on the central axis, pulling the whole design together, may also be based on a knowledge of the master-plan for Wilton drawn up by Jones and de Caux in 1637. The architectural

Right] Robert Adam was only rarely given the chance to practise external architecture on a monumental scale, but his south front at Kedleston Hall in Derbyshire, designed about 1765, shows what he might have achieved in this sphere. The central section is clearly based on Roman triumphal arches like those of Titus and Constantine, which Adam had studied closely during his time in Italy. But it is given a 'picturesque' quality by the curving flights of stairs leading up to it, giving a foretaste of the circular domed saloon behind: a subtle interplay of geometrical shapes.

Left] Statues of classical deities stride forward purposefully from the entablature of Adam's south front at Kedleston, as if to roam the landscaped park with its temples and pavilions, lakes and cascades.

ornament here is as sparing as in Palladio's own work, and the solemn Roman character of the house is enhanced by the use of a dun-coloured brick instead of stone for the walls, and even for the rusticated basement. Besides the large saving in cost, Lord Leicester could find justification for this in the writings of Vitruvius, and in many of Palladio's own buildings.

Holkham was a particularly important influence on the most prolific Palladian architect of the mid-eighteenth century, James Paine. The main blocks of several of his houses echo Kent's wings, and others, like Nostell Priory in Yorkshire and Kedleston Hall in Derbyshire, aimed at a complete Villa Mocenigo plan. At Kedleston only two of his four projected pavilions were completed, on the entrance side of the house, and Paine was dismissed by Lord Scarsdale in favour of Robert Adam before the completion of the garden front and before work had started on the interior. There can be no better illustration of the change of taste that took place in England in the 1760s than a comparison between Paine's conventional Palladian north front and Adam's Neoclassical south front, still startling today with its monumental centre section (screening his domed saloon) clearly inspired by the Arch of Constantine in Rome.

Left] A vision of Arcadia based on the paintings of Claude: the view across the lake to Flitcroft's Pantheon at Stourhead in Wiltshire. The planting, the making of the lake, and the erection of the many buildings around it, was begun by the banker Henry Hoare about 1744, and few English gardens laid out on picturesque principles have survived so completely. The tour of the grounds was conceived in terms of a series of carefully contrived viewpoints framed by trees, as if bringing the landscapes of Claude, Salvator Rosa and Poussin literally to life.

Right] Nicholas Revett's Music Temple of 1781 on an island in the lake at West Wycombe Park, Buckinghamshire, with the east portico of the house behind it. West Wycombe is an extreme example of a country house conceived as a series of picturesque incidents in the landscape rather than as an architectural entity. Its façades, screened from each other by plantations, are stage sets, just as much as the follies and 'eye-catchers' which surround it. Here its owner, Sir Francis Dashwood, could entertain his guests, dressed as bacchanals and satyrs, to *fêtes champêtres*, or people his garden with the musicians and revellers familiar from the paintings of Watteau.

The Vale of Venus at Rousham in Oxfordshire, with the Lower Cascade designed by William Kent in the 1730s. It was Kent who, according to Horace Walpole, revolutionized English landscape gardening, replacing the formal parterre with the serpentine lines of 'pleasing nature'. Of the 'opening and retiring shades of Venus's Vale', Walpole wrote: 'the whole is as elegant and antique as if the Emperor Julian had selected the most pleasing solitude about Daphne to enjoy philosophic retirement'.

Children often have more in common with their grandparents than their mothers and fathers, and so it is with architects. Despite Adam's passionate advocacy of the latest 'archaeological' styles based on the finds at Herculaneum and Pompeii, there is more than a hint of Vanbrugh in his plea for movement rather than 'correctness' in architecture – in his own words: 'the rise and fall, the advance and recess with other diversity of form, in the different parts of a building, so as to add greatly to the picturesque of the composition'. The way the curving flights of the staircase at Kedleston set off the colossal weight of the great Corinthian columns, and the shallow curve of the dome, are masterly, and cause one only to regret how few other opportunities Adam was given to produce works of architecture on so grand a scale. However, it was as an interior designer that he was to make the most impact on English country houses, and the exteriors of these – Syon, Osterley, Harewood, Newby, Nostell and Saltram among them – bear remarkably few signs of what lies within.

By the second half of the eighteenth century, most of the great Whig families who were to govern England until the Reform Bill of 1832 had in fact built their country seats, and were now more likely to be redecorating outmoded interiors, perhaps adding a wing, but above all landscape gardening and building follies and temples, boat-houses and cascades. Adam's own reference to 'the picturesque of the composition' shows how buildings were by this time appreciated more for their appearance in a landscape setting than for their purely architectural merits. Kent had been one of the pioneers of this way of thinking. Trained as a painter himself, he was one of the first to attack the idea of formal parterres, clipped topiary, straight avenues, canals and walled enclosures. In Horace Walpole's words, 'he leaped the fence, and saw that all Nature was a garden'; and it was he who realized at Rousham in Oxfordshire and at Claremont in Surrey Addison's vision of 'a whole estate thrown into a kind of garden by frequent plantations'.

The appreciation of landscape painting, and particularly the works of Claude, Poussin and Salvator Rosa, were at the heart of this development. At Holkham, significantly, there was a whole Landscape Room filled with canvases by these and other masters, and it is evident that the comparative austerity of many Palladian houses was meant to be softened by the 'natural' setting created round them: Capability Brown's serpentine lakes and smooth rounded hills, his carefully asymmetrical clumps of oak and chestnut, and his ha-ha walls constructed so that cattle and deer should appear to be grazing on the same green lawns that led up to the very windows of the house. To walk round such a park was to experience a series of three-dimensional pictures comparable to, if not actually derived from, the ideal compositions of the Old Masters. Even the façades of some houses, like West Wycombe in Buckinghamshire, were conceived as separate 'eye-catchers', framed by plantations which made it impossible to see more than one side of the building at any one time. Nicholas Revett's portico at West Wycombe, though built as the entrance front, was always known as the Temple of Bacchus after its prototype at Telos illustrated in Stuart and Revett's *Antiquities of Ionia*. At its dedication in September 1771, a procession of 'Bacchanals, Priests, Priestesses, Pan, Fauns, Satyrs, Silenus etc all in proper habits and skins wreathed with vine leaves' made a sacrifice to the god before repairing to the lake for more 'paeans and libations' and 'discharges of cannon' from several boats.

The bridge, lake and Pantheon at Stourhead, seen from the medieval Bristol Cross, erected by Henry Hoare in 1765 at the start of the tour of the gardens. By this date Stourhead was already one of the most celebrated landscapes in Europe.

The marriage of gardening and architecture as a setting for eternal fêtes was nowhere achieved with such success as at Stourhead in Wiltshire, where Henry Hoare II, the son of Colen Campbell's patron, laid out some of the most celebrated pleasure grounds in England from about 1740 onwards. Flitcroft's buildings, including the Temple of Hercules based on the Pantheon and the Temple of Apollo based on the Round Temple at Baalbec, framed by dark hanging woods and reflected in the dark waters of the lake, recall the *capriccio* paintings bought by English Grand Tourists from artists in Rome like Giovanni Panini and Giovanni Battista Busiri, depicting their favourite monuments of classical antiquity painted to order in idealized landscape settings.

While it would be wrong to suggest that country-house building became of secondary interest to gardening in the second half of the eighteenth century, it is true that exteriors generally became plainer and a matter of less concern than interiors. Palladian models continued to be used by architects like James Wyatt and Henry Holland, though each developed highly individual styles indoors. Only with the great castles of Belvoir and Penrhyn in the early nineteenth century were the romantic aspirations of Vanbrugh and Adam aroused once more. They are beyond the scope of this book for, by the time they were built, the concept of 'rooms of state' was almost dead and the battle of the styles was so various and so complex that each deserves a tome to itself. We have looked at the outward appearance of the country house and its architectural development; we have seen something of its landscape setting; it is time to mount the stone stairs to the front door and begin our tour.

THE LIBRARY
COLLEGE OF FURTHER EDUCATION
NORTHAMPTON

2 Halls

Opposite] The great hall at Cotehele, built by Sir Piers Edgcumbe some time before 1520 and little changed since his day. The practice of hanging arms and armour on the walls of the hall arose because this was the place of assembly where a lord of the manor and his retainers would gather not only to eat but to prepare for attack in time of war: only later was it to become a merely decorative custom. The solid oak roof-timbers, the whitewashed walls and rough stone floor, wonderfully preserve the atmosphere of the early sixteenth century.

A 'bobbin-turned' oak chair at Cotehele, so called after its elaborately turned struts and rails, carved with an infinity of knobs and rings.

Of all the interiors that go to make up the British country house, the hall has the longest pedigree. Throughout the Middle Ages it was the chief room, and originally perhaps it was the only one: a stone barn-like structure in which a whole feudal community assembled, ate and slept, with a variety of lesser timber buildings around it, encircled by a stockade. Even today many of the grandest houses in England, from Elizabethan 'prodigy houses' like Hardwick to Palladian palaces like Holkham and Houghton, bear the name 'Hall' rather than 'Castle' or 'House', a distant echo of such primitive beginnings.

The early medieval hall invariably had a central hearth from which smoke rose, to escape from a louvre high up in the rafters overhead. There were thus two essential prerequisites for the building of such a room: it should be as high as possible (for a low ceiling might catch fire) and it should be on the ground floor. First-floor halls are occasionally to be found in Border fortresses, raised on vaulted stone basements which made them easier to defend, but generally the hall was adequately protected by a courtyard and gatehouse, sometimes on both sides, as at Haddon in Derbyshire, built as early as 1350.

The hall was used for a variety of functions. Assemblies and calls to arms were made here in time of danger, but here also the lord would dispense justice through his manorial court, receive distinguished guests, or hold feasts and entertainments to celebrate family marriages or christenings often with the help of travelling bands of players and musicians. From day to day too this was where the entire household ate, seated on benches at the long refectory tables which can still be seen in Oxford and Cambridge college halls. And just like dons today, so a landowner and his family would sit at a 'high table' placed crossways at one end of the hall on a raised dais, surveying their servants and tenants 'below the salt'.

Despite the survival of this custom in university life, the family had already begun to eat separately in a solar or great chamber beyond the hall as early as the fourteenth century. In the *Vision of Piers Plowman*, of about 1362, Langland writes 'wretched is the hall . . . each day in the week there the lord and lady liketh not to sit. Now have the rich a rule to eat by themselves in a privy parlour . . . or in a chamber with a chimney, and leave the chief hall that was made for meals, for men to eat in.' But whether the family were there or not (and they would return for feast days and other great entertainments), the dais remained the focal point of the hall. The stair turret that led up to the solar gradually became an oriel window, flooding it with light, and damp and draughts were counteracted by panelling or wall-hangings round the dais with a central canopy over the owner's seat. As wall-chimneypieces gradually replaced central hearths, so these were often placed at the upper end of the hall, as at Cotehele, and sometimes even behind the high table.

Early on, great halls were generally aisled, that is to say built with two rows of posts or stone pillars to support the roof. It was only the increasing skill of carpenters towards the end of the thirteenth century that resulted in wide span roofs – first arch-braced and then

hammerbeam – rendering these posts or 'speres' unnecessary. One of the wonders of the Middle Ages was Hugh Herland's magnificent timber roof of Westminster Hall, completed in 1401, which was the inspiration for many a country-house carpenter-architect over the next two hundred years.

At the opposite end of the hall from the dais there were generally three doors on the short end wall, that in the centre leading down a long corridor to the kitchen (detached from the hall in case of fire), and those on either side to the buttery and pantry where drink, bread and table utensils were dispensed. The two main entrance doors to the hall, leading to the courtyards either side, were also situated nearby on the long walls, so that the traffic and draughts at this end of the room would have been considerable. It was for this reason that the idea of the screen was developed. At first a movable partition between the two 'speres' nearest the end wall, it later became a more solid affair with two openings and a gallery above for musicians. Food could be brought in a formal procession from the kitchen accompanied by fanfares as it entered the hall. The screen itself was often made of linenfold panelling and elaborately painted like the rood-screens of contemporary churches.

The decoration of the great hall was in general far more colourful and less purely architectural than it became at a later date. Stonework would always be white- or colour-washed, and plastered walls were often lined out in red or ochre to look like ashlar blocks. Woven hangings or wainscot would line the dais and the blank wall above it would often have a great painting – Dives and Lazarus being a favourite subject since it symbolized the landowner's own munificence to the poor and needy. 'Arrases' or tapestries were hung in the halls of the richest owners, with the windows generally high above them where the embrasures would not interfere with the benches and tables lining the walls. But painted hangings were cheaper and therefore commoner. They were also easily movable at a time when great nobles were constantly travelling between the castles and manors on their widespread estates. Arms and armour were also hung on the walls of the hall, not just because a lord's retainers gathered here to defend themselves in times of danger, but because in peacetime a check could be kept on the whereabouts of weapons that were valuable as well as dangerous. Originally, shields painted with the coats-of-arms of the baron and his squires, and helmets surmounted by their crests, would have been among them, and the display of heraldry as well as martial trophies became one of the most persistent conventions in the decoration of halls, surviving centuries of changing tastes and styles.

Coats-of-arms became a favourite motif in wall-painting at an early date but their vivid colours were also ideally suited to stained glass. In the tall oriel window lighting his dais, a landowner could arrange a whole family tree of heraldic shields representing a succession of marriage alliances – a secular equivalent to the 'Tree of Jesse' windows found in medieval cathedrals. This obsession with heraldry was not simply sentimental and romantic, as it became in the eighteenth century with Horace Walpole's enthusiasm for the 'true rust of the Barons' war': it was a statement of power and influence specially designed to impress the visitor in the first room he entered.

The primacy of the hall was bound to be threatened by the gradual withdrawal of the family to eat privately in their own apartments. At Hardwick, built in the 1590s, the hall is

Robert Smythson's great hall at Hardwick in Derbyshire, completed in 1597. Revolutionary in its planning, the hall's entrance is on the central axis rather than at one end, while the room is placed symmetrically at the core of the house. The classical columns, carved by the mason William Griffin, are after engravings by the Italian Renaissance architect, Sebastiano Serlio, and replace the old medieval idea of a timber screen. Bess of Hardwick's arms above the chimneypiece, by the master-plasterer Abraham Smith, are supported by life-size stags, an appropriate image for what was essentially a hunting lodge on however grand a scale.

still a large two-storey room, but it is considerably smaller than the High Great Chamber and gallery at the top of the house where Bess of Hardwick dined in state, held masques and received the Queen's envoy almost in the style of a foreign ambassador. Large numbers of servants still ate here and the room had also to be an impressive starting point for the processional route by which visitors (and food from the neighbouring kitchen, accompanied by beadles, butlers, pages and clerks) ascended the broad staircase to the upper floors. So the Hardwick arms are given pride of place above the chimneypiece, guarded by lifesize plaster stags and surmounted by a countess's coronet lest any should remain unaware of the rank and noble origins of the proprietor.

But the hall at Hardwick was revolutionary in other ways. To begin with, the architect Robert Smythson placed it on the central axis of the house in the interests of symmetry, with the main door entering in the middle of the screens passage; it had no dais for even the idea of the high table had now been abandoned; it had a flat ceiling since there were now rooms above it; and finally, where one might have expected an elaborate wooden screen, it had a gallery supported by four carved stone Doric columns of remarkably pure classical design, based on an engraving by Serlio. This gallery may on occasion have been used by musicians, but it was also the only means of communication between Bess of Harwick's own private dining room and withdrawing room on the first floor. From the balcony she could check on the seemly behaviour of her household below, and one can imagine the hush as this indomitable widow, dressed in mourning for her four husbands, passed and re-passed on her imperious way.

Not many houses before the Civil War could rival the sophistication or the novel classicism of Hardwick. When the 1st Earl of Dorset came to remodel Archbishop Bourchier's great hall at Knole in 1605-8, he employed the King's Plasterer Richard Dungan to put in a flat ceiling below the medieval roof timbers, decorated with 'fretts' in a typically geometric Elizabethan style. But at the same time William Portinton was commissioned to build the gargantuan carved oak screen, which (like those at Hatfield and Audley End) is almost a throwback to medieval precedent with its elaborate heraldry, once picked out in the gaudiest colours.

Already by this time the upper servants had, like the family, left the hall and were eating in a separate parlour. The revolution in architecture brought about partly by Inigo Jones and John Webb, but still more by economic necessity in the Restoration period, encouraged a more compact 'double-pile' plan – particularly following Dutch precedents. In these 'gentry houses' the kitchen was swept away below stairs, with a servants' hall adjoining it. The entrance hall was in danger of becoming for the first time merely a vestibule on the Continental model – where visitors and tradesmen, perched on high-backed *sgabello* chairs, awaited an interview with His Grace or begged to present a petition to Her Ladyship.

The Marble Hall at Petworth, dating from 1692, is an instance of this. A comparatively small-scale introduction to so vast a house, it is saved from banality by the highly architectural quality of the design with over-large mouldings, bracketed frieze, splayed door and window surrounds, all very much in keeping with the west front of the house and all suggesting the hand of William III's Huguenot architect, Daniel Marot. The owner of

Opposite] The great hall at Knole is part of Archbishop Bourchier's house, built about 1460, though much altered by Thomas Sackville, 1st Earl of Dorset, who put in the chimneypiece, the oak panelling, the plasterwork ceiling below the earlier timber roof, and the ornate oak screen, between 1605 and 1608. The ceiling with its geometrical pattern of squares and octagons, and the deep arcaded frieze, are by the King's Plasterer Richard Dungan, and the screen – one of the last of its kind – was carved by William Portinton, likewise described in the accounts as the King's Carpenter. Its pairs of caryatids and panels of elaborate grotesque ornament (*above*) are based on Flemish pattern-books such as those of Wendel Dietterlin and Marten de Vos. The private orchestra which Lord Dorset maintained at Knole must often have performed behind the lattice windows of the musicians' gallery.

The 'Proud Duke' of Somerset's arms and supporters – the bull and unicorn – above one of the chimneypieces in the Marble Hall at Petworth, probably designed by Daniel Marot. The carver John Selden was paid £50 for the overmantels and the elaborate door and window surrounds in this room in 1692, the year before William III's visit to the house. As a waiting place for servants and visitors, and as an introduction to a family's rank and status, it was usual for a hall to be prominently decorated with its owner's coat-of-arms: painted on the backs of hall chairs, engraved on brass lockplates, or carved in stone, wood or plaster.

Petworth, the 'Proud Duke' of Somerset, not surprisingly insisted on having his arms and their supporters, the bull and unicorn (revealing his royal cousinage), carved by John Selden larger than life above the chimneypiece at either end of the room.

Sir Roger Pratt's slightly earlier experiment in combining hall and staircase, at Coleshill House in Berkshire, resulted in a more monumental interior than this but found few imitators because the main rooms in country houses, including bedchambers, were no longer on the upper floors, as they had been in the Elizabethan period but on the *piano nobile* or main floor, as recommended by the Italophile Lord Burlington in the early eighteenth century. Thus there was no need for a grand staircase. Yet the old English tradition of the great hall was in the end too strong to be resisted. At Ragley in Warwickshire, Robert Hooke provided a two-storey hall with an almost equally large saloon beyond it on the central axis, flanked by four separate *appartements* in the French manner, looking back to Hardwick and forward to the great stone and marble Palladian halls of Houghton and Holkham. Part of the reason for this conservatism was the empirical tradition of English country-house building. Instead of tearing down his ancestors' old-fashioned buildings and starting from scratch, a landowner would remodel an existing hall, add a new wing to it, and case his father's brick in stone or his grandfather's stone in brick, according to the fashion of the moment. It suited his purse better, for such expenditure could come out of annual income, and it also preserved the idea that this was his family's ancient seat, not merely the expensive whim of a *nouveau riche*.

Looking from the Marble Hall at
Petworth down the length of the house
to a giant classical bust in the North
Gallery. Axial vistas were a favourite
concept of the Baroque period, and by
the early 1690s, when Petworth was
being rebuilt, no house was complete
without its enfilade of doors stretching
out on either side of the central hall and
saloon. This alignment was intended not
only to impress by its length and
diminishing perspective, but to form an
ideal setting for the formal processions
and ceremonies that were part of a
nobleman's everyday life.

Left] The Painted Hall at Chatsworth in Derbyshire with Louis Laguerre's painted scenes from the life of Julius Caesar on the walls, and an assembly of the gods on the ceiling, all of 1692–4. As originally built by William Talman for the 1st Duke of Devonshire, there were twin curving flights in place of the present straight staircase and no gallery. In combining hall and staircase, perhaps following the example of Hugh May's famous staircase at Windsor Castle, Talman anticipated the still more exciting spatial possibilities grasped by Vanbrugh at Blenheim and Castle Howard.

Right] The ceiling of the great hall at Blenheim Palace, Oxfordshire. The idea of a huge clerestory lantern, 67 feet high, may have been derived from Elizabethan houses like Wollaton in Nottinghamshire, and it gave Vanbrugh the chance to provide a fitting central mass to the entrance front, as well as a hall of epic proportions to be equipped as a guard chamber worthy of Britain's greatest military hero. The ceiling itself, painted by Sir James Thornhill in 1716, shows Marlborough victorious, with the battle order at Blenheim spread for view. But the Duchess suspected the artist of sharp practice in charging the same for the *grisaille* trophies as for the coloured 'historical part', and soon afterwards dismissed him in favour of Laguerre.

53

At Boughton in Northamptonshire, Ralph, 1st Duke of Montagu, several times Ambassador to Louis XIV, masked the medieval great hall with a new range of state rooms in the French château style and brought the painter Louis Chéron back from Paris to paint a vast *Assembly of the Gods* on a coved ceiling, inserted just below the old open timber roof. At Chatsworth, the Painted Hall also occupies the same site as the Elizabethan great hall, though here Louis Laguerre's murals of 1692–4 showing scenes from the life of Julius Caesar strike a more old-fashioned martial note.

Vanbrugh and Hawksmoor's halls are among the most remarkable and original achievements in the history of English architecture. Just as the fantastic skylines of the English Perpendicular cathedrals may have influenced the bristling silhouettes of Blenheim and Castle Howard, so the picturesque qualities of earlier great halls and screens may have inspired the verticality of their entrance halls, the vistas through arches to flanking staircases and corridors, the deliberate changes of axis and the delight in massive architectural ornament. Of the two, Blenheim is the most consciously backward-looking, with a deliberate 'castle air' in the immense thickness of the side walls punched through with arches to the staircases either side. The gallery high above the door to the saloon was probably intended for musicians and consciously evokes the minstrels' gallery of earlier times. Originally the walls were intended to be covered with arms and armour, great wheels of swords, criss-crosses of spears and muskets, and whole standing suits of armour on brackets between the upper arches matching Sir James Thornhill's military trophies between the windows of the lantern. The same consciously heavy fortress-architecture can be seen in Vanbrugh's later hall at Grimsthorpe in Lincolnshire, though the huge clerestory windows at Blenheim flooding the room with light give a less crushing effect: the liberation scene from *Fidelio* rather than the dungeon.

By contrast, the hall at Castle Howard is light, festive, Italian in inspiration, perhaps the first English interior of its kind to be conceived as a temple of the arts of peace, rather than war. Music is again a dominant theme: painted musicians lean over balconies, just as their real-life counterparts must have serenaded from the galleries and staircases. Apollo entertains the nine Muses with his lyre, while the Elements, the Continents, the Rivers and the Signs of the Zodiac present a whole cosmic order, presided over by the Sun – high in the gilded dome from which Phaethon and his horses tumble in disarray.

Much of the playfulness and lightness of touch is undoubtedly due to the Venetian artists Giovanni Pellegrini and Sebastiano Ricci recently brought back by an ambassador to Venice, the 1st Duke of Manchester, and the plasterers Bagutti and Plura who introduced a first taste of the Rococo here many years before it became the accepted style in England. It was indeed the foreign connotations of Baroque buildings like Castle Howard that led to the downfall of Baroque in England. While its exuberance and ostentation perfectly suited the absolute rule of a German elector or an Italian Grand Duke, it was viewed in this country with suspicion and identified increasingly with Tory and Jacobite patrons looking over the water to the exiled Pretender's court at Saint-Germain. Instead, Lord Burlington and his *protégés* Colen Campbell and William Kent discovered a purer source of Italian architecture in the designs and writings of the Renaissance architect Palladio, which were themselves

Opposite] More like a Baroque cathedral than a room in a private house, the hall at Castle Howard is all the more astonishing for being one of Vanbrugh's earliest works of architecture. Although the dome and cupola, the crowning glory of the house, were completed in 1706, the decoration of the hall took another five or six years. Despite the twin staircases and long corridors opening into it, Vanbrugh claimed to have experienced 'bitter stormy nights, in which not one candle wanted to be put in a lanthorn, not even in the Hall which is as high . . . as that at Blenheim'.

Opposite] The Stone Hall at Houghton in Norfolk, one of the supreme expressions of William Kent's Palladian style. Like Inigo Jones's hall in the Queen's House at Greenwich, built exactly a hundred years earlier, it is a perfect cube – 40 feet high and 40 feet square – with a balcony at first-floor level supported on brackets and linked to an adjoining staircase.

The keynote of Kent's decoration, completed in about 1730, was the series of classical Roman busts of emperors and senators placed on brackets round the room, and complemented by Rysbrack's carved stone bas-reliefs above the chimneypieces. Noble and masculine in its restraint, it provided a perfect transition from Campbell's exterior to the progressively more colourful and more luxurious rooms beyond. Only the tumbling putti playing amongst the garlands of the cove (*above*) strike a lighter note. Humorous touches such as these prevent Kent's work from ever becoming over-heavy or grandiloquent, while the skill of his Italian plasterer Giuseppe Artari matches the boldness and originality of the design.

based on the classical Roman treatises of Vitruvius. If the Palladians had the sanction of antiquity, they could also claim to represent a native style of English architecture, for had not Inigo Jones introduced the style to England a century earlier? Patriotism and politics thus entered the artistic arena and the Whig magnates, whose triumph came with the Hanoverian Succession, began to build themselves versions of Palladio's villas, hugely enlarged in size, and with the pavilions that had once been barns and cow-byres now turned into chapels, libraries or vast domestic offices.

Sir Robert Walpole, First Lord of the Treasury for over twenty years, personified this patriotic Whig attitude to architecture. At Houghton Hall in Norfolk, designed for him by Campbell and decorated by Kent, the Stone Hall is a greatly expanded version of Inigo Jones's hall at the Queen's House, Greenwich. A perfect cube, it also conforms to those rules of 'harmonic proportions' that Lord Burlington urged – serene and static compared with the movement and drama of Castle Howard. Much of the carving is by John Michael Rysbrack, the finest English sculptor of the day, and the plasterwork by Giuseppe Artari includes portraits of Sir Robert and his family in medallions in the cove. Houghton was primarily a hunting lodge where Walpole and his political allies spent weeks at a time enjoying the pleasures of the table and the chase, so the stags' and boars' heads, foxes' masks, hunting horns and powder flasks, entwined with vine leaves, are appropriate.

Isaac Ware in his *Complete Body of Architecture* of 1756 gives a good idea how such rooms were used in the eighteenth century. While he allows that town houses may have small vestibules, in the country the hall must be 'large and noble' since it 'serves as a summer-room for dining; it is an anti-chamber in which people of business, or of the second rank, wait and amuse themselves; and it is a good apartment for the reception of large companies at public feasts'. Mrs Delany, describing the hall at Dangan in Ireland in 1733, records it as being so large that 'very often breakfast, battledore and the shuttlecock and the harpsichord, go on at the same time without molesting one another'.

A notable feature of Palladian halls like Houghton is their restrained colouring. Stone and marble predominate, again making an easy transition from the exterior to the interior of the house. Warmth in such a room was not a prime consideration, though a blazing log fire in the chimneypiece would have kept those waiting to be received by the great man from freezing altogether. Sculpture was considered more fitting than pictures in such an architectural setting, although sets of large-scale sporting pictures by John Wootton are set in plasterwork frames in the entrance halls at Badminton, Althorp and Longleat.

The Marble Hall at Holkham in Norfolk, only a few miles away from Houghton, is still grander in conception – and still colder, for no fireplace was provided. Both Kent and his patron Lord Leicester (an amateur architect of considerable skill) played a part in the design of the room, which was based on Palladio's interpretation of a Temple of Justice described by Vitruvius. Unusually, the ascent to the *piano nobile* was contrived inside the hall itself and not by an exterior staircase and perron as at Houghton. The basilican plan, with the steps cascading out of the narthex (or apsed end), and the great peristyle of eighteen fluted alabaster columns round the gallery, copied from the Temple of Fortuna Virilis in Rome, makes this one of the noblest interiors in any English house.

Right] The Marble Hall at Holkham in Norfolk was originally designed by William Kent, but only completed in 1762, long after his death, by its owner Thomas Coke, Earl of Leicester, himself a skilled amateur architect. Its basilican plan is based on Palladio's interpretation of a Temple of Justice described by the Roman architect Vitruvius, the ceiling is taken from a design by Inigo Jones, and other features from Desgodetz's *Edifices Antiques de Rome*. Yet instead of being merely scholarly or archaeological in feeling, it is a unique and monumental work of art, as breathtaking today as it must have been to contemporaries.

Left] Vistas through fluted alabaster columns in the Marble Hall at Holkham. The peristyle of Ionic columns was derived from the Temple of Fortuna Virilis in Rome, and there could be no better source for a house which was itself intended to be a temple of the arts – an appropriate setting for the Greek and Roman sculpture and the Italian Old Master paintings acquired by Thomas Coke during his Grand Tour.

Overleaf] The Marble Hall at Kedleston in Derbyshire, conceived by Robert Adam as an ancient Roman atrium, top-lit so as to resemble an open colonnaded courtyard. The statuary figures of classical gods and goddesses, and painted bas-reliefs depicting scenes from Homer, replace the images of ancestors and the trophies of military and civil prowess which might have occupied a similar position in the villa of a first-century Roman senator. The magnificent alabaster columns were dug from the family's own quarries at Ratcliffe-on-Soar, and were only fluted *in situ* as an afterthought.

Already in the archaeological correctness of the hall at Holkham one can see the seeds of Neoclassicism emerging. But it was Robert Adam's years in Italy and his assiduous study of the latest discoveries made at Herculaneum, at Spalato and in Rome itself, that gave him a revolutionary new vocabulary of ornament with which to impress potential clients. Lord Scarsdale, the builder of Kedleston in Derbyshire, was among the first of these, and Adam's Marble Hall there dating from the late 1760s is among his finest creations. At first sight, it has much in common with that at Holkham: the fluted columns of Derbyshire alabaster from the family's own quarries at Ratcliffe-on-Soar, the coved ceiling, and the niches between the columns containing copies of the most famous statues of antiquity. But the delicacy of the ornament, brilliantly realized by the plasterer Joseph Rose the younger, is new and daring. The winged gryphons and anthemion in the frieze, the tripod perfume-burners, rosettes and paterae, chains of husks and thin acanthus tendrils, are taken from Etruscan wall-paintings and terracotta vases, but adapted with the greatest skill and taste.

Adam's strength was in his refusal to be too academic, and his love of movement in architecture as against the static 'rule-book' designs of many Palladian architects. At Kedleston, the way the columns march right into the far wall of the Marble Hall, leading the spectator through to the domed saloon beyond, can be compared with Lord Burlington's own Assembly Rooms at York where the colonnade continues all round, producing an effect of deadening weight. In other hands, the chimneypieces and overmantels would seem too feminine and pretty, crushed by the giant columns which frame them, but Adam makes such unexpected juxtapositions endlessly exciting by his sense of balance and scale.

Syon House in Middlesex, which he remodelled soon afterwards for the Duke of Northumberland, was used more as a summer Thames-side villa than a full-blown country house, and here Adam was free to indulge some of his most advanced ideas. As so often, forces of circumstance led to ingenious and satisfying solutions. The excessive length of the hall, for instance, was reduced by the recesses at either end, one a semicircular apse, the other square, with steps up to the ante room beyond a screen of Doric columns. The balanced irregularity is fascinating; in Adam's own words, 'the inequality of the levels has been managed in such a manner as to increase the scenery and add to the movement, so that an apparent defect has been converted into a real beauty'. The colours are kept deliberately cool so as to contrast with the richness of what is to come, but the black and white marble floor significantly echoes the pattern of the ceiling, their bold diagonals helping to achieve the change of axis necessary for the visitor entering the front door on the long wall.

Military trophies play a small part in the decoration of the hall at Syon, but in the ante room beyond, intended as a second hall for those of higher rank to wait in, they are the dominant motif, as they are in Adam's hall at Osterley nearby. The ante room is an astonishing contrast to the hall: a lavish re-creation of the guard-chamber of an Imperial Roman palace decorated with a riot of colour and gilding. The keynote is given by the twelve columns of *verde antico*, brought back from Rome by the Duke of Northumberland and supposedly found on the bed of the river Tiber. These are given solid gilt Ionic capitals and a honeysuckle frieze above, breaking out over the columns in a Baroque rather than a characteristically Neoclassical fashion, and surmounted by gilded statues after the antique.

The scagliola floor, again echoing the compartments of the ceiling, is in the richest colours: yellow, red, blue, chocolate and greenish grey.

So elegant are the panels of plaster shields and helmets, quivers of arrows and bundles of *fasces*, that it is hard to recognize in them the descendants of the medieval great hall hung with real weapons. Yet only a few miles away, at Strawberry Hill, Horace Walpole was already busy decking his 'Gothick' rooms with ancient and not-so-ancient arms and armour, in an effort to re-create a 'mansion of the olden time'. On a grander scale, William Beckford's Fonthill Abbey in Wiltshire, begun in 1796, was swift to follow, and the nineteenth century brought with it a consuming nostalgia for the past, from Thomas Hopper's neo-Norman style at Penrhyn Castle in North Wales to the mock-Elizabethan of Thomas Willement's Charlecote Park in Warwickshire. But the great age of private country-house building was over, and the real heirs of the tradition were the Gothic Revival town halls of William Burges, E. W. Godwin and Sir Gilbert Scott. Here, again, the hall became both a symbol and setting of the life of the community, though peopled with mayors and burgesses rather than knights and squires: a prosaic development maybe, but conceived, like so many aspects of English art and architecture, as part of a deeply romantic attitude to life.

Right] The entrance hall at Syon House, Middlesex, designed by Robert Adam in 1762, with Luigi Valadier's bronze version of the *Dying Gaul*, purchased in Rome in 1773, in the foreground. Adam took advantage of the long, thin proportions of this room (probably the site of the refectory in the old medieval convent) to provide recesses at either end: one semicircular containing a life-size cast of the *Apollo Belvedere*; the other rectangular but containing curving flights of stairs flanking the *Dying Gaul* and leading up to the main apartments. These and the diagonal patterns of floor and ceiling create a strong sense of movement and drama that is typical of Adam's empirical approach.

Left] 'Classic form, romantic overtones, exquisite ornament' – all these characterize Adam's remarkable synthesis of grandeur and simplicity in the hall at Syon. Restrained colouring – blacks, whites and pale shades of stone – form a transition from exterior to interior and contrast with the richness to come, while Joseph Rose's delicate plasterwork evokes the refinement of imperial Roman architecture.

3 Staircases

The simplicity of sixteenth-century staircases, built of wood or stone according to regional practice: that at Little Moreton Hall in Cheshire (*above*), dating from the 1570s, is made of great wedges of solid oak let into a central newel post, while that at Haddon in Derbyshire (*opposite*) is of stone, worn away by the feet of generations of Vernons and Manners and their retainers. The dog-gate, with its primitive self-closing mechanism, is Jacobean.

No room has greater dramatic possibilities than the staircase. If the great hall of a country house is like the first act of a play, announcing with appropriate fanfares the themes of dynastic pride, of culture based on wealth and position, the staircase (which so often follows it) is a second act in which the plot thickens. Tension and expectations mount with our footsteps, for who knows what splendours lie ahead, what changes of axis, what vistas through landings and galleries? Few architects have been able to resist its challenge to represent movement and excitement in purely visual terms.

Yet the earliest staircases, built by master masons and carpenters before the Renaissance, give remarkably little indication of what was to follow. The narrow spiral stair, whether built of stone, brick, or wood as at Little Moreton Hall in Cheshire, was the usual means by which the family ascended from the dais end of the great hall to their solar or great chamber on the first floor. That at Oxburgh in Norfolk dating from 1482 is a marvel of the bricklayer's art with its central core of smoothly rubbed Tudor brick and fine white mortar, the steps worn away by generations of feet. Such a staircase was practical in terms of construction: indeed the great triangular wedges of oak or of stone with their inner angles piled on top of each other were virtually self-supporting. But it was also a hangover from the narrow turret-stair of the medieval castle, built for reasons of defence. Only one person at a time could mount to the first floor, where he and a whole company of assailants could be easily repulsed by a single armed guard. Even today it is a strange feeling to dine in state at the high table of an Oxford or Cambridge college hall, and then, with portly dons in flowing robes, to squeeze up a little lime-washed spiral staircase leading from the dais to the senior common room (a latter-day solar) for dessert.

As the family started to withdraw more from the communal life of the great hall, and as the great chamber increased in importance, so the staircase became broader and grander. In the relative peace brought by the Tudors, defence was no longer the prime consideration and arrow-slits could be replaced by glazed mullion-and-transom windows. At Haddon in Derbyshire a cascade of wide stone steps flows down into the great hall from the first floor, turning at inconsequential angles like a river finding its own course – apparently more the result of evolution than of planning. The nearest equivalent appears to be the 'night stairs' in the transepts of many abbey churches and minsters in the north of England by which the monks in procession arrived at their early offices direct from the first-floor dorter. At the bottom of the Haddon staircase a dog-gate, closed by a weight and pulley mechanism, kept the hounds and mastiffs, fed on bones and scraps thrown down from the long tables, from joining politer and more civilized company above.

Robert Smythson's main staircase at Hardwick has a far greater upward impulse. Beginning in a comparatively low dark space on the ground floor it becomes progressively higher, lighter and straighter until, with a sudden 180-degree turn, it reaches the door of the

High Great Chamber on the second floor. Nothing could have provided a more impressive ceremonial approach either for Bess of Hardwick's more distinguished guests or for the formal processions accompanying the food which wound their way up from the great kitchen, preceded by beadles, clerks, servants and pages.

From an early date tapestries hung on the walls of the staircase at Hardwick, ruthlessly cut to fit the irregular shapes of the walls where necessary – an extravagance that few other houses could afford. Above the door to Bess of Hardwick's private apartments, on the first-floor landing, the plasterer Abraham Smith provided the fearsome helmeted head and torso of a moustachioed warrior flanked by grenades – perhaps based on an engraving by Marten de Vos – for this was where a sentry would have stood during the days and slept at night, on a straw pallet described in the inventory taken after Bess's death in 1601. Nor was security forgotten on the second floor where the entrance to the great rooms of state is guarded by a carved oak door with an elaborate metal lock of a Late Gothic type, perhaps acquired from some dissolved monastery.

Smythson's extraordinarily precocious use of 'picturesque' principles in architecture found few imitators among his contemporaries. The tunnel-vaulted flights of the Roman staircase at Burghley, built in 1563 by a Flemish stonemason named Hendrik for Queen Elizabeth's faithful Secretary William Cecil, would not have disgraced an Italian Renaissance palace and are equally revolutionary in their way. But on the whole the staircase was to become the special province of the joiner rather than the stonemason in England, unlike in other countries. At Hatfield, built by Cecil's son Robert, 1st Earl of Salisbury, his architect Robert Lyminge designed the staircase round three sides of an ample square (the same width as the great hall) with a landing on the fourth side. This arrangement was to become standard practice in the early seventeenth century, as were his arcaded or strapwork balustrades and tall newel posts crowned by heraldic beasts and figures – as at Blickling.

Such newel posts had a practical origin, for they once continued up the whole height of the staircase at the angles, providing a structural 'cage' to hold the heavy oak treads in place. A stair of this form can still be seen at Robert Cecil's earlier and simpler hunting lodge at Cranborne in Dorset. But the growing ability to cantilever treads out from the walls made it possible to dispense first with the upper parts, and then with the lower too. Henceforward they became purely decorative, carved as often as not with the crest or supporters of the family arms, continuing the display of heraldry first encountered in the great hall. As late as the 1760s, Horace Walpole described a new staircase at Boughton, built in the Chinese Chippendale style, as 'the descent of the Montagus' because of the arms emblazoned on the end of every tread. The newel posts on the staircase at Knole, dating from 1605–8, are carved with sleek spotted leopards holding shields with the Sackville arms, and these have stone counterparts crowning the gables of the Stone Court outside.

But the great importance of the Knole staircase is that it has preserved its original scheme of painted decoration by Paul Isaacson, Master of the Painter Stainers Company, and probably the same Paul 'Jackson' who painted the hall screen at Greenwich for Queen Elizabeth I in 1594. Here one can sense something of the appearance of Elizabeth's and James I's vanished palaces of Nonsuch, Oatlands and Theobalds. The marbling and graining

Opposite] Shafts of sunlight stream down from great mullion windows in the south tower to light the upper reaches of the staircase at Hardwick Hall, completed in 1597. Robert Smythson, Bess of Hardwick's architect, was one of the first to exploit the full dramatic possibilities of the stair as a processional route: long gentle flights suddenly turn steeply back on themselves to reveal new vistas, light succeeds dark, and high open landings follow low-ceilinged passages. Mounting the last few steps to the door of the High Great Chamber we can feel something of the same sense of awe and exhilaration that must have struck Bess's contemporaries.

is crude but wonderfully boisterous, and there are *grisaille* scenes of the six Virtues, based on Flemish woodcuts, that look forward to the later allegories of the Baroque. But the most charming detail is the *trompe-l'œil* balustrade on the outer walls complete with newel posts and leopards, which gives an illusion both of symmetry and of larger scale to the ascent.

Both wood-carving and plasterwork reached new heights in England after the Restoration, encouraged not only by the availability of French and Dutch pattern-books, and the arrival of foreign craftsmen like Grinling Gibbons, but also by the feverish haste to rebuild London after the Great Fire in 1666. At Sudbury in Derbyshire, the plasterers Robert Bradbury and James Pettifer and the wood-carver Edward Pierce had all previously worked on Wren's City churches. Their efforts combined to make the staircase here one of the most splendid in any Carolean house: the sumptuous wreaths of fruit and flowers in the ceiling, surrounding Antonio Verrio's painting, are matched by the swirling acanthus pattern of the carved balustrade – which can also be found in communion rails of the same period. Pierce's inspiration may have been the designs of Jean Le Pautre, pirated by a London printer Robert Pricke for his *Architect's Store-House* of 1674, while Bradbury and Pettifer would have known the famous engravings of Van Campen's Town Hall at Amsterdam, with their details of the Quellin brothers' naturalistic carving.

There have been arguments as to the decorative treatment of carved woodwork in the seventeenth century. Some of Grinling Gibbons's finest limewood carvings were obviously never intended to be painted, but he and his contemporaries more often worked in softwoods, leaving the knots and joins to show, and knowing that these would later be disguised by some form of paintwork. The staircase balustrade at Ham House in Surrey, similar to that at Sudbury though slightly earlier, and with rectangular panels of military trophies instead of acanthus, was originally grained and partly gilded. Others may have been painted white so as to match the plasterwork decoration of ceiling, cornice and walls – almost invariably limewashed at this date. One interesting detail at Sudbury is that the carved baskets of flowers on the newel posts are removable and can be replaced by lamps at night. Lanterns on staves could, at an earlier date, have been held by the heraldic beasts at Hatfield and Knole.

Joiners' and carvers' staircases became increasingly more elaborate towards the end of the century, often using walnut instead of oak, as at Drayton House in Northamptonshire, where the cantilevered spiral is an extraordinary feat of engineering. Elegant turned balusters, often of three different patterns to each tread, a hand-rail with marquetry 'stringing', and half-landings of so-called '*parquet de Versailles*', can be found in Baroque houses by provincial architects like William Thornton of York, the Bastards of Blandford or the Smiths of Warwick. At Beningbrough Hall in Yorkshire, Thornton even incorporates the monogram of his patrons John and Mary Bourchier and the date 1716 in marquetry on the landings, and introduces curious panels of carving apparently imitating wrought-ironwork at intervals in the balustrade.

Wrought-iron balustrades had themselves become fashionable in the greater houses (where stone staircases were again the order of the day) largely through the genius of the French blacksmith Jean Tijou and his work for William III at Hampton Court. But native

Opposite] The great staircase at Knole in Kent, of 1605–8, is one of the first in England to be conceived as a room in its own right, worthy of an ambitious architectural scheme and not merely a means of passing from one floor to another by the most convenient route. The painted decoration by Paul Isaacson includes a *trompe-l'œil* version of the balustrade on the outer walls, complete with the Sackville leopards carved on the newel posts (*below*), the supporters of the 1st Earl of Dorset's coat-of-arms.

smiths such as John Gardom and Robert Bakewell in Derbyshire, and the Davies brothers in Wrexham, were soon able to emulate his *repoussé* scrolls and 'cloths-of-estate'. Bills and accounts tell us that such ironwork was often painted blue, dark green or chocolate brown, with gilt enrichments.

The King's Staircase at Hampton Court was influential not only because of Tijou's ironwork, but because of Verrio's ceiling and wall-paintings depicting William III in his favourite guise as Hercules – the first great Baroque scheme of painted decoration in England. Not to be outdone, the Whig patricians who had brought him to the throne were soon celebrating their own virtues and family history in terms of mythology. Laguerre's Grand Staircase at Petworth is largely concerned with the story of Prometheus' punishment for stealing the secret of fire from the gods – an appropriate subject since this part of the house had been badly damaged by fire in 1714. But it also shows the Duchess of Somerset as Juno riding in her chariot attended by her ladies, saved from total pomposity by her very English-looking spaniel. High up in the ceiling, an assembly of the gods, apparently omitting none of the known inhabitants of Mount Olympus, made a suitable approach to the 'Proud Duke's' own apartments on the first floor.

Ralph Montagu's staircase at Boughton is much more pure and academic, with Chéron's feigned stone bas-reliefs on a high base that is 'channelled' in the French manner. The heavy iron balustrade is also simple, with only its little twisted tails giving some sense of movement. The reason for this highly architectural treatment may be that, with its external door leading into the north arcade, it was on occasion used as a hall. But Hawksmoor's superb staircase at Easton Neston in Northamptonshire also has *grisaille* decoration by Thornhill, its restraint more effective than the high colouring and slightly absurd gesticulations of the 'sprawling saints of Verrio and Laguerre', as Pope described them.

William Talman's stairs at Chatsworth, spilling out into the Painted Hall, and Vanbrugh's pairs of staircases at Blenheim and Castle Howard, flanking his entrance halls and providing extraordinary vistas and effects of space and light, are truly Baroque in a European sense and may ultimately derive from Hugh May's famous staircase at Windsor built for Charles II, sadly destroyed in the early nineteenth century. But they were to have few successors. The triumph of the Palladians after the accession of George I meant that most English country houses, like the Italian villas and *palazzi* which they sought to imitate, were built with a *piano nobile* (literally 'noble floor') on which all the main rooms were situated, including the state bedchamber. These rooms provided the 'circuit' that was necessary both for visiting gentry to view the house, and for the country balls and entertainments which were so much a part of eighteenth-century life. An elaborately decorated staircase was not only unnecessary in these circumstances, it might also have aroused expectations of the smaller rooms on the first floor which could in no way be fulfilled. Thus the staircases at Chiswick and at Mereworth in Kent are reduced to tiny spirals leading off the central rotunda. The only staircase of importance at Holkham is that in the hall – in concept an exterior stair that would (in kinder climates than the raw East Anglian coast) have swept up to a portico or perron, like that at Kedleston. Nor is it a surprise that at Kedleston itself the main internal staircase was never finished or decorated.

Carvers and joiners in the Restoration period achieved new heights of technical skill, particularly influenced by Dutch and Flemish immigrants like Grinling Gibbons. The cantilevered flights of the great staircase at Sudbury Hall in Derbyshire (*opposite*) date from 1675, and the carver Edward Pierce, who worked on many of Wren's London churches, charged £112.15s.5d. for the balustrade (*above*) of luxuriant scrolling acanthus, made of pine and apparently always intended to be painted. The equally rich plasterwork by Robert Bradbury and James Pettifer now frames decorative paintings by Louis Laguerre added about 1691.

Triumphs of the Baroque: assemblies of
the gods on the staircase ceilings at
Petworth by Louis Laguerre (*left*), and
Boughton by Louis Chéron (*right*)
beckon mere mortals to ascend and gain
the heights of Parnassus. Both artists
probably came to England at the
invitation of Ralph, Duke of Montagu,
several times ambassador to Louis XIV
and the owner of Boughton. But while
Chéron followed the more strictly
classical and academic style of Le Brun,
Laguerre's work is in a bolder, more
illusionistic vein – a whirlpool of
fluttering draperies and limbs, billowing
clouds and fitful sunbursts.

Naturally, the number of old houses whose main rooms still lay on the upper floors (as at Chatsworth), and the sheer strength of native tradition, meant that there were a number of notable exceptions to this rule. As already suggested, rain, cold and wind made Palladio's open porticoes and loggias less than welcoming for visitors in a typical English winter, and the usual means of entry to such a house was therefore by a central sub-hall in the rusticated basement, as is still the case at Houghton. Here, that arch-Palladian architect Colen Campbell provided two large skylit staircases flanking the main axis and rising the full height of the house. One of these, sparsely decorated, was intended for the servants, but the other was elaborately decked out by William Kent who strengthened the impression of an internal courtyard by the sash windows which look into it from adjoining corridors, and by the *tempietto* at ground-floor level, supporting a huge bronze cast of the Borghese Gladiator – one of the antique statues most admired by English visitors to Rome. Kent's painted decoration, in stone colours with some gilding, is studiously two-dimensional in effect, avoiding the false perspectives of the Baroque scene painters, while the heavy balustrade and pedimented doorcases (still highly architectural) are in solid mahogany, now for the first time being imported in large quantities from the West Indies.

Nostell Priory in Yorkshire, whose plan may also derive from a design by Colen Campbell, has the same pair of skylit staircases flanking the central axis. But the difference is that both are highly ornamented, with Rococo plasterwork by Joseph Rose and Thomas Perritt, probably designed by the executant architect James Paine. An early visitor, Dr Pococke, describes these as 'two grand staircases, one leading to the apartments in the attick story for the family, the other for strangers' – referring to the rooms on the second floor (above the *piano nobile*) which they approached. The family staircase is appropriately decorated with medallion portraits of Sir Rowland and Lady Winn and their offspring over the doors on the top landing, and fanciful portrait heads of Henry VIII and Queen Elizabeth (from whom the Winns originally gained their monastic lands and wealth) incorporated in the ceiling of the skylight.

Plasterwork trophies were particularly appropriate decorations for staircases where the squares and rectangles of picture frames hardly assorted well with the sharp diagonals of balustrades and their answering dado rails. Some of the achievements of the Italian *stuccadores* working in England – Bagutti and Artari on the staircase at Wimpole Hall in Cambridgeshire, or Giuseppe Cortese at Lytham Hall in Lancashire – are among the most graceful and festive of country-house experiences. But even the madness of a local plasterer far away from metropolitan fashion, like John Jenkins of Exeter who crowded the staircase walls at Powderham Castle with everything from rabbits' heads to cupids' bows, have a bucolic charm that is suitable for a room of passage, even if it might be difficult to live with.

Another wonderfully eccentric character, the carver Luke Lightfoot, made a staircase for Earl Verney at Claydon House in Buckinghamshire that is a marvel of the inlayer's art, using walnut and oak, mahogany, yew, boxwood, ebony and even mother-of-pearl in patterns on every tread. Really a throwback to the Baroque, despite Joseph Rose's chaste Neoclassical plasterwork on the walls, the Claydon staircase also has a scrolling wrought-iron balustrade of singular beauty, whose ears of corn tremble in anticipation at the lightest footfall. One of

Opposite] William Kent's staircase at Houghton Hall in Norfolk, dating from the 1730s, looks back a hundred years to the simple Palladian classicism of Inigo Jones. Massive mahogany balusters support a wide ramped handrail, still with its original glass lanterns, while Kent's *chiaroscuro* decorations, the sash windows looking into it from the upper landings, and Le Sueur's bronze gladiator in the centre (*above*), give the staircase the feeling of an open courtyard in a richly-appointed Renaissance *palazzo*.

The staircase at The Vyne in Hampshire, designed in 1770 by its owner John Chute, an amateur architect and friend of Horace Walpole. A triumph of art over circumstance, it fills a long narrow space, 44 by only 18 feet, yet has all the mystery and drama of an Italian Baroque stage set. The engraved designs of the Bibiena family may indeed have influenced Chute, different as they are from the Palladian prototypes still popular among most of his contemporaries.

the most interesting staircases in any English house, that at The Vyne in Hampshire, is just as backward-looking but at the same time infinitely more refined and cultivated. This is the more remarkable because it was designed and built for himself by a squire of moderate means, John Chute, who as a friend of Horace Walpole and a member of the 'Committee of Taste' which advised him on the decoration of Strawberry Hill, was more used to producing Gothick decoration of a particularly flimsy variety. But Chute took his cue from John Webb's portico at The Vyne, built in the 1650s and the earliest of its kind in England. He had been an assiduous Grand Tourist and his classical staircase inserted behind this portico, at the very centre of the old house, is based on an intimate knowledge of the work of the Bibiena family – perhaps the most famous of Italian Baroque stage designers. An order of giant Corinthain columns (in reality quite small) marches round the upper landing, giving an impression of grand scale, while the temporary concealment of the upper flights gives a feeling of mystery and drama that is rarely found in the static designs of more conventional Palladians.

The rhythm of carved and turned balusters on staircases at The Vyne (*left*) and Uppark (*right*). The skill of eighteenth-century carvers is shown in the infinite variety of patterns carried out in every kind of soft and hard wood. According to Richard Neve's *City and Country Purchaser*, published in 1726, such balustrades should cost no more than threepence a yard.

The staircase and hall at West Wycombe Park, Buckinghamshire, designed by John Donowell about 1754–5. The sense of theatre, achieved by removing the walls between the two rooms and replacing them by screens of columns, must have appealed to the owner of the house, the eccentric Sir Francis Dashwood, who enjoyed dressing up as his namesake St Francis of Assisi, or performing as the high priest of Bacchus attended by nymphs, fauns and satyrs. The stairs themselves are remarkable in being made of mahogany, inlaid with satinwood and ebony, and are perhaps by a cabinet maker who turned to architectural decoration on finding that marquetry furniture was no longer fashionable.

The essential asymmetry of the staircase had always been a thorn in the flesh of English architects since Roger Pratt's brave attempt to combine it with a centralized hall at Coleshill in Berkshire in the 1670s. In the late eighteenth century several attempts were made to revive this idea using the French form of an 'imperial' staircase with a central first flight, returning in two balancing flights to left and right. At Blickling the Earl of Buckinghamshire, newly returned from his embassy to Catherine the Great (for which his good looks were said to have fully equipped him), appropriately remodelled Robert Lyminge's original Jacobean staircase '*à l'impériale*', moving the latter's balustrades and carved newel posts to the hall on the central axis. Like other conservative landowners of the period, he commissioned a firm of local architects (the Ivorys of Norwich) to produce neo-Jacobean cornices and dados – not to mention carved wooden bas-reliefs of Queen Elizabeth and her mother Anne Boleyn, who was reported to have been born at Blickling – to fill the niches above the landings.

The horseshoe staircase at Attingham Park in Shropshire, designed by the Prince Regent's architect John Nash, is a more sophisticated answer to the same problem. Added in an apsed projection beyond the existing entrance hall and picture gallery, it achieves an effect of great elegance in the minimum space, perhaps owing something to contemporary French designers such as Percier and Fontaine. The fluted walls give the impression of being inside a giant column, while another tongue in cheek note, typical of Nash, is struck by the almost invisible 'jib-doors' on the upper landing, that might fool the unwary guest looking for his bedroom into thinking he had come on a fruitless mission.

With the eclecticism of the early nineteenth century it is less easy to generalize about staircases, and it would be invidious to make a choice between the neo-Norman of Thomas Hopper's Penrhyn in North Wales, the austere Greek Revival of Sir Charles Monck's Belsay in Northumberland, the South German Baroque of William Burn's Harlaxton in Lincolnshire or the extraordinary Gothick fantasy of William Burges's Cardiff Castle. It is time to struggle up the last few steps and grasp the handle of the door that awaits us on the upper landing – our adventure has only just begun.

Opposite] The circular staircase at Attingham Park in Shropshire, designed by the Prince Regent's favourite architect John Nash in 1805 and with curving 'horseshoe' flights influenced by contemporary French architects such as Percier and Fontaine. Entered from a long rectangular picture gallery and decorated in the same Pompeian red, its walls are fluted, giving the feeling of being inside a giant Corinthian column.

THE LIBRARY
COLLEGE OF FURTHER EDUCATION
NORTHAMPTON

4 Great Chambers and Saloons

Opposite] Evening sunlight in the High Great Chamber at Hardwick. The great painted frieze is the masterpiece of Bess of Hardwick's plasterer, Abraham Smith. Appropriately for a hunting lodge, it depicts Diana and her maidens, larger than life, frozen in their pursuit of stag and boar among the tall trees of an enchanted forest, while Venus chastising Cupid (*above*) represents Spring, after an engraving by Marten de Vos.

There is no mistaking a hall or a staircase, a library or a bedchamber: their functions are immediately apparent even if they have subtly changed over the centuries. But what of the medieval solar, that became the great chamber of the Elizabethan house, was transformed into a saloon in the Baroque and Palladian periods and ended up as a picture gallery in the early nineteenth century? Can such a room be said to have a coherent history?

As will already have become clear, the development of the country house is largely concerned with the retreat of the family as private rooms became steadily more public, and comfort and seclusion became increasingly prized. The move out of the great hall to the solar was largely accomplished by the opening of the Tudor period, and from here it was a short step to the withdrawing room, the bedchamber and beyond that the dressing room, cabinet or closet. Thus the great chamber had already assumed a semi-public role by the reign of Elizabeth I and, despite changes of name, it was to remain a room with certain definite characteristics: highly architectural in treatment, a magnificent setting for great gatherings rather than for everyday life, and essentially masculine in feeling, as opposed to the feminine attributes of the withdrawing room beyond. The German word *prunksaal* or show-room perhaps describes it best.

Large-scale works of art adorned its walls, first tapestries, then family portraits (a logical continuation of the heraldry in the hall and staircase), then Old Masters bought on the Grand Tour. A set of seat furniture, again monumental in scale, might stand with tables round the walls, and increasingly these would be designed by architects rather than cabinet-makers or upholsterers. The only major change of use came in the early eighteenth century when separate dining rooms came into fashion, and the family would only eat on high days and holidays in the saloon. But this made little difference to the furnishing of the room since tables, chairs and other paraphernalia would invariably have been brought in and set up by servants on such occasions.

There is perhaps no room that gives so vivid a picture of sixteenth-century country-house life as the High Great Chamber at Hardwick. Already more a public than a private room (for Bess of Hardwick had her own Low Great Chamber on the floor below), it is an apartment built on a huge scale, whose human inhabitants are made to feel still more dwarfed by the giant divinities of the plasterwork frieze, above the set of Brussels tapestries of the story of Ulysses which probably dictated the dimensions of the room. Hardwick was built primarily as a hunting lodge, and from the roof, with its banqueting houses in each tower, one could watch the parties of horsemen, hounds, falconers and archers moving off down the long straight forest rides radiating from the house. So the High Great Chamber frieze shows Diana and her nymphs embarking on the chase through the leafy trunks and branches of an enchanted forest.

But this was also a room where spectacular feasts would be prepared for distinguished

visitors, and so the Seasons are also present distributing their bounty: Ceres representing Summer pouring out her cornucopia, and Flora as Spring bidding flowers and plants to grow, flank the bay window. In the bay itself stands (as it has since Bess's day) the famous eglantine table, whose marquetry top is inlaid with boards for various games of cards and dice, the Hardwick arms supported by stags, and the mysterious but beautiful couplet:

The redolent smelle of eglantyne
We stagges exalte to the divine.

A canopy may have been erected at the far end of the room, opposite the door from the staircase, when Bess received or dined in state, and one was certainly here in the time of her son and daughter-in-law, the 1st Earl and Countess of Devonshire, who also introduced the velvet-covered farthingale chairs embroidered with flowers, emblems and devices to match it. The colours of needlework, tapestry, plasterwork and rush-matting are now faded and infinitely romantic, but the original effect must have been startlingly colourful.

A state of something like armed neutrality existed between Bess of Hardwick and Elizabeth I who was rightly suspicious of the former's ambitions for her granddaughter and ward, Arabella Stuart, a possible claimant to the throne. It might therefore seem surprising to find the Queen's arms carved in marble over the great chimneypiece, with the Tudor dragon replacing the more familiar unicorn. But the royal arms appear in a similar position in great chambers all over the country, from the palaces of leading courtiers to the remote manors of obscure squires, until at least the mid-seventeenth century – symbolizing the landowner's position as the sovereign's representative, whether as justice of the peace, sheriff or lord lieutenant of his county. Here justice was administered in the king's name, rents and taxes gathered, and writs for service in the local militia issued.

As at Hardwick, the frieze is the dominant feature of the great chamber at Knole (rechristened the ballroom in the nineteenth century): writhing sea-monsters, chimeras and other weird creatures are represented, but this time in carved wood rather than plaster, while elaborate panelling replaces the earlier tapestries. The marble chimneypiece and overmantel are of a very different order, however. The work of Cornelius Cuer (presumably a Fleming by origin), who carved the tomb of Mary Queen of Scots in Westminster Abbey, they show not only a remarkable technical assurance, especially in the delicate *sgraffito* carving of the local Sussex marble, but also an awareness of the latest French fashions. The trophy of arms guarded by sphinxes seems to derive from Jacques du Cerceau, while other features look further back to the craftsmen of the School of Fontainebleau.

The elaborate pattern of the panelling at Knole suggests that the room may not originally have been hung with pictures, though the full-length family portraits by Larkin, Peake, Van Dyck and Dobson must have arrived early on in its history. They were to become a standard ingredient of the great chamber in the seventeenth century. When there were not enough to go round, as at Drayton in Northamptonshire, the owner Lord Peterborough did not hesitate to have wholly imaginary likenesses of his Mordaunt ancestors painted wearing armour or peers' robes of a primitive type which it was hoped would pass for medieval.

With the Double Cube Room at Wilton we reach not only one of the most celebrated of

Opposite] The Double Cube Room at Wilton, attributed to Inigo Jones and John Webb. Completed about 1653, it is among the first English interiors to be based on Palladio's 'harmonic proportions', with a deep cove – or *volta a conca* – filled with decorative painting by Edward Pierce, and a ceiling by Emanuel de Critz, strongly influenced by Rubens. This sumptuous Italianate *salone*, reflecting the cultivated court circles of Charles I, must have seemed revolutionary at a time when the backwoods squires of Wiltshire were still panelling their great chambers with old-fashioned wainscot. Van Dyck's haunting portraits of the Herberts, including the huge family group on the end wall – the largest picture he ever painted – were brought down to Wilton from London after the Restoration, though they look as if they must always have belonged here.

all English interiors, but also an architectural turning-point – even if its importance was not to be fully realized for the best part of a century. There has been controversy over Inigo Jones's exact role at Wilton and that of the architect Isaac de Caux who also laid the Earl of Pembroke's extraordinary Italianate garden. But there can be no real doubt that the idea of a grand *salone* following Palladio's own rules of 'harmonic proportion' – 60 feet long by 30 feet wide by 30 feet high – must have originated with Jones. Pembroke's close friendship with Charles I, cemented by their common interest in art-collecting, enabled him to use almost exclusively artists and craftsmen employed on the royal palaces, not least the court-painter Van Dyck who was specially commissioned to produce a series of full-length portraits for the room, and the gigantic family group (his largest ever canvas) which fills the west wall. If there was ever a moment that the great chamber emerged from its chrysalis, reborn as the saloon, it was under the sad, proud gaze of these Van Dyck cavaliers and their ladies, so few of them to survive the Civil War and Commonwealth.

Few country-house builders after the Restoration could emulate the princely scale of the Double Cube, the sumptuous effect of its ceiling-paintings by Emanuel de Critz, or the great pedimented doorcases surmounted by life-size reclining putti. But the idea of the coved ceiling, hardly known in England before Jones, the chimneypiece with an overmantel painting in a tabernacle frame (more French than Italian in origin, and now thought to have been based on the engravings of Jean Barbet), and finally the carved festoons of drapery, fruit and flowers which enrich the panelling – all these were to find their way into the country houses of Hugh May, William Winde and Sir Roger Pratt after 1660. It is also in the architectural writings of Pratt that the new name of the 'saloon' can be seen to have gained common currency.

The saloon could still be relatively small, like that at Sudbury dating from the 1670s. But it was now a strictly symmetrical set-piece with the pantheon of Vernon family portraits (many of them by John Michael Wright) contained within a whole series of tabernacles, echoing the overmantel. Each of these is like a miniature reredos in a City church, and it is significant that the carver Edward Pierce not only worked regularly for Wren but was the son and namesake of the carver employed on the Double Cube Room at Wilton.

By the end of the seventeenth century it was generally accepted that the saloon should be larger and higher than the rooms that succeeded it, and often as large as the hall itself – the two rooms (as at Robert Hooke's Ragley) being placed on the main axis of a so-called 'double-pile' house, with apartments in the French sense, each consisting of withdrawing room, bedchamber, dressing room and closet, projecting at the four corners of the house. Mark Girouard has called this central axis of hall and saloon the 'state centre', which is a useful definition though it would have meant little to an architect or patron of the time.

Even Vanbrugh's Blenheim, which breaks so many rules in its quest for drama and movement, conforms to this basic layout, with the saloon in the centre of the garden front on axis with the hall. Pope's celebrated quip on being shown the house – '. . . 'tis very fine, but where d'ye sleep and where d'ye dine?' – has real point, for, just like the High Great Chamber at Hardwick over a century earlier, this Brobdingnagian interior was intended to be the main eating room on state occasions, and still is. East-facing, over 30 feet high, and

Opposite] The First State Room or great chamber at Boughton in Northamptonshire, hardly changed since William III's visit to the house in 1693. The arrangement of furniture round the edge of the room and the sombre green colour of the walls, described in contemporary documents as 'drab', with the mouldings of the deep cornice painted in *trompe l'œil*, are typical of formal Baroque interiors. The tapestry cartoon of the *Holy Family* after Raphael came to the house by virtue of the 1st Duke of Montagu's position as William III's Master of the Wardrobe and director of the Mortlake tapestry works.

without a fireplace in the interests of symmetry, one can hardly imagine a less inviting room in which to enjoy a meal, that must have been brought nearly a quarter of a mile from the kitchen wing. Laguerre's life-size spectators leaning over balconies round the walls hardly help to induce a feeling of intimacy. Perhaps in caricature of Louis XIV's Escalier des Ambassadeurs at Versailles, they include a positively Hogarthian chaplain and other members of the Duke's household whose appearance is more amusing than decorative.

Blenheim and Castle Howard, whose first-floor saloon was sadly destroyed by fire earlier in this century, underline the novelty of a great Palladian house like Houghton, begun in 1723 before either of them was completed. Sir Robert Walpole no longer needed his saloon to dine in, as a separate room for that purpose had been introduced by William Kent on the *piano nobile* – a grander version of the parlour or everyday dining room provided on the ground floor. Instead of panelling and horsehair-covered chairs, usually chosen because they would not retain the smell of food, he was therefore free to have the marvellous wall-hangings of crimson Utrecht velvet, which still miraculously survive, and seat furniture (again designed by Kent) upholstered in the same material.

The cut velvet was chosen particularly as a background for some of the larger Italian pictures from Walpole's collection, eventually to be sold *en bloc* to Catherine the Great of Russia. Even if the major masterpieces were only later brought down to Houghton from his London house, this idea of the saloon at Houghton primarily as a picture gallery was to be of immense importance for the future. But in his magnificent decoration, Kent also strove to give it the character of a truly Italian *salone*, based on his intimate knowledge of the palaces and villas of Rome and on his admiration for Palladio and Inigo Jones. There are conscious references to the Double Cube Room at Wilton in the pedimented doorcases with their pairs of putti, themselves reflected by the gilt frames of the pier tables, each with a putto riding on a giant shell.

The coffered ceiling gives an impression of great altitude, without having to hang the pictures so high they cannot be 'read', and the tremendous scale of the cornice, probably based on a fragment illustrated in Desgodetz's *Edifices Antiques de Rome*, binds the various elements together in a masterly way. The chairs and settees would of course have been disposed symmetrically round the walls, and their carved decoration incorporates lion-heads taken from the cornice, and shells from the pier glasses and tables. The first large Vauxhall mirror plates were being introduced in England at this date, and Kent used them to great effect between the windows, where pictures would have been invisible by day and where they reflected candlelight into the room by night.

Kent was also concerned with the decoration of Holkham, only a few miles away, although here Lord Leicester himself and the builder Matthew Brettingham the elder also played an important part. Mounting the marble staircase of the hall and pausing at the entrance to the saloon, the grandeur of their conception becomes apparent: through the columns of the portico beyond the great obelisk can be seen, over a mile away at the head of its straight avenue, while behind, through the window above the main entrance, is the column to Coke of Norfolk, Lord Leicester's successor, at the opposite edge of the park nearest the sea. Such axial planning, one legacy of the Baroque that was not despised by the

Opposite] The saloon at Blenheim Palace. Still used as a dining room by the family on grand occasions, as it was in the 1st Duke of Malborough's day, it is one of the few 'great chambers' not to have been turned into a drawing room at a later date. Laguerre's painted decoration peoples the room with spectators, leaning over balconies or tumbling out of *œils de bœuf* (*above*) – a reminder that 'dining in state' at this period was still very much a public event.

Palladians, is enhanced in crossing the saloon by the vista that opens up from one end of the house to the other, through the enfilade (or alignment of doors) along the garden front. Standing in front of the central window of the saloon, it is possible to see from the chapel in one wing to the library in the other.

As at Houghton, large-scale subject pictures dominate the room: a Rubens *Flight into Egypt* on the west wall balanced by Van Dyck's *Comte d'Ahremberg* on the east. But in the next generation portraits were also introduced flanking the door to the hall: Coke of Norfolk, painted by Gainsborough in the rough country clothes he insisted on wearing even to the House of Commons, and his close political ally Charles James Fox. The wall-hangings here are of a crimson Genoese velvet, with a specially wide repeat, bought in Italy on the Grand Tour and perfect in scale and richness for what can almost be seen as a secular chancel after the nave of Lord Leicester's basilican hall.

In a great Palladian mansion, built from scratch, it was comparatively easy to provide a saloon of appropriate scale, but in a smaller and older house it could present problems. Sir Matthew Fetherstonhaugh, just returned from the Grand Tour, decided he must have such a room at Uppark in Sussex and, probably with the help of the architect James Paine, created an interior of singular beauty – though at the cost of reducing the bedrooms above it to mere garrets with their windows at floor level. The plasterwork ceiling of about 1770, once again coved to achieve greater height, is in the new Neoclassical taste made popular by Adam but still has a Rococo prettiness and delicacy of touch, while the two marble chimneypieces, attributed to Sir Henry Cheere, are in sienna and white marble imported from Italy. The decoration of the room, long thought to be original, probably dates from the time of Sir Harry Fetherstonhaugh, a friend of the Prince Regent, who commissioned Humphry Repton to make several alterations to the house about 1812. The dwarf bookcases flanking the door to the hall must be of this date, together with the off-white and gold colour scheme, perhaps influenced by Henry Holland's contemporary essays in the Louis Seize manner at Althorp and Woburn.

Robert Adam's most unusual and spectacular saloon is that at Kedleston, a circular domed pantheon lit by an oculus that comes as an overwhelming surprise whether entered from his atrium-hall, based on the Baths of Titus, or from his garden façade, based still more ambitiously on the Arch of Constantine. Such freedom in 'lifting' the most admired works of classical architecture and transporting them to English soil recalls the capriccio paintings of Giovanni Panini and of Adam's own friend and tutor C.L.Clérisseau, which regroup such famous monuments according to picturesque principles. Some 'ruin pieces' of this kind, by Clérisseau himself, decorate the upper walls of the rotunda at Kedleston above the deep niches. Every surface here is curved, from the massive mahogany doors and their pedimented doorcases to the pairs of caned benches which are the only pieces of furniture. Adam made one concession to the English climate in the form of the cast-iron stoves from the Carron Iron Works set into the niches flanking the hall door and balanced by false 'stoves' of bronzed plasterwork on the opposite walls. These could be cunningly stoked from the servants' staircases behind without disturbing the gossip of the dowagers attending Lord Scarsdale's receptions.

Opposite] The saloon at Houghton Hall with deep crimson cut velvet from Utrecht used for the wall-hangings and chair covers, contrasting with the sombre stone colours of the adjoining hall. The use of solid West Indian mahogany, parcel gilded, for the massive doors and doorcases, window surrounds, settees and chairs (*below*), marks the first use of this wood on a large scale in an English country house. It is always said that Sir Robert Walpole, as Prime Minister, introduced a tax on mahogany only after Houghton was completed.

Left] The spirit of classicism: a brooding Homer from one of Thomas Carter's marble chimneypieces in the saloon at Uppark. The study of Homer and Virgil, Plato and Cicero, was at the heart of the eighteenth-century connoisseurs' attempt to create a new Augustan Era.

Right] The architectural character of the saloon inspired some of the noblest ceiling designs of the age. The true coffering at Holkham, probably by William Kent in collaboration with the 1st Earl of Leicester (*above*), contrasts with the false at Uppark, attributed to James Paine (*below*), where the central oval, though flat, gives the impression of greater height. The gilding at Holkham is almost certainly original, while that at Uppark dates from the first decade of the nineteenth century.

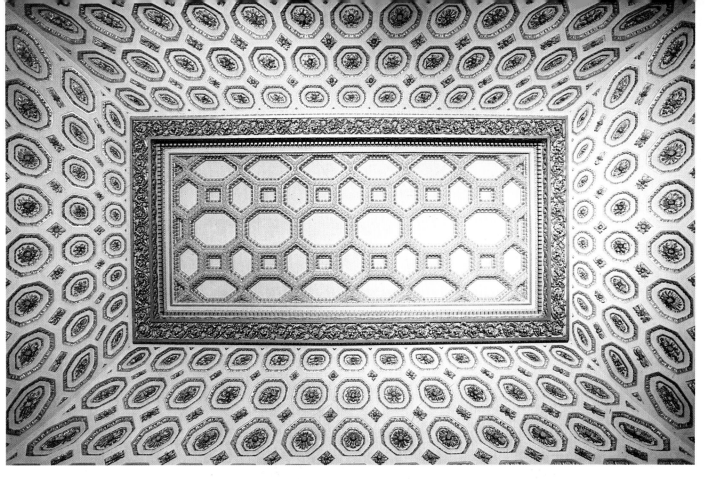

The austerity of the Kedleston rotunda was originally mitigated also by the Axminster carpet, of which only a fragment sadly remains. This repeated the pattern of the coffering in the dome, in stone and yellow colours complementing the gilding and warm off-white of the paintwork. Lit by Adam's many-branched wall-lights (adaptations of the famous antique bas-relief in the Vatican Museum known as *The Aldobrandini Marriage*), and thronged with ladies in the wide panniered dresses that we know from the portraits of Reynolds and Gainsborough, the saloon must have presented a spectacle not unworthy of its imperial Roman antecedents.

But it was only in a house the size of Kedleston, where the withdrawing room could vie with the saloon in scale, that such purity and monumentality were possible. In a house like Saltram in Devon, the new saloon that Adam designed for the Parker family in 1768 had in some ways to combine the functions of both rooms. His triumph, repeated in at least a dozen other houses all over England, was to humanize rooms of almost super-human proportions by his use of colour, texture, uniformity of ornament, and the subtle balance of different elements – pictures, furniture, doorcases, chimneypieces – thought of as one single entity.

At Saltram the carpet is again one of the key elements. Echoing but not exactly repeating the pattern of the plasterwork ceiling, it is, after two hundred years, still brightly coloured: not the washed-out pastels that are so often regarded as 'Adam colours' but strong, clear blues, pinks and greys with touches of red and black to deepen the effect. The blue damask of the wall-hangings and the paint colours of the ceiling are no longer original, but they follow the architect's watercolour designs in the house and must be close to his intentions.

It is easy today to take such colours for granted, but for their time they were revolutionary. Before the Adam brothers, ceilings had almost invariably been painted in one colour, however elaborately decorated, and indeed the high relief of Rococo plasterwork cast enough light and shadow of its own. But the shallower ornament of Neoclassicism, produced so much more easily from moulds, needed the help of colouring to give it depth, and Adam readily found precedents for this not only in newly excavated Greek and Roman temples but in the colour theories of Rousseau, which assumed a natural harmony between different tones in much the same way as Palladio had assumed a harmony in certain mathematical ratios. Pinks and greens; blues and reds; greens, yellows and blacks are all favourite Adam combinations, based on such thinking, and their use in the English country house must have seemed as strange and novel as Lord Burlington's neo-Palladianism fifty years earlier.

But it is Adam's attention to detail at Saltram that is so astonishing. The same honeysuckle, gryphon and tripod motifs appear in carpet and ceiling, cornice and chimneypiece, on chair frames and candlestands, shutter panels and dado rails, even on the gilt brass door furniture, where the keyholes are hidden by exquisite miniature vases. As at Houghton and Holkham, the furniture, probably made by Thomas Chippendale to Adam's design, would have stood round the walls, with two settees flanking the chimneypiece and balancing the pier tables opposite. Their graceful serpentine forms prove that he was by no means averse to the curved line. The necessity for only two doors left the corners free for gilt candlestands surmounted by Matthew Boulton's splendid blue-john candelabra.

The saloon at Uppark, created by Sir Matthew Fetherstonhaugh about 1770, is one of the most hauntingly beautiful rooms of its date. The coved ceiling, achieved by raising the floor level of the rooms above, has delicate plasterwork in the Adam manner though still with a Rococo lightness of touch characteristic of the architect James Paine's later manner. The bookcases and the white and gold decoration were introduced by Sir Harry Fetherstonhaugh, the Prince Regent's friend, in 1814. The room remained untouched during the long widowhood of his wife, the dairymaid, whom he married in 1825 when he was over seventy.

Left] A pantheon designed for parties: the dome of Robert Adam's circular saloon at Kedleston, 42 feet in diameter and 55 in height. After the insistent rectangularity of the Marble Hall, everything here is curved, from the ruin paintings by William Hamilton and the *grisailles* by Biagio Rebecca, down to the doors and doorcases, the chairs and settees, and the cast-iron stoves made to Adam's design at the Carron Iron Works. These stoves, standing like altars in the niches either side of the door to the hall, were stoked from the passages behind by servants who could thus remain invisible. They are crowned by splendid bronzed plasterwork urns *à l'antique* (*right*), made by Joseph Rose who also provided two false 'stoves' in plaster to match the real ones, in the niches opposite.

The garniture of Zoffoli bronzes on the chimneypiece were bought by Matthew Parker on his Grand Tour and have always stood here, while the pictures are largely copies of Old Masters which not only suited his purse better but could be enlarged or reduced in size to achieve a perfectly balanced picture-hanging. The later stigma attached to copies was scarcely felt in the eighteenth century, and indeed it was often thought a mark of better taste to acquire versions of great pictures by Raphael, Guido Reni or the Carraccis than to buy originals by less well-known artists.

The idea of the saloon as a picture gallery perhaps reached its summit at Corsham Court. Sir Paul Methuen's collection, mainly formed during his time as ambassador to various European courts, was inherited by his cousin in 1757 and brought down to the Elizabethan family seat in Wiltshire, where Capability Brown not only laid out the grounds but also remodelled one wing of the house as an appropriate setting for the pictures. With additional Old Masters bequeathed by another relative, the Revd. John Sanford, in the early nineteenth century, these rooms remain one of the supreme expressions of Augustan taste and connoisseurship. Canvases in carved and gilt eighteenth-century frames are crammed on to the walls, but also carefully balanced in terms of size and shape. Because they leave so little of the walls visible, the brightest red silk damask was chosen as a background. This is almost precisely the colour of the walls in Zoffany's famous picture of *The Tribuna of the Uffizi Gallery* (in the Royal Collection), filled with admiring English Grand Tourists, and it is also the red that Sir Joshua Reynolds specified for the galleries of the Royal Academy during his time as President. The carved and gilt borders which hide the nails fixing the silk are carefully cut round the mouldings of the chimneypiece and doorcases, another example of that attention to detail that is characteristic of the golden age of English craftsmanship.

Far more houses were remodelled or extended, like Corsham and Saltram, than were totally rebuilt as the century drew to a close. So the idea of a saloon on the main axis was gradually lost, and as the age of museums dawned its very name became rarer. Sir Richard Colt Hoare's picture gallery at Stourhead, completed in 1802, is a saloon only in name, though built as a separate pavilion on one side of Colen Campbell's original Palladian villa, balanced by a library on the other. The balance of the picture-hanging is again all-important, and the acquisition of a huge altarpiece by Cigoli, *The Adoration of the Magi* from the church of San Pietro Maggiore in Florence, to hang above the chimneypiece, confirms the latter's role as a kind of secular altar – a source of physical if not spiritual warmth. A pair to the big Maratta *Self-Portrait with the Marchese Pallavicini*, on the left, was not easily found so Colt Hoare commissioned a *Caesar and Cleopatra* from Anton Raphael Mengs, then considered the leading history painter in Rome. The dark green of the walls may have been chosen because of the high proportion of landscapes which the Hoare family particularly appreciated, and which in turn influenced the layout of the famous gardens at Stourhead. The furniture by Thomas Chippendale the younger owes something to contemporary French *ébénistes*, in particular the work of Georges Jacob. Later top-lit picture galleries, like those at Attingham and Somerley in Hampshire, have something of the character of the eighteenth-century saloon, but are also close in function to the long gallery – that equally persistent English phenomenon to which we must now turn.

Opposite] The picture gallery at Attingham, designed by John Nash in 1805 to house the collection formed by the 2nd Lord Berwick. It is placed on the central axis with the entrance hall, fulfilling all the functions of a saloon in an earlier Palladian house, and with large-scale Italian pictures that also look back to a previous generation of Grand Tourists. But in other respects the Attingham gallery anticipates nineteenth-century museum architecture. Its ceiling is the earliest one to use curved cast-iron ribs, made at Coalbrookdale a few miles away down the River Severn; its colour scheme of Pompeian red walls with porphyry scagliola columns and prophyrized doorcases anticipates Soane's Dulwich Gallery; while the white marble chimneypieces with their Egyptian flavour (recalling Nelson's recent victory of the Nile), and the Italian and French Empire furniture, reflect the increasingly international interests of the British in the Waterloo period.

THE LIBRARY
COLLEGE OF FURTHER EDUCATIO
NORTHAMPTON

5 Long Galleries

If country houses in England were to a large extent heirs of the great medieval monasteries dissolved by Henry VIII, their long galleries are almost the only rooms that pay obvious tribute to an ecclesiastical past. Just like the cloisters which preceded them, they were primarily places for exercise in cold or rainy weather. At Lacock Abbey in Wiltshire, the astute financier William Sharington, who acquired the old nunnery in 1539, actually retained the cloisters as the central courtyard of his house, adding two long galleries above the northern and southern walks. Woburn Abbey in Bedfordshire now gives the appearance of a wholly eighteenth-century building, despite its name, and it is surprising to find that its long gallery and corridors also occupy the site of Cistercian cloisters, like those which still survive in ruins at the abbeys of Fountains and Rievaulx.

The cloister tradition, enhanced by a new awareness of the Italian Renaissance courtyards of Bramante and Brunelleschi (known more from woodcuts than from personal experience), was adapted for courtyard houses like Burghley in Northamptonshire in the sixteenth century – and even for Giacomo Leoni's remodelling of Lyme Park in Cheshire, in the early eighteenth – where open arcades on the ground floor support galleries above. Later still, at Horace Walpole's Strawberry Hill and in James Wyatt's alterations to Wilton of 1801, the wheel has turned full circle and galleries are built to masquerade as cloisters: stone-floored and fan-vaulted – though decorated with classical rather than medieval statuary – and a setting for crinolines instead of cassocks.

Even when built as projecting wings to non-courtyard houses, the earliest long galleries in England seem often to have been built above covered walks or arcades, like that at The Vyne in Hampshire which was only later enclosed with windows and doors facing the garden. Daniel Mytens' famous portraits of the Earl and Countess of Arundel, now at Arundel Castle, painted in the early seventeenth century, show galleries behind each sitter: an open arcade filled with classical sculpture behind the Earl, with an arch at the far end giving a view south over the Thames; and a mullion-windowed long gallery behind his wife, hung with portraits and culminating in a view over a parterre garden. These two interiors may well have been at Arundel House in the Strand.

The first-floor gallery at The Vyne, built by William Lord Sandys, Henry VIII's Lord Chamberlain, between 1515 and 1528, has claims to be the earliest in any English house. Seventy-four feet long by only sixteen feet wide and a dead-end rather than a room of passage, it is entirely panelled with superbly carved linenfold, incorporating the arms, crests, badges and devices of all Sandys' relations and political allies, among them Cardinal Wolsey. Grained in the early nineteenth century, this heraldic decoration must once have been picked out in vivid colours, making pictures, tapestries and other furniture largely redundant. In an inventory of 1541 it contained only one Spanish folding chair, two small wooden tables, a small cupboard and two Turkey carpets – presumably to go on the tables.

Opposite] The long gallery at Little Moreton Hall, dating from the 1570s: a masterpiece of Elizabethan joinery. The arch-braced roof is structurally ingenious, yet at the same time highly decorative, with the braces between the purlins (or main timbers) curved and cusped like the cogs of gigantic wheels. The plasterwork in the gables at either end represents 'the Sphere of Destinye whose governor is Knowledge' (*above*) and 'the Wheele of Fortune whose ruler is Ignorance', two contrasting figures from the frontispiece of Robert Recorde's *The Castle of Knowledge*, a mathematical treatise published in 1556.

The 'prodigy houses' of the Elizabethan period ushered in the golden age of the long gallery. For courtiers like Sir Christopher Hatton and the Cecils, who hoped for advancement by entertaining the Queen and her ever larger retinue, it was essential to have interiors big enough to contain such numbers well away from the hall, which was now the domain of the servants. Placing the gallery on the very top floor, above the great chamber and withdrawing room, meant that it could be flooded with light. Montacute House in Somerset, at 172 feet the longest of all, has windows on all four walls, including semi-circular oriels at either end that push out still further – a spectacular feat of engineering. Taking exercise here was not unlike being in a garden (or rather a bird wheeling above one), and cannot have been much warmer despite the provision of two chimneypieces.

Though a few feet shorter than Montacute, the long gallery at Hardwick is still more monumental with its vast height and projecting lantern-like bays. The dimensions of the room, like those of the adjoining High Great Chamber, were dictated by the Flemish tapestries: a set of thirteen representing the story of Gideon which Bess of Hardwick had acquired from Sir Christopher Hatton's heirs in 1592. Though she paid over £300 for these – a huge sum – Bess followed many of her contemporaries and successors in treating them simply as wallpaper on which to hang portraits of past kings and queens as well as members of her own family. These and others added by her son and daughter-in-law, the 1st Earl and Countess of Devonshire, still hang three deep against the tapestry – witness to the wonderful profligacy of the age.

The over-life-size proportions of the Hardwick gallery are stressed by the simple geometry of the plasterwork ceiling, the painted strapwork frieze that runs above the tapestries, executed by a Flemish painter, John Ballergons, and the great marble chimneypieces and overmantels with statues of Justice and Mercy by Thomas Accres. The latter suggest that Bess of Hardwick may herself have sat in judgement here on occasion, with the portraits of sovereigns and ancestors giving additional weight to her pronouncements. It was here too that the formidable old lady received Elizabeth I's commissioner, Sir Henry Brouncker, when he arrived unexpectedly in 1603 to investigate the potentially treasonable marriage-plans of Lady Arabella Stuart.

The furniture listed in the gallery in 1601 included the tables in the bay windows with their magnificent Ushak and Shah Abbas table-carpets, a chair or couch of state on the central pier between the windows, and a small number of other chairs and stools. But the chief glory of the room was the series of embroidered cushion covers for the window-seats representing scenes as various as the Judgement of Solomon, Diana and Actaeon, 'the fancie of a fowler', the Hardwick arms and the entrance front of Elizabethan Chatsworth. Most of these were probably the work of Bess's own team of needleworkers, though they include other examples of professional work, some thought to be French.

Few of Bess of Hardwick's contemporaries could afford to furnish their long galleries with either tapestries or pictures, and the tradition of elaborately carved panelling was thus more enduring. Her Derbyshire neighbour Sir John Manners formed a gallery at Haddon about 1600 with particularly beautiful arcaded panelling featuring peacocks, his family's unusual crest, in the frieze. The room is more intimate than Hardwick in its proportions,

Lord Sandys' long gallery at The Vyne, probably the earliest in any English country house, has superb linenfold panelling of the 1520s (*opposite*), contrasting with the tapestry-covered walls of the gallery at Hardwick dating from the end of the century (*above*). Among the family portraits, Bess of Hardwick's likeness by Rowland Lockey, dressed in her widow's weeds and pearls, gives some idea of the old lady's forceful personality.

Left] It was in the long gallery at Hardwick that the Countess of Shrewsbury (better known as Bess of Hardwick) received Queen Elizabeth I's envoy Sir Henry Brouncker in 1603, when he was sent north to investigate the potentially treasonable marriage plans of the old lady's granddaughter, Arabella Stuart. Even such a seasoned courtier must have been overwhelmed by the scale and splendour of such surroundings, hardly known in the royal palaces of the period. 166 feet in length, the room was probably designed specifically to take the set of thirteen Flemish tapestries telling the *Story of Gideon*, woven for Sir Christopher Hatton in 1578 and bought by Bess of Hardwick from his heirs in 1592. Family portraits have hung against the tapestries since at least the early seventeenth century, a wonderfully extravagant idea typical of the taste of the time.

Right] Smaller and less opulent than Hardwick, but just as beautiful in its way, the panelled long gallery at Haddon Hall was built by Sir John Manners and his wife Dorothy Vernon probably in the first decade of the seventeenth century. With mullion windows on three sides and three great bay windows overlooking the terraced garden, the room has a light and airy feel, enhanced by the lime-washed plaster ceiling and the silvery grey tones of the oak panelling. The Vernon boar's head crest and the Manners peacock alternate in the frieze with roses and thistles, symbolizing the union of England and Scotland which came with the accession of James I in 1603.

110 feet long and only 15 feet high. The huge mullion windows on both sides, and the three projecting bays on the south overlooking Sir John's terraced garden (where real peacocks fan their tails), give it a warmth and light that is enchanting on a summer's day when the silvery oak floorboards are dappled in sunlight and the delicate rippling plasterwork of the ceiling seems almost like the trellis above a garden walk.

Indeed, the intimate relationship between long galleries and gardens deserves to be stressed. Almost invariably their bay windows and oriels were planned to provide the best vantage points over the intricate knot-gardens, terraces and walled enclosures below – only bettered by the prospect from the roof above, used in fine weather as a sort of outdoor gallery and often provided with banqueting houses, as at Hardwick, where desserts and sweetmeats could be served.

The Cartoon Gallery at Knole has a still more elaborate ceiling than that at Haddon, decorated with botanical emblems by the plasterer Richard Dungan based on the woodcuts of some late sixteenth-century herbal. The room derives its name from the Mytens copies of Raphael's famous tapestry cartoons which have hung here since 1701; before that it was known as the 'Matted Gallery' and its wide Jacobean oak floor-boards must have been covered by the loose-woven rush matting still made to the traditional pattern for Hardwick and Blickling.

As remodelled by Thomas Sackville, 1st Earl of Dorset, between 1605 and 1608, Knole can boast no less than three long galleries, each of them leading to an 'apartment' consisting of bedchamber, dressing room and closet: in other words conceived as rooms of passage as well as places for exercise. But physical recreation was not forgotten. The deep bay in the Leicester Gallery not only contains an early billiard table, but a rope suspended through a hole in the ceiling is attached to a seventeenth-century 'dumb-bell' in the attics above. This weighted mechanism provided the same sort of exertion as pulling a bell rope in a church tower, but without causing any noise.

Other long galleries of this date, like the Audit Gallery at Boughton, contained 'shuffle-boards' for playing a version of shove-halfpenny with heavy brass counters rather than coins. These tables, often of immense length, and made with one gigantic plank of oak, can only have been assembled in the room. Early inventories also list skipping ropes, battledores and shuttlecocks, spinning wheels and tops among the items likely to be found in a long gallery. Here the young could work off their energy and the portly could keep their livers in order by bouncing up and down on the springs of an 'exercising chair' – like a leather-covered concertina.

The Brown Gallery at Knole illustrates another more educational aspect of such rooms, already sensed at Hardwick. Here on the long south wall, hung cheek by jowl, are a huge series of uniform portraits – largely imaginary likenesses of medieval kings and remote family ancestors – by Jan van Belkamp, a Flemish artist working in England in the early seventeenth century. Together these provide a complete chronological survey of English history from the early Plantagenets to the early Stuarts, with the addition of some heroes of the Reformation such as Luther, Melanchthon and Pomeranus, after Holbein and Cranach. It is easy to imagine the tutors to the Sackville children using such a history lesson in pictures

The Cartoon Gallery at Knole, called after the six large copies of Raphael's famous tapestry cartoons which have hung here since 1701. The room was remodelled by the 1st Earl of Dorset between 1605 and 1608 as a suitably grand approach to the King's Room, the best bedchamber in the house. A marvellous rippling effect of light and shade is given by the serpentine ribs of Richard Dungan's plasterwork ceiling, enclosing botanical emblems taken from a sixteenth-century herbal, while the Corinthian pilasters framing the bay windows, and the deep recess opposite the chimneypiece, are ornately carved with 'grotesques' – including caryatid figures, birds, monkeys and garlands of fruit and flowers – probably derived from Raphael's decoration of the Vatican *loggie*.

to instill a sense of traditional virtues and family pride in their young charges.

Ceilings too could be educational, though to work out all the allegories, emblems and devices in a ceiling as complex as that of the long gallery at Blickling would be to risk a permanent crick in the neck. Sir Henry Hobart, James I's Lord Chief Justice and the builder of the house, had just the sort of legal mind that would delight in such a crossword puzzle, and it was probably he who instructed the plasterer Edward Stanyan to base his design on plates in Henry Peacham's *Minerva Britannia or a Garden of heroical devices . . .* published eight years earlier in 1612. Heraldic achievements and symbols of the Five Senses and of Learning are thus mingled with less familiar images: 'a virgin naked on a dragon sits' symbolizing '*pulchritudo feminae*'; a rhinoceros (one of the earliest depictions of the animal in English art) curiously representing the poet, who ought apparently to be thick-skinned; and the goddess Athene being drawn from the axe-cleft head of Zeus oddly illustrating the Christian tag 'all wisdom comes from God'.

The gallery at Blickling must originally have been panelled, though it is now lined with bookcases tactfully introduced in the 1860s by one of the pioneers of the Arts and Crafts Movement, John Hungerford Pollen. One of the finest collections of rare books in England was thereby united with one of the most intellectually ambitious schemes of decoration to have survived from the seventeenth century. Another impressive gallery later adapted as a library is that at Lanhydrock in Cornwall, whose length is accentuated by a shallow tunnel-vaulted plaster ceiling with spectacular pendant bosses. But perhaps the most romantic of all is that at Chastleton House in Oxfordshire, whose deeper tunnel vault is an intricate web of daisies, roses and fleur-de-lis in their hundreds, as fine as the embroidered coverlets and crewel-work hangings still to be seen in the rooms below.

Whereas long galleries, lit from both sides, were ideal for the thin ranges of a courtyard house or for the top storey of a tall Jacobean manor like Chastleton, they were more difficult to place in the compact 'double-pile' houses built after the Restoration. The gallery at Ham House occupies one of the uprights of the original H-shaped building with bay windows at each end overlooking the garden and forecourt. The fluted classical pilasters date from as early as 1639, but the pantheon of twenty-two family portraits in identical 'Sunderland' frames were introduced in the 1670s, when the room also contained four globes (two of which still survive with their original leather cases), four stools or 'squobbs', and 'seavon boxes carv'd and guilt for tuby roses'. This sparse furnishing and the absence of a chimneypiece proves it was still primarily a room for exercise and parade rather than for comfort. The Earl of Sunderland, who gave his name to the type of Dutch-inspired 'auricular' picture frames so popular in Charles II's reign, had a similar oak-panelled gallery at Althorp in Northamptonshire, hung with pictures of court beauties by Van Dyck and Lely – which were obviously more to his taste than the mock-medieval ancestors of a previous generation.

In contrast to Ham and Althorp, the monumental long gallery at Sudbury in Derbyshire seems (like other features of the house) to be a conscious throwback. It occupies the whole of the garden front on the first floor of the house and its magnificent ceiling by Bradbury and Pettifer, though in the up-to-date idiom of Wren's City churches, seems to vie with the

Opposite] The chief glory of the long gallery at Blickling is its ceiling, one of the most elaborate surviving examples of Jacobean plasterwork. Until recently the identity of its creator was unknown, but a bill of December 1620, which has only just come to light, reveals that he was a London craftsman, Edward Stanyan, many of whose emblems and devices were taken from Henry Peacham's *Minerva Britannia*, published eight years earlier. Peacham intended such symbols 'to seede at once both the mind and eie by expressing mystically and doubtfully our disposition. . . .', and such an intellectual approach must have appealed to the owner of Blickling, Sir Henry Hobart, who was also James I's Lord Chief Justice. The gallery was converted into a library in the nineteenth century by the 8th Marquess of Lothian and his architect John Hungerford Pollen.

triumphs of the earlier Jacobean plasterers. Large busts of Roman emperors flanked by shells and palm branches fill the coved frieze, and may have been chosen to complement the equally chronological survey of family portraits below, many of them by John Michael Wright.

Such reckless use of the most important space in the house was not to be attempted again, and later houses like Erddig, Easton Neston and Wimpole experimented with smaller galleries on the main axis running from front to back of the house on the first floor, and offering splendid views down the long avenues and canals in each direction. This solution satisfied the craving for symmetry and axial planning so central to the Baroque, but it was incompatible with the great two- and three-storey entrance halls conceived by Vanbrugh at Blenheim and Castle Howard.

Opposite] The long gallery at Sudbury Hall in Derbyshire is something of a rarity for a Charles II house. Completed in 1676, it has a superb plasterwork ceiling and frieze by Robert Bradbury. The busts of moustachioed Roman emperors in the cornice (*below*) may have been intended to complement the pantheon of family portraits, many of them by John Michael Wright, hung on the panelled walls beneath.

It may seem surprising to find that no long gallery was planned for a house the size of Castle Howard. Yet its place was to a large extent taken by the dramatic corridors, each pair totalling almost 300 feet in length, which open into the hall at its four corners and owe something to Wren's aisles of St Paul's with their saucer domes and arches, niches and recesses. By one of those strokes of genius that only rarely accompanies the overlay of one generation's taste on another, the 4th and 5th Earls of Carlisle filled these corridors in the later eighteenth century with the Greek and Roman sculpture they had acquired in Italy on the Grand Tour, on altars, pedestals and antique mosaic tables. The result, probably very different from the builder's intentions, remains one of the most perfect syntheses of art and architecture in any English house.

Unlike Castle Howard, Blenheim sprang as it were 'fully armed' from Vanbrugh's fertile imagination, with a four-square plan for the main block that allowed for important side elevations: that on the east containing the private apartments (and overlooking the 'privy garden'); that on the west entirely occupied by the 'Great Gallery', two storeys in height, and intended to be worthy of a Prince of the Holy Roman Empire, who must have known the work of the great Viennese architects Hildebrandt and Fischer von Erlach. But in the event this end of the house was only a shell by the time of Vanbrugh's final quarrel with the Duchess in 1716, and it was not until 1722–5 that the room was completed to the designs of his assistant Nicholas Hawksmoor, with plasterwork by Isaac Mansfield. The original intention to hang it with pictures was abandoned after 1729 when the famous Sunderland library was inherited and bookcases were then installed to house the thousands of volumes collected by the Great Duke's son-in-law. The room today is not unlike Hawksmoor's Codrington Library at All Souls College, Oxford, but somehow lacks the sense of drama and movement that characterizes Vanbrugh's earlier work.

If the long gallery did not prosper greatly in the Baroque period, the ascendancy of the Palladians after 1714 should by rights have dealt it a death-blow. Nowhere does such a feature occur in Palladio's own designs either for villas or for town houses. But such was the strength of native tradition that even such a stickler for the rules as Lord Burlington contrived to find precedents for rooms of differing shapes opening into each other, and offering axial vistas, in the planning of the Roman baths as described by Vitruvius. In his villa at Chiswick the whole of the garden front is taken up by a rectangular *tribuna* with apsed ends, linked by open arches to a circular vestibule on one side and an octagonal one on the other. But what is entirely new about this gallery is its emphasis on sculpture: niches in the apses contain statues of Mercury, Venus, Apollo and a Muse; great porphyry urns stand on pedestals flanking the door to the garden; the doorcases have broken pediments for busts; and the decoration as a whole is highly sculptural in the Italian mode so brilliantly mastered by Burlington's protégé, the young William Kent.

What Burlington proposed in miniature was not immediately executed by his followers on a grander scale, and the first large Palladian houses, Houghton and Wanstead, conspicuously lacked long galleries in their search for pure harmonic proportions based on the cube. Completed in 1753, the statue gallery at Holkham in Norfolk, however, closely follows the Chiswick plan of a tribune flanked by vestibules – which also act as links to the

Opposite] Classical coffering by Hawksmoor in the long gallery at Blenheim (*above*), and by Kent in the statue gallery at Holkham (*below*). The infinite variety of such ornament shows how little English architects depended on the slavish copying of pattern-books.

Right] One of Vanbrugh's long corridors flanking the great hall at Castle Howard. These were filled with classical statues, busts and sarcophagi collected by the 4th and 5th Earls of Carlisle in the mid-eighteenth century.

family and strangers' pavilions beyond. The genesis of the design is complicated, but the owner of Holkham, Thomas Coke, 1st Earl of Leicester, having consulted both Kent and Burlington, seems to have worked out the plans himself in collaboration with Matthew Brettingham, the executant architect. With its life-size statues in deep niches, busts on brackets and wonderfully restrained architecture, it breathes new life into the old concept of the long gallery – now brought down on to the *piano nobile* and forming part of the regular circuit of state rooms opened for the balls and assemblies which were then an essential part of social and political life. As for the Greek gods and goddesses, the Roman senators and matrons shipped from the warm waters of the Mediterranean to this cold north Norfolk coast, what a much more distinguished spiritual ancestry they provided than the dull seventeenth-century Cokes whose portraits Lord Leicester could banish to back passages and attic bedrooms with impunity.

Leicester's contemporaries were swift to follow his lead. In 1754 his particular friend the 2nd Earl of Egremont commissioned Matthew Brettingham to enclose an open arcade at the north end of Petworth House, so as to make a gallery for his own collection of antique sculpture – mostly sent from Rome by the dealer Gavin Hamilton, having been through the hands of the famous 'restorer' Cavaceppi. Such collections were of course of variable quality. More by good luck than judgement, Lord Egremont acquired one bust of great beauty in a 'job lot' – an Aphrodite later convincingly attributed to Praxiteles – but for the most part his acquisitions were reworked Roman copies of Greek originals. These might not have borne close inspection, but they looked the part crowded together on pedestals and brackets, emerging and retreating into niches on the long wall of the gallery, and testifying to their owner's culture and taste at a time when a classical education, and a thorough knowledge of Greek and Latin, were considered indispensable components of a gentleman's education.

One of the most passionate and scholarly collectors of antiquities on the Grand Tour was the young William Weddell, whom Batoni painted in Rome in 1765 with the *Laocöon* and other statues he particularly admired in the background. On his return Weddell commissioned Robert Adam to extend the old house at Newby in Yorkshire, which his father had bought, and in particular to add a sculpture gallery as a separate wing on axis with his new long library.

Although the Newby gallery is tripartite like that at Holkham, the contrast between the two succinctly illustrates the revolution in taste brought about by Neoclassicism. Whereas Holkham is a product of the Renaissance, achieving its effect by balanced proportion and light, Newby is an imaginative attempt to reconstruct the appearance of an actual Roman interior on the evidence of Herculaneum and the Catacombs. The comparatively low square vestibules at either end are joined to the rotunda by deep arches, heavily coffered, which exaggerate the height of the central dome. Below it stands the famous *Barberini Venus*, the most celebrated piece in the collection, and in an apse at the far end of the gallery, seen from the library, is a gigantic bath of white and purple *pavanazzo* – an appropriate symbol, for the unfortunate Weddell died in 1792 of a seizure in the then fashionable Roman Bath in the Strand. The statues, sarcophagi, vases and tripods at Newby relate to each other

A Jacobean long gallery transformed into a masterpiece of Neoclassical design: Robert Adam's gallery at Syon House in Middlesex, completed in 1769. While orthodox Palladians might have found the proportions of such a room grotesque, Adam responded to the challenge and produced one of his most original and sublime inventions. The groups of pilasters flanking the bookcases, and the 'triumphal arch' motifs of the chimneypieces, help to regulate the perspective, while the circles, octagons and squares of the ceiling seem to expand its width – in reality only 14 feet. Soft opalescent greens, pinks and greys are also carefully contrived after the primary colours of the preceding rooms to give an atmosphere of informality, since this was intended to be a retiring room for the ladies where they might find books and cards, sewing boxes and games tables 'to afford great variety and amusement'.

Overleaf] James Wyatt's Gothic vaulted galleries at Wilton House were intended as a conscious reference to the cloisters of the medieval abbey built on the same site. Completed in about 1814, they also contain much of the classical statuary acquired in France and Italy by the 8th Earl of Pembroke. Evidently nothing was thought amiss in this radical mixture of the styles, which looks forward to the eclecticism of the later nineteenth century.

and to the scale of the gallery so perfectly that it is possible they were chosen specially to fit a scheme by Adam formulated in the early 1760s. Certainly the exquisite decoration and mastery of spatial effects is characteristic of the architect's early career, before his office became over-extended and his work somewhat repetitive.

Another triumph of these years, against all the odds, was his remodelling of the Jacobean gallery at Syon in Middlesex, 136 feet long but only 14 feet wide and high. To orthodox eyes such proportions would have seemed grotesque, but Adam's powers of synthesis resulted in one of the most original and beautiful Neoclassical rooms in England. In his own words, the room was to be used 'for the reception of company before dinner and for the ladies to retire to after it – for the Drawing Room (which lay between it and the Dining Room) prevents the noise of the men being troublesome. It is (therefore) finished in a style to afford great variety and amusement.'

The thin pilasters, delicately painted by Michelangelo Pergolesi, recall the traditional use of pilastered wainscoting to break up a long wall in the seventeenth century, but at the same time the groups of four on the inside wall are echoes of Adam's favourite triumphal arch motif and stand on wave-moulded bases like ancient sarcophagi. Real fragments of antique burial vases, terracotta pots in circular recesses flanking the chimneypieces, painted roundels of Percy ancestors, leather-bound books, even convex and concave 'porthole' mirrors flanking the central bays, contribute to the 'variety and amusement' without in any way disrupting the harmony of the whole. Adam's endlessly inventive classical ornament, picked out in soft pinks and greens – one of his favourite colour schemes – was admired even by Horace Walpole who deplored such 'filigree' elsewhere.

For later Neoclassical architects Adam's approach was not serious or archaeological enough. The young Charles Heathcote Tatham, a pupil of Henry Holland, was one of the most uncompromising 'hawks' of this new generation, specializing in the design of mausolea which have been described as 'almost brutalist in their exaggeratedly simple forms'. Tatham's meeting with the 5th Earl of Carlisle in Rome in 1795 led to one of his most important commissions: the remodelling of Sir Thomas Robinson's west wing at Castle Howard as a gigantic long gallery, with a museum room at one end and a chapel at the other – perhaps a consciously didactic progress from paganism to Christianity. Tatham's line-drawings for the gallery, which were published in 1811, are in the austere style of John Flaxman and Johann Tischbein (whom he had met in Italy). They show a room which is a remarkable precursor of Karl Friedrich Schinkel's public buildings in Berlin and the interiors of Sir Robert Smirke's British Museum in London, with a touch of neo-Egyptian in the tapered 'pylons' of the chimneypieces and the great lotus-leaf chandeliers, perhaps inspired by Vivant Denon's *Voyages dans la Basse et la Haute Egypte* published in London in 1802. The central domed rotunda was never given its statues and niches, and the early introduction of full-length Baroque portraits somewhat detracted from the purity of Tatham's intentions, but the room is still a fascinating instance of the narrow borderline between private and public 'gallery' in the early nineteenth century.

The increase in the number of visitors to country houses may have had something to do with this. The 3rd Earl of Egremont, Turner's great patron, decided to extend his father's

Antique and Neoclassical sculpture in the galleries at Petworth (*opposite*) and Chatsworth (*above*). Still used for exercise on rainy days, like its Elizabethan and Jacobean predecessors, the early nineteenth-century sculpture gallery also afforded opportunities to study 'high art' in idealized surroundings – a role it was soon to share with the great public museums.

North Gallery at Petworth with another parallel 'aisle' in the 1780s, and then with a further square bay in 1823, specifically to house his modern British paintings and sculptures. His intention was both to foster native artists, to whom he offered constant hospitality, and to bring them into contact with the Old Masters already in the collection. Anyone who called at Petworth was welcome to visit the gallery, and it was constantly filled with copyists, foreign visitors, *cognoscenti* and the downright curious. Architecturally, the room was undistinguished, but with its pictures hung two and three deep against Pompeian red walls, its skylights (introduced before 1837), and its huge marble figures and groups by Flaxman, Westmacott, Rossi and Carew, it must have offered an experience not unlike a visit to the Royal Academy at the same period.

The 6th Duke of Devonshire's interest in modern sculpture was not confined to the British School and his skylit gallery at Chatsworth, designed by Sir Jeffry Wyatville, is filled with works by Canova, Thorwaldsen and their Roman contemporaries. The columns and plinths, pedestals and table tops, demonstrate his passion for coloured stones of every kind, perhaps first inspired by those of his native Derbyshire: rosewood, moss-agate, alabaster and blue-john. The careful placing of the statues – including the seated figures of Madame Mère (Napoleon's mother) and her daughter Pauline Borghese facing each other either side of a huge malachite clock given by the Czar – shows the 'Bachelor Duke' to have been one of the most sensitive connoisseurs as well as one of the most opulent collectors of his day. The sculpture gallery in many ways took over the function of the old long gallery built by the 1st Duke of Devonshire, which was now converted into a library as large and comfortable as a London club's. Wyatville's new wing was built on axis with this room, so that those who looked up from their books could see through five sets of double doors, via the ante library, Dome Room, state dining room and sculpture gallery to the far end of the orangery, beyond which lay the private theatre. It provided a promenade on a rainy day as sensational in its way as the long gallery at Hardwick, built by the Duke's ancestress, the redoubtable Bess, over 250 years before.

The sculpture gallery at Chatsworth was one of the last to be built in an English country house, for the Victorians preferred to expend their energies on baronial halls and ballrooms. The billiard room was the long gallery's true heir as a place for indoor exercise. But as a strictly male preserve, it no longer played a central role in the life of the family. With children tidied away to the nursery, estate business and politics being discussed in the study, and needlework and feminine diversions in the boudoir, country-house life became more compartmentalized, and the long gallery as a melting-pot of different generations and ranks, different pursuits and parleys, became a thing of the past.

6 Dining Rooms

Sir Robert Walpole's Marble Parlour at Houghton was one of the first dining rooms to be included among the state apartments of an English country house. William Kent's sumptuous Italianate decoration is Bacchic in theme, like so many later dining rooms, with the ribs of the ceiling (*opposite*) decorated with gilded vine leaves and bunches of grapes.

There can be few houses in the world today that cannot boast a dining room, so it comes as a surprise to find what a comparatively short pedigree such rooms have, and what an even shorter life-span has been enjoyed by that apparent prop of western civilization – the dining room table. We have already seen the family eating in two rooms: the great hall in the Middle Ages and the great chamber in the Tudor and Elizabethan period. But in the constant search for privacy and greater comfort that has always been the lot of country-house owners (never more so than today when the vast majority are open to the public), a third room emerged as the usual place for meals to be served.

The first, extraordinarily precocious step towards this can be seen in Bess of Hardwick's Low Great Chamber, and the adjoining Paved Room, called the 'Little Dyning Chamber' in the inventory of Hardwick taken in 1601. These were on the floor below her main rooms of state, which could be sealed off and unused when she was not entertaining important guests, or in the winter when the penetrating Derbyshire cold would have made them untenable. True to its name, the first was of course merely an alternative great chamber with all the other uses that that implies. The bay window, one of the lightest spots in the house, may well have been where Bess's ladies sat to produce much of the famous embroidery that still survives at Hardwick, to the accompaniment of lute music, games and other entertainments going on in the rest of the room.

The square Paved Room, however, was situated at the top of a flight of stairs leading immediately up from the great kitchen on the ground floor – a far more convenient arrangement than in most eighteenth-century houses where the dining room occupied a distant wing reached by subterranean passages or even open colonnades. The room was panelled and therefore tolerably warm, and contained a 'long drawing table' (that is, with a leaf or leaves that could be drawn out to make it bigger), a 'turkie carpet' to go on it, a chair and stool of 'turkie work' – presumably for the old lady and her granddaughter Arabella Stuart – and fourteen 'joyned stools' for her immediate companions and attendants. Above the chimneypiece, the plasterer Abraham Smith modelled a life-size Ceres with overflowing cornucopia in a verdant landscape recalling the paintings of Primaticcio and the School of Fontainebleau; this must have been considered particularly appropriate decoration for a room where nature's bounty was to be enjoyed to the full.

In the early seventeenth century everyday eating rooms of this sort became known as parlours, but they rarely received any decoration beyond the simplest panelling and were not part of the progression of state rooms 'above stairs'. A permanent table like that at Hardwick was virtually unknown, and oval gateleg tables, which could be folded up and put away after use, were the usual rule. At Knole, a list of seating arrangements between 1613 and 1624 shows that meals were served in three rooms at once: the hall for the lower servants; the great chamber for the family; and the parlour (now called the Poet's Parlour)

for the upper servants. On the other hand the Countess of Dorset records that she and her husband dined in the parlour sometimes in winter, or when they were alone and not entertaining guests.

The 'Marble Dining Room' at Ham House is described thus in an inventory of 1677, probably the earliest known use of the phrase, and occupied a central position on the ground floor of the house, flanked by the Duke and Duchess of Lauderdale's own apartments. The room originally had a black and white marble floor in the Dutch manner, and its gilt-leather wall-hangings, which still survive, would also have been practical – not retaining the smell of food, which was always a risk with tapestries. The furniture included three oval tables made of cedar wood (perhaps also chosen for its sweet-smelling properties), and eighteen walnut chairs with caned seats, rather surprisingly not supplied with squab cushions. These would normally have stood round the walls when not in use. The Grand Duke of Tuscany, visiting Althorp in this same decade, commented on the informality with which the company dined at two oval tables, all seated on stools, where elsewhere his rank would have entitled him to an arm-chair. Two cedar side-tables with marble tops occupy recesses flanking the central door, one with a marble cistern under it, and these are early precursors of the sideboards which would become an inevitable part of the furnishing of dining rooms in the following century. The overdoor paintings after Polidoro, showing putti with pan-pipes, satyrs and goats, also prefigure the type of Bacchic decoration so favoured by Georgian architects, carvers and plasterers.

Confusingly, the Marble Dining Room at Ham is essentially a parlour (for it was not part of the run of ornately decorated state rooms on the first floor), while the Marble Parlour at Houghton in Norfolk is the first real dining room in an English country house, taking its place on the *piano nobile* of this outsize Palladian villa. Sir Robert Walpole, the builder of the house, was as passionately addicted to hunting as to politics, and twice yearly held his famous Norfolk 'congresses' here, a mixture of local gentry and great Whig patricians who were entertained, in Lord Hervey's words, 'up to the chin with beef, venison, geese, turkeys etc. and generally over the chin in claret, strong beer and punch'.

Everyday life at Houghton went on in the 'rustic' or ground floor: here the 'hunting apartment' contained Sir Robert's 'supping parlour' as well as a breakfast room. But when entertaining on a large scale, and presumably during the 'congresses', he and his cronies would have used the splendid new dining room and picture cabinet (completed in 1732) which William Kent provided, where the architect Colen Campbell had originally planned the usual Baroque arrangement of bedchamber, dressing room and closet. Kent's decoration here is remarkably architectural, with an order of fluted Ionic columns which, on the inside wall, suddenly turns into marble, with great arches on either side of the chimneypiece leading into recesses fully lined with different coloured marbles specially imported from Italy: black and gold *porto venere* for the skirtings and the pedestals to the columns, *brèche violet* for the shafts of the columns and pilasters, a mottled white and grey for the walls, and pure Carrara for Rysbrack's splendid chimneypiece. Practical as well as magnificent, the serving tables in these recesses must have seen many an overflowing gilt wine-fountain and the huge cisterns have washed countless glasses before recharging them for loyal, and not so loyal, toasts. Another eminently practical reason for these alcoves was the provision of a door between them (immediately behind the chimneypiece) which emerged at the top of the servants' staircase, allowing them to come and go unseen.

In its decoration, the Marble Parlour at Houghton is a veritable temple to Bacchus. Rysbrack's overmantel depicts a sacrifice to the god after a painting by Titian with fat garlands of vines decorating the fireplace surround, and tumbling over the sides of a basket supported by two panthers above. More vine leaves, tendrils and bunches of grapes feature in the cornice, the overdoors and Kent's ceiling, painted in the style of Raphael's 'grotesques' and one of his most successful essays in the genre. As elsewhere at Houghton, the oil-gilding on the mahogany doors, the frieze and ceiling ribs was on a hitherto unparalleled scale, and struck the diarist Mrs Lybbe Powys as 'magnificently glaring' in 1756, after over twenty years of wear and tear. In these splendid surroundings Sir Robert's oval walnut dining table, made so that it can expand to seat sixteen, looks plain and somewhat utilitarian; it may well have come from his 'supping parlour' below in the 'rustic' – the servants setting up small tables with cloths and bringing the chairs out from their usual positions round the walls when this state dining room was in use.

Important Old Master paintings were not to be wasted on the walls of an eating room. Some contained portraits, but others were hung with large Snyders hunting pictures or still lifes with dead game, by Flemish artists like Jan Fyt and Jan Both or their English follower Francis Barlow. Snyders' *Stag and Boar Hunts* at Easton Neston might seem too bloodthirsty to encourage the appetite, but the eighteenth-century squire was less squeamish than his descendants reared on the niceties of Jane Austen. They are in any case relieved by the playful Rococo frames given them by a plasterer – perhaps the Dane Charles Stanley – complete with hunting horns and nets, foxes' masks, and bows and arrows, all engagingly asymmetrical so as to accommodate Hawksmoor's earlier doorcases. To complete the sporting theme, a version of Titian's *Diana and Actaeon* occupies the central oval of the ceiling.

The state dining room at Holkham represents a development of Kent's arrangements for service in the Marble Parlour at Houghton. Here an arched sideboard niche, or exedra, on the inside wall has small jib-doors each side leading to the servants' stair, and the mirrored panels on the reveals of the arch allow the butler and footmen to survey the table even if standing outside these doors. The niche, an idea later taken up by Adam at Kedleston and Saltram, also gave added prominence to the display of gold and silver plate massed on the sideboard in the French manner, and known there as the *buffet*. Sometimes these would also contain formal pyramids of apricots, peaches, grapes, even the odd pineapple, grown in the hothouses that country-house owners were now erecting in their walled gardens. Placed between the great Marble Hall and the statue gallery, the dining room at Holkham was necessarily severe and monumental in its decoration, taking its key from the two colossal Roman heads of Juno and the Emperor Lucius Verus above the two fireplaces. But the bas-reliefs of Thomas Carter's Sicilian jasper chimneypieces introduce a lighter note, depicting Aesop's fables of the Fox and the Wolf, and the Bear and Bee-hive: both on the appropriate topic of nourishment. The splat-back dining chairs with leather seats, probably supplied by

William Bradshaw, are of a favourite eighteenth-century type. But it is interesting that the backs are not carved, for once again they were intended to be placed round the walls and only pulled forward when folding mahogany dining tables were brought in by the servants and covered with cloths in preparation for an important dinner.

The North Italian *stuccadores* who flocked to England in the early eighteenth century, beginning with Artari and Bagutti, encouraged a native school of plasterers who were soon their equals in technique, even if they depended on architect's drawings rather than their own designing skills. Dining rooms were the scenes of some of their major triumphs, again because of the frequent lack of suitable pictures to adorn their walls. The dining room from Kirtlington Park (now in the Metropolitan Museum, New York) was designed by James Sanderson and carried out by Thomas Roberts of Oxford, while that at Felbrigg Hall in Norfolk was designed by James Paine and carried out by Joseph Rose the elder, the uncle of Adam's still more celebrated plasterer.

Paine's room at Felbrigg, dating from 1752, is one of the most satisfying Rococo interiors in England. The theme is Bacchic as usual, but the lions' pelts and garlands of oak and ivy leaves which creep round spears, guns and hunting horns, over the doors and in the ceiling, are executed with such sinuous grace that they evoke the enchanted woodlands of Watteau and Pater. At Carton in Ireland in 1779, a visitor remarked on the 'French horns playing at breakfast and dinner', and their inclusion in the decoration of a dining room may partly refer to this kind of music, often performed at mealtimes in an adjoining room. The pale lilac colour of the walls at Felbrigg may well be original, and provides a wonderfully soft, warm background for the plasterwork picked out in off-white, and the bronzed plaster busts on brackets. While the panelling of seventeenth-century 'parlours' tended to be grained or marbled in dark colours, or sometimes painted a 'drab green' like the state rooms at Boughton, the Palladians favoured light colours, particularly white, perhaps because their dining rooms were almost exclusively used in daylight. At Bulstrode in 1740 dinner was served at 2.00 p.m., tea at 8.00 p.m. and supper at 10.00 p.m.; but as the century wore on, dinner (the main meal of the day) grew later and later, until in the Regency period luncheon was gradually introduced to fill the long gap until the evening.

Whereas there is little provision for lighting in the dining rooms at Houghton and Holkham, an eagle with wings outspread in the centre of the ceiling at Felbrigg was evidently meant to hold the chain of a chandelier in its talons, and a series of eight small oval mirrors or 'sconces' are set into plasterwork frames, two on each wall, intended to reflect candlelight back and forth round the room. Most unusually, these sconces are 'hung' from slender links of chain – perhaps a reference to the fetterlock of the Windham family crest. Felbrigg was of course a comparatively small house where one might be expected to sup as well as dine in the same room. This was rarely true of Adam's dining rooms like those at Syon, Kedleston and Saltram, which were used only when the family were 'holding state'. On the other hand, they also came into commission for the 'routs' and county balls which were increasingly a feature of rural life, and had to accommodate the crowds of guests who might previously have dined in the saloon – now used for dancing. More space too was demanded for the great panniered and crinolined dresses that were considered *de rigueur*.

The Square Dining Room at Petworth, despite its seventeenth-century appearance, was formed in 1794–5 by the 3rd Earl of Egremont, Turner's great patron. Here he assembled many of the splendid Van Dycks commissioned by his ancestor, the 10th Earl of Northumberland, and one can imagine the artists, sculptors and writers who thronged the house in his day gathered to enjoy the hospitality of his 'open table'. Apart from the large 'Monteith' bowl in the centre, made by David Willaume in 1710, the silver on the table was all commissioned by Lord Egremont from Paul Storr between 1807 and 1814.

THE LIBRARY
COLLEGE OF FURTHER EDUCATION
NORTHAMPTON

125

James Paine's Rococo dining room at Felbrigg Hall in Norfolk (*right*), designed for William Windham in 1752. The pale lilac colour of the walls, with the elder Joseph Rose's flowing plasterwork trophies of the chase picked out in white, may represent the original decorative scheme. Seventeenth-century family portraits, mostly by Lely, look surprisingly at home in the company of John Cheere's bronzed plaster busts, made specially for the room – and the casts of famous antique sculptures bought on the Grand Tour, including (*above*) the *Belvedere Antinous* and the *Dying Gaul*.

The dining room at Sledmere in Yorkshire, dominated by Romney's double portrait of Sir Christopher and Lady Sykes, *The Morning Walk*. The room probably dates from the 1740s, though with Neoclassical plasterwork added by Joseph Rose the younger about 1789. 'I intend', wrote Sir Christopher, 'to finish very slowly, as I wish the work to be well done, neat and simple rather in the Old than the New Style, nothing Rich & Gawdy, but suiting to plain Country Gentlemen', approving Rose's design for the dining room as 'something uncommon'. The armchairs are in the 'Chinese Chippendale' taste, and a bed in the same style also survives in the house.

'Inexplicable splendours of Ionian white and gold': the Great Dining Room at Syon House, designed by Robert Adam about 1763. His screens of Corinthian columns with niches behind them reduced this long, thin room to manageable proportions, the central section becoming almost a triple cube, 66 by 21 by 21 feet. At this date small folding tables would have been brought in by footmen at the appointed hour, and there is therefore no long dining table permanently set up.

At Syon, the dining room was conceived as the third in the progression of five great rooms, each differently treated in terms of decoration. After the stone colours of the hall (a suitable transition from the exterior), comes the deep blue, green and yellow scagliola of the ante room, the white and gold of the dining room, the crimson damask of the drawing room, and finally the progression to secondary colours in the pinks and greens of the gallery. Describing the dining room in his *Works in Architecture*, Adam draws attention to the difference in French and English attitudes: whereas the former rarely had their eating rooms on the main enfilade, and did not devote great attention to their decoration because they left promptly after meals, in England they 'are considered as the apartments of conversation, in which we are to pass a great part of our time – this renders it desirable to have them fitted up with elegance and splendour, but in a style different from that of the other apartments. Instead of being hung with damask, tapestry etc., they are always finished with stucco, and adorned with statues and paintings, that they may not retain the smell of victuals.' Curtains were included in this general ban on textiles in dining rooms, their places at Syon being taken by richly carved shutters in the deep window recesses, but carpets were not. The superb Moorfields carpet for the room, dated 1769 and echoing the ceiling, still exists, but is now in the drawing room – perhaps as the result of an early change of heart, for it seems to have been here even in the late eighteenth century.

The colour scheme of parchment white and gold, ultimately French in origin, had been used in Rococo interiors of the previous generation like those at Woburn and Petworth, and Adam also used Palladian harmonic proportions for the room, reducing it to a triple cube by the simple device of apses at either end, screened off with Corinthian columns. The antique statues in niches, complemented by Cipriani's *trompe-l'œil* bas-reliefs above, even seem to look back to the Holkham sculpture gallery. Yet the true novelty of the Syon dining room lies in its noble attempt to re-create the life-style of Imperial Rome at its height – an idealized vision that was at one with the thinking of the great Whig philosophers and historians of the age, Burke and Gibbon.

The dining room at Kedleston, also dating from the late 1760s, is more conventional in form, with the wide apsed sideboard recess invented by Kent at Holkham. Adam's drawing for the display of plate in this niche includes salvers perched precariously on the open lids of knife-boxes, exquisite bronze and ormolu vases by Matthew Boulton, and a tripod perfume burner designed earlier by his rival for the Kedleston commission, James 'Athenian' Stuart, all arranged on three tables with curving marble tops, and with pedestals for wine-fountains and cisterns in between: a culmination of the Baroque *buffet* in the most advanced vocabulary of Neoclassicism. To judge by the other surviving designs for the room, the walls were to be an ochre colour not often used for state rooms, for yellow was generally held to be a bad background for pictures. Wellington's friend Mrs Arbuthnot described the yellow damask hung by the Iron Duke at Apsley House in London as 'just the very worst colour he can have for pictures and will kill the effect of the gilding' – a view shared by the painter Sir Thomas Lawrence, who replaced his own yellow paper with a 'rich crimson'.

However, the Kedleston colour was probably more in tone with the soft 'Quaker brown' recorded in the dining room at Fawley Court in Oxfordshire in 1771, while the yellow

shown in Adam's designs for ceiling and cornice must have indicated gilding rather than the yellow paint which has replaced it. Like Antonio Zucchi's roundels in the ceiling, the paintings on the walls are more decorative than great works of art, with large-scale Snyders still–lifes characteristically on the upper tier and Claudian landscapes by Zuccarelli and others below – easy on the eye and, for once, the digestion. But what is particularly remarkable is the way they are inset into uniform plasterwork frames of the normal 'Maratta' type, so that Adam's precisely balanced picture hanging has survived to this day. Knowing the *penchant* of owners for moving paintings, selling some and buying others in every new generation, perhaps he did this with a conscious eye to posterity.

Adam's later career saw a tendency to abandon the primary colours he had always advocated for state rooms, and to introduce even to these the subtle combinations of secondary colours with which his name has become synonymous: 'pea-green', pink, and the clear blue which he habitually described as '*couleur de ciel*', with a notable absence of gilding. The dining room at Saltram in Devon, dating from 1780–1, was an earlier low-ceilinged Palladian room with a conventional Georgian bow window, two of whose sashes he blocked so as to form a sideboard recess, with copies of 'Etruscan' amphoras in niches each side. The predominant greens of the decoration, perhaps partly chosen because of the strong reds and blues of the preceding rooms, are picked up by the tones of Zucchi's leafy picturesque landscapes, once again in fitted plasterwork frames – those above the doors actually recessed into the walls.

The furniture here, all of it carefully designed by Adam to provide a wholly unified interior, is painted to match the colours of the rest of the room. The pier glass and pier table, and the urn-shaped wine coolers on pedestals flanking the sideboard, have painted medallions by Zucchi and his wife Angelica Kauffmann which tie them in with the painted roundels and 'fans' of the ceiling – in fact executed twelve years before as part of an earlier library scheme. The splendid Axminster carpet by Thomas Whitty closely follows the design of the ceiling, and is made to such precise dimensions that the legs of the chairs and pier table, and the marble hearth-stone, approach but do not quite touch its edge. A carpet of this sort was never, of course, intended to have a large dining table permanently set up on it, so that its complete design and subtle tonality – introducing browns and blacks which pick up the dark mahogany of the chairs, the 'Etruscan' urns and the 'stone-ware' Wedgwood vases on the mantlepiece – could be appreciated to the full. Though no examples now survive, it was often the practice in the eighteenth century to lay a painted oil-cloth exactly matching the central reserve of such a carpet, before dining tables were brought in and arranged by the footmen. The miraculous state of the Saltram carpet today may be partly due to that, and partly to the fact that the Parkers generally took their meals in a smaller parlour on the first floor, only rarely using the state rooms.

French influence, that recurring refrain in English decoration, brought a return to white and gold as a favourite colour scheme at the very end of the eighteenth century, with Henry Holland's chaste Louis Seize interiors at Althorp and Woburn, and with furniture bought at the Revolutionary sales or made by Parisian *émigrés* working in London. The dining room at Uppark in Sussex is a reflection of this taste, though designed about 1812 by Holland's friend

Opposite] Adam's niche or exedra at one end of the dining room at Kedleston was intended for the display of silver and gold plate, in the old tradition of the Baroque buffet. Side-tables with curved backs and marble tops were set with knife-boxes, salvers and *maronnières* (or chestnut vases), and in the centre a famous ormolu tripod perfume-burner after a design by Athenian Stuart, while wine fountains and cisterns were placed on pedestals between them. In front of the fireplace stood a magnificent plate-warmer in gun-metal and gilt bronze (*below*) by the Swedish-born metalworker Diederich Nicholas Anderson.

Sporting themes are commonly found in country-house dining rooms. At Uppark in Sussex (*left*), the Lewes Cup stands in the centre of the dining table, a relic of Sir Harry Fetherstonhaugh's day when races, often attended by the Prince Regent, were held on the Downs in front of the house, while bronzed plaster bas-reliefs of horses by Garrard are placed over the doors. At Deene Park in Northamptonshire (*right*), the Earl of Cardigan, leader of the Charge of the Light Brigade, is portrayed on his famous horse 'Ronald' above the chimneypiece, while the rest of the room is hung with Ferneley's pictures of his hunters, some of them painted in the park at Deene. Talk at such dining tables must have centred largely on outdoor pursuits, hunting, shooting and fishing, particularly after the ladies' departure for the drawing room.

and pupil, the landscape gardener Humphry Repton, and his architect son John Adey Repton. The owner of the house, Sir Harry Fetherstonhaugh, was a close friend of both the Prince Regent and the Duke of Bedford, and his political and sporting interests are both evident in the remodelled room: Wedgwood black basalt busts of the Duke, Charles James Fox, Napoleon and William Bastine, a Sussex poet of the period and one of Fox's keenest supporters, are placed above the niches at either end of the room, while between them are bronzed bas-reliefs of horses by Garrard – complemented by race-cups won at the regular meetings held on the downs in front of the house. As well as these, there is a Grand Tour element in the series of Vernet pictures representing the *Four Times of Day*, acquired in Italy by his father, Sir Matthew. The panelling and alcoves at either end of the room are basically seventeenth century, but the Reptons fitted the latter with grey marble shelves for the display of plate and lined them with mirror glass, carefully set at an angle so that the reflections should be multiplied in perspective.

A fascinating touch of Regency whimsy is the stained-glass 'rose window' in the service lobby at the far end of the room, seen through double doors. 'The principal object', Repton wrote, 'will be figures in clear obscure [chiaroscuro] from a pure classical source, as my son has made sketches from the marbles imported from Athens by Lord Elgin . . . by candlelight the effect will be magic, as all the light may proceed from this window with Argand lamps adjusted from behind.' The dark passage behind, where the servants struggled with this newly patented type of oil-lamp, still exists.

By the time the Uppark dining room was completed, the fashion for a permanent long table in the centre had caught on. Tradition has it that this was the table on which the young Emma Hart danced, soon after she had been 'discovered' by Sir Harry in London in 1780 and before her meeting with his friend (and her future husband) Sir William Hamilton. The solid comfort of the leather-covered Regency dining chairs tells of long hours spent enjoying the famous cooking of Sir Harry's French chef, Monsieur Moget, or, over port and brandy, discussing horses and hustings long after the departure of the ladies.

The sporting instincts of the country-house owner were indulged to the full in the early years of the nineteenth century, when hunting, shooting and the breeding of thoroughbred racehorses became fine arts. Ben Marshall, John Herring and John Ferneley could not quite rival the achievements of their predecessor, George Stubbs, but there are few country houses without examples of their work, and these were, as often as not, destined for dining rooms where they were a suitable accompaniment to the racing trophies and selling plates displayed on sidetables and as centrepieces. A typical example of a sporting dining room can be seen at Deene Park in Northamptonshire, with its massive Ferneley portraits of Lord Cardigan's hunters grazing in the park: pictures that are almost literally brought to life by the view from the windows opposite, to the groups of horses across the lake that still pose nonchalantly against the vivid green turf and under the clumps of ancient oaks and chestnuts.

The concepts of comfort and cosiness, long prevalent in the decoration of drawing rooms, were slow to be accepted for dining rooms where meals were still very much a ritual, with a formal procession in order of rank and importance – 'leading in' – and a half-way

'Like dining in a great trunk, and you expect the lid to open,' was how the 6th Duke of Devonshire described the Great Dining Room at Chatsworth (*above*), designed for him by Sir Jeffry Wyatville about 1830. The massive side-table in the Kentian style, between the two chimneypieces (*opposite*), was specially made for a display of plate including a pair of candelabra by Paul Storr, the finest silversmith of the period, dated 1813–14.

point indicated by the hostess when 'turning' (to address the left-hand neighbour rather than the right) was obligatory.

'Answers perfectly, never feeling over large' – thus the 6th Duke of Devonshire decribed the colossal Great Dining Room at Chatsworth, designed for him by Sir Jeffry Wyatville, and completed in 1832, the year of the Reform Bill. The first dinner given in the room was for the thirteen-year-old Princess Victoria. It was her first experience of a dinner with grown-up people and anyone else might have felt intimidated in such magnificent surroundings. The Duke's passion for rare hardstones ruled here as much as in the neighbouring sculpture gallery. The dado is of local Derbyshire marble, the columns flanking the doors at each end of Breccia and Porto Santo, and the table-tops of red Swedish porphyry and Siberian jasper, the latter a gift from the Tsar during the Duke's embassy to Russia. Instead of the Baroque and Rococo revival of Wyatville's interiors at Windsor, the Great Dining Room was designed in a pure Neoclassical style worthy of Charles Percier and Pierre Fontaine. Its gently curved ceiling with coffering like great snowflakes made it, again in the Duke's words, 'like dining in a great trunk, and you expect the lid to open'. A particularly French feature is the way the huge pier glasses are matched by two equally gigantic mirrors on the opposite wall above the two chimneypieces. The latter's comparatively low proportions are redeemed by Sir Richard Westmacott's large marble *bacchantes* which flank each fireplace. Perhaps surprisingly, the Duke found these extraordinarily life-like figures, so scantily clad in vine garlands and goat-skins, 'too composed and sedate . . . I wanted more abandon, and joyous expression'.

Just as these statues were intended to look back to the revelry of Sir Robert Walpole's Houghton 'congresses', so Paul Storr's magnificent salver and candelabra, on the massive Kentian sideboard between them, consciously evoke the *buffet* displays of the late seventeenth century – the chargers and ewers, wine fountains and cisterns, made by Huguenot smiths like Willaume and Archambo. And if tradition is the key to an understanding of the English country house, perhaps the 6th Duke's ingeniously constructed orchestra gallery, over the vestibule just outside the dining room door, offers a parallel with the minstrels' gallery above the great hall screen at Knole, where the 1st Earl of Dorset's musicians played minuets and galliards rather than mazurkas and galops.

Thomire's gilt-bronze vestal virgins at Woburn (*above*), and Storr's silver shepherd boys at Chatsworth (*opposite*), show how a display of plate continued to be an essential element in the early nineteenth-century dining room.

137

7   Withdrawing Rooms

From the Regency period onwards the 'drawing room' has become almost a generic term for a room with no other specific use – in Repton's words, a 'general living room'. Today, with the withdrawal of families into smaller, more comfortable quarters, the 'state apartments' of many English country houses look like an endless succession of drawing rooms, with the furniture arranged to give some semblance of a lived-in look, but with few clues as to their original purposes. In particular, it has become hard to differentiate between saloons and drawing rooms, and to see how in the seventeenth and eighteenth centuries these would have quite distinct characteristics both in terms of use and decoration.

As usual, the idea of such a room developed from the search for privacy and comfort, hard to find in the medieval castle. As a first step the bed was moved from the great chamber to a privy chamber beyond. Then, as the former became used for eating in place of the great hall, an intermediate room evolved as a place to 'withdraw' after meals, even to dine in private on occasion, before the advent of the parlour. Fifteenth-century inventories refer to almost any small room leading off the great chamber as a 'withdraughte' or plain 'draughte', but by the end of the century this was almost always an ante room to the bedchamber, like that at Charlecote in Warwickshire in 1496, where the upper or personal servants slept on straw pallets outside their master's door.

Tapestries, or cheaper canvas hangings painted to resemble them, almost inevitably covered the walls of such rooms, as in the adjoining bedchambers. Not only did these provide a certain amount of warmth and insulation from damp, they could also be easily rolled and transported to suit the peripatetic life led by most courtiers and 'marcher barons', before the relative peace established by the Tudors. Some of the smaller rooms at Cotehele in Cornwall, which are lined with loosely-hung tapestries, hitched up over the doors, and simply furnished with an oak table and stools, could just as well be recreated in another castle, or even in a tent during some military campaign.

The 'prodigy houses' built during the reign of Elizabeth were altogether more permanent, and in them the drawing room became, for the first time, the repository of some of the owner's finest works of art, a role it was never to lose. The 'Withdrawing Chamber' at Hardwick not only contained the famous 'sea-dog' table after designs by du Cerceau, perhaps the finest surviving piece of Elizabethan furniture in England, but also a 'Cubberd with tills [i.e. drawers] carved and guilt' – probably the cabinet of very architectural form on the wall opposite the chimneypiece – in which Bess of Hardwick evidently kept some of her more valuable jewels and other treasures. The room had two alternative sets of hangings, probably for summer and winter: a set of tapestries of 'the storie of Abraham' and the magnificent patchwork appliqué wall-hangings of the Virtues, some of which still survive. Many of the materials used for these hangings, 'of cloth of golde, velvett and other like stuff', were taken from medieval church vestments, plundered at the Dissolution of the

Opposite] The withdrawing room at Hardwick still contains many of the pieces of furniture listed here in an inventory of 1601, seven years before Bess of Hardwick's death. These include the famous 'sea-dog' table, after designs by Jacques Androuet du Cerceau, with winged chimeras symbolizing speed resting on the backs of tortoises (*below*) – illustrating the old tag *festina lente*, or 'make haste slowly'.

Monasteries or the Protestant purge after the reign of Queen Mary. Even with the hangings there was still room for pictures, including a portrait of Mary Queen of Scots, who spent several years of her captivity at Hardwick Old Hall and Chatsworth under the guardianship of Bess's husband Lord Shrewsbury, and a naïve but charming representation of Penelope and Ulysses which has claims to be the earliest documented subject-picture in an English house.

The ceiling of the withdrawing room at Hardwick was lowered in the nineteenth century, but it was still considerably smaller than the High Great Chamber and long gallery which it adjoined; likewise Bess's own withdrawing room on the floor below was smaller than the Low Great Chamber across the gallery of the hall. Despite its size this room was still more crowded than its grander equivalent 'above stairs'. Cupboards, iron-bound coffers and marquetry chests, chairs and stools covered in damask, velvet or leather, needlework cushions and even 'a foote turkie Carpet' (a great rarity for its day) are all listed in the 1601 inventory. In effect it could have vied with the clutter of a Victorian drawing room, and no effort was made to produce the kind of unified decorative scheme which became popular in the following century.

Because of the difficulty of adapting an older house to the Baroque concept of a 'state apartment', two drawing rooms are listed on the first floor of Ham House in 1677. The North Drawing Room, which lay between the great dining room or saloon (now destroyed) and the long gallery, was largely decorated in 1637 by Franz Cleyn, who painted the overdoors of playing boys and designed the splendid Mannerist panelling. During their remodelling of Ham after the Restoration, the Duke and Duchess of Lauderdale introduced the set of gilt chairs carved with dolphins, perhaps bought by the Duchess in Paris in 1670, the Persian silk carpet and the ivory-veneered cabinet, which must have been regarded as particularly precious and exotic. The latter may have been the cue for the white and grey marbling of the panelling, at a time when white paints were extraordinarily expensive compared to the usual dark greens and browns.

Exoticism was still more the key to the smaller Blue Drawing Room between the gallery and the Queen's Bedchamber. Instead of tapestries, the wall hangings here were originally of green silk and velvet, but these were changed by 1683 to 'blew Damask inpain'd wt [i.e. in alternating panels with] blew velvet embroidered wt gold, mounted wt Silk & Gold fringe'. Paned hangings of this kind occur in countless contemporary inventories, and can be seen in Dutch pictures of the period, but apart from those at Ham (whose bright blue damask has now faded to a mellow brown) hardly any have survived. The panelling in the rest of the room is boldly grained in brown on a gilt ground, perhaps to simulate olivewood, and the furniture was either imported Chinese lacquer, like the cabinet-on-stand now in the room, or japanned like the remarkable caned chairs with the Lauderdales' cypher and coronet applied in silver on their backs.

To some extent this 'Anti-roome to ye Queen's Chamber', as it was rechristened in the Ham inventory of 1683, had more the character of a dressing room than a drawing room – there was even a japanned close stool concealed in a cupboard in the inside wall – but Oriental furniture is found in several other withdrawing rooms at this period. The Chinese

Drawing room details: a marble therm figure of the 1640s from a chimneypiece at Wilton (*opposite*) and an engraved brass lockplate in the Balcony Room at Dyrham (*above*), perhaps by the London locksmith Henry Walton whose trade card is among the Blathwayt papers still at the house. As the scale of rooms diminished away from the hall and saloon on the central axis, so their decoration grew more ornate, with attention given to the smallest refinements.

THE LIBRARY
COLLEGE OF FURTHER EDUCATION
NORTHAMPTON

Opposite] The Velvet Drawing Room at Saltram, with a detail of its Rococo plasterwork ceiling (*below*). The comfort and warmth of such a room, dating from the 1740s, is revealed by contemporary letter-writers like Mrs Delany and Lady Grey, who describe evenings of ladies' *causerie*, music-making, reading aloud, sewing, silhouette-cutting and other genteel occupations in such surroundings. The gilt papier-mâché border framing the red velvet, and cut to fit round the intricate mouldings of Thomas Carter's chimneypiece, is a particularly nice detail.

tea table in the Balcony Room at Dyrham was already in the room in 1700, united with the Venetian blackamoor torchères, which must have seemed suitably bizarre companions. The latter were a gift to William Blathwayt from his uncle Thomas Povey, whose son reported back from Dyrham in December of that year: '... your pictures have a great share in the decoration as the two Black Boys have a proper Place on Each side of an Indian Tambour in one of the Best Rooms.' Of course, the term 'Indian' at this date covered any Oriental import, which came by way of the East India Company's trading stations.

The Balcony Room at Dyrham served as a withdrawing room leading to William Blathwayt's own apartment on the first floor. Its very architectural panelling, with Ionic pilasters raised on tall plinths, may have been based on Dutch engravings like those of Pieter Post, although Blathwayt's architect at this time was a Huguenot, Samuel Hauduroy, who also practised as a decorative painter. Traces of Hauduroy's original marbling in deep purple colours have recently been discovered under later graining, but the gilding of the capitals, cornice and doorcases is much as he intended.

As William III's Secretary at War, Blathwayt had his own apartments at the Dutch royal palace of Het Loo, and his close ties with Holland, which began as a young man in Sir William Temple's embassy, may explain the charming Hondecoeter picture of ornamental fowl above the chimneypiece, the Dutch flower-pieces, and the 'flower pott in ye chimney of Delf' – the companion to some magnificent pyramid tulip vases elsewhere in the house. The 'landscape mirror' above the marble bolection chimneypiece is a typical feature of a Baroque interior, often supplied with candle branches each side like a pier glass, while another nice detail is the way the carved door frames, boldly carved with acanthus, match the frames of the overdoors in the style of Jean-Baptiste Monnoyer. The brass locks and hinges on the doors themselves, probably by the London smith Henry Walton whose trade card still survives in the house, are works of art in their own right. Pierced and engraved with tulips, daffodils, roses and strawberries, these again reflect Blathwayt's botanical interests and are reminders that the formal garden at Dyrham, engraved by Johannes Kip in 1712, was one of the finest in England.

To travel from the homely Dutch-influenced rooms at Dyrham to the palatial Italianate interiors of Houghton and Holkham is as much a 'culture shock' today as it must have been to contemporaries who witnessed Lord Burlington's revolution in taste and the rise to power of the Whig magnates. For the sake of symmetry, the saloons of both these houses were flanked by drawing rooms, about two thirds their size and again based on harmonic proportions. Those at Holkham, which have been least altered (though the Great Drawing Room is now confusingly known as the South Dining Room), are 30 feet by 22 feet, and both are hung with crimson silk damask which gives a smoother, more even background than the bold pattern of the cut wool velvet in the saloon. At Houghton, the drawing room was originally hung with a plain green silk velvet which provided a similar contrast.

This difference in hangings is a pointer to the different characters of saloons and drawing rooms, which tends to be forgotten today when both are arranged along the same lines. The former, with their great coved ceilings, massive doorcases and vast pictures, were always arranged formally as befitted their position on axis with the hall, as part of the 'state centre'

of the house; the latter, with their more intimate scale, lower ceilings and double-hung pictures of much more human proportions, could be used quite informally on occasion, but immediately returned to formality with chairs regimented round the walls once its occupants left. Mrs Delany, the Duchess of Portland's friend and companion, gives a vivid insight into this 'double life' in her account of the drawing room at Bulstrode in Buckinghamshire being prepared for a visit by Princess Amelia, one of the daughters of George III: 'all the comfortable sofas and great chairs, all the piramids of books (adorning *almost every chair*), all the tables and *even the spinning wheel* were banish'd for that day, and the blue damask chairs set in prim form around the room, only one arm'd chair placed in the middle for Her Royal Highness . . .' With all the furniture-moving that was needed in a great house, it was not surprising that many of the larger households maintained a 'Groom of the Chambers' to supervise a regiment of footmen.

Silk damask hangings like those at Holkham were extremely popular for drawing rooms and crimson was a favourite colour, partly because of its warmth, partly because it was considered an ideal background for Italian pictures – especially enhancing the rich, glowing tones of the Bolognese School so dear to the heart of the English Grand Tourist. Chair covers and curtains would inevitably be made from the same material as the wall-hangings to give a unity to the room. Despite the flourishing state of the Huguenot silk-weavers in Spitalfields this was likely to be an expensive business, so savings were often made by covering the backs of chairs in a cheaper material (since they generally stood against the wall), or leaving gaps behind the bigger pictures. Another alternative was the 'Flower'd Red paper' originally used in the drawing room at Felbrigg and only later replaced by real damask. This must have been similar in character to the flocked wallpapers supplied by Thomas Chippendale to Nostell Priory, fragments of which have recently been discovered. Papers like this, made in England, are known to have been exported both to France and the United States in the late eighteenth century. But still more elaborate examples of printing came back from France, such as the Réveillon design called *Les Deux Pigeons* found in the Palladio Room at Clandon Park in Surrey, which dates from the 1780s and incorporates five or six different colours.

Plain silk velvets were often imported from Genoa in the same shipments that brought statues, scagliola table tops and Batoni portraits acquired on the Grand Tour, and these were likely to be used in drawing rooms, as at Houghton, in contrast to the multicoloured or patterned cut-velvets bought for saloons. That in the Velvet Drawing Room at Saltram is a particularly beautiful deep crimson, with the nails fixing it at the edges concealed by a pierced gilt papier-maché border of a scrolling Rococo pattern that adds greatly to the richness of the effect, climbing round the complicated outlines of the chimneypiece and doorcases. Fillets of this sort, sometimes in carved wood, sometimes simply gilded rope, 'framed' expensive wall-hangings just as one might frame a picture or looking glass.

Balanced picture-hanging, emphasized by the placing of seat furniture below the dado rail, was considered essential in drawing rooms like those at Saltram, Holkham and Felbrigg. The chairs, supplied by the cabinet-maker Benjamin Goodison at Holkham and by the upholsterer John Bladwell at Felbrigg, often came in sets of six armchairs with two

Opposite] The White and Gold Room at Petworth was remodelled in the 1750s by the 2nd Earl of Egremont, English ambassador at the Peace of Augsburg, and a *bon viveur* who developed a taste for Parisian luxury at a time when the Rococo style in England was more popular for furniture and textiles than for architectural decoration. The carved wall-panels or *boiseries*, close to engravings by Nicolas Pineau, may have been designed by Matthew Brettingham the elder specially to frame the celebrated 'four Countesses' by Van Dyck, among his most beautiful female portraits. Their presence here once again underlines the feminine attributes of the drawing room after the essentially masculine character of the dining room.

Music is a theme constantly found
in the decoration of drawing rooms,
suggesting that this was where it was
most often to be heard. Musical
instruments, carved almost entirely in
the round, can be found at Petworth
both in the Carved Room (*left*), where
Grinling Gibbons's trophies were
described by Horace Walpole as
'worthy of the Grecian age of Cameos',
and in the White and Gold Room
(*opposite above*) dating from sixty or
seventy years later.

At Kedleston the 1st Lord Scarsdale's
love of music was such that Robert
Adam provided a special music room
adjoining the drawing room, where an
organ designed by the architect still
survives (*opposite below*), in company
with a contemporary Kirckman
harpsichord and a set of eighteenth-
century kettledrums.

settees for the long walls. They would be less massive and architectural than those intended for the saloon, with completely upholstered backs and seats – sometimes fixed with parallel rows of brass nail-heads which matched the fixing of the wall-hangings; sometimes with carved seat rails matching the moulding of the dado rail. Immense care was also taken with picture frames, whether of the standard 'Maratta' type or elaborately carved Rococo frames to complement the pier glasses between the windows.

The French fashion for overmantel mirrors was practically unknown in English drawing rooms until the end of the century, though an exception to this rule is the White and Gold Room at Petworth. This remarkable Rococo interior was remodelled in the 1750s by Matthew Brettingham for the 2nd Earl of Egremont, probably based on engravings of panelled rooms by Nicolas Pineau. The trophies of musical instruments carved over the doors and in the white marble chimneypiece suggest that it was not only used as a withdrawing room leading to the King of Spain's Bedchamber, but also as a music room, where the sound would reverberate and not be muffled by wall-hangings or tapestries. *Boiseries* of this type existed in some London houses, including the Duke of Norfolk's and Lord Chesterfield's, but are extremely rarely found in English country houses.

At Kedleston Adam also provided a music room, still complete with its original organ and kettle drums, adjoining the drawing room. The latter, with its wall-hangings of blue damask rewoven to the original pattern in recent years, was the first room in the main block to be completed, and followed James Paine's original plans. The great pedimented doorcases and Venetian window, all in Derbyshire marble, may indeed be Paine's rather than Adam's. On the other hand, the latter's drawing for the ceiling still survives, dated 1762, and is in the loosely flowing style of Hatchlands and other early commissions received after his return from Rome in 1758. The elegant caryatid figures in the corners of the cove are echoed in Michael Henry Spang's monumental chimneypiece, and it seems that Adam originally visualized much smaller and more Neoclassical settees with similar caryatids. However, his design for these (actually executed for the 'bluestocking' Mrs Montagu's London house) was entirely altered by the carver John Linnell, who produced – presumably with Lord Scarsdale's knowledge – four monumental sofas with mermaids, tritons and dolphins, reminiscent of Sir William Chambers's coronation coach recently made for George III. The sofas were delivered in 1765 and may explain Adam's surprisingly Rococo design for the two girandoles made in the same year.

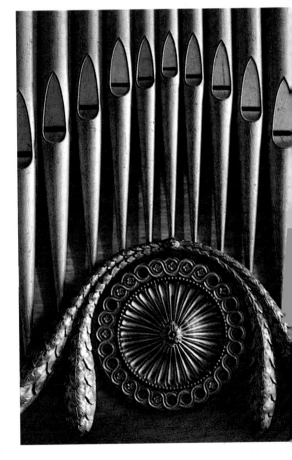

The convention that architects should design only the permanent fixtures in a room such as pier glasses and tables, leaving carvers and upholsterers to provide the movable furniture, was one that Adam and Chambers were both to question. In a famous letter written to Lord Melbourne in 1773, Chambers complains that 'Chippendale called upon me yesterday with some Designs for furnishing the rooms which upon the whole seem very well but I wish to be a little consulted about these as I am really a very pretty connoisseur in furniture ...' The divided responsibility could certainly result in some strange anomalies. For instance, Linnell also supplied a pair of small folding card-tables for the drawing room at Kedleston, charming and beautifully made in themselves but dwarfed by Adam's pier glasses under which they stood, and by the room in general. Their presence here, with no seat furniture

The tritons, mermaids and dolphins of John Linnell's magnificent settees in the drawing room at Kedleston may derive from furniture carved by the Venetian Andrea Brustolon, seen and admired by many of the Grand Tourists on their Italian travels.

but the four massive sofas, again proves how chairs were likely to be brought in and out of a drawing room by the servants as and when they were needed.

Adam's drawing room at Syon was designed for a patron, the Duke of Northumberland, who did not need persuading that he wanted the last word in Neoclassical decoration. The architect himself described it as 'a splendid with-drawing room for the ladies, or *salle de compagnie*, varied from the others by the form of its ceiling which is wood and painted in compartments'. Instead of going directly back to antique Roman precedents, Adam for once preferred a Renaissance source for this remarkable ceiling: the vault decorations by Raphael and Giovanni da Udine at the Villa Madama near Rome. The small octagons contain *paterae* with bright red and blue grounds painted on paper by Angelica Kauffmann, which Chambers rudely referred to as 'a myriad skied dinner plates'.

The minute detail of the decoration and its 'debased' source well illustrate the femir attributes of a drawing room as opposed to the more strictly classical, masculine characteristics of the dining room. At Syon it is saved from being finicky by the exquisite precision of the craftsmanship: the white marble chimneypiece is applied with ormolu mounts of superb quality by Matthew Boulton, and the door and shutter panels are by a woodcarver of equal skill, while the pilasters of the doorcases have grotesques in gilded lead on an ivory background – unique in Adam's *œuvre*. The tops of the massive gilt pier tables are adapted from antique mosaics said to have been discovered in the Baths of Titus and would originally have been balanced by settees on the opposite wall with armchairs round the rest of the room. All these are upholstered in the same Spitalfields brocaded silk as the wall-hangings: crimson relieved with a delicate silver-grey floral pattern.

Tapestries never wholly went out of fashion for drawing rooms, unlike in France where they were almost exclusively reserved for bedrooms and boudoirs. Brussels tapestries after Teniers' designs are used for a ground-floor drawing room at West Wycombe, floral Soho ones at Hagley Hall, and sets by Neilson from the Gobelins factory (after designs by François Boucher) for Newby Hall and Osterley, both under Adam's supervision. The chairs and settees designed by him for these two drawing rooms had tapestry covers made *en suite*, just as the upholstered furniture in other drawing rooms inevitably matched the wall-hangings and curtains.

Cupid and Psyche attended by putti with garlands and flowers: a detail of the chimneypiece in the music room at West Wycombe Park. The most elaborate chimney surround in the house, it has been attributed to Sir Henry Cheere whose statuary yard at Old Palace Yard, Westminster, was at its peak in about 1749–50 when this room was built. The doorcases here are, most unusually, carved in the same combination of Siena and Carrara marbles, and one can sense in this rich display something of the enthusiasm for Italian art and architecture that obsessed its owner, the first Sir Francis Dashwood.

Benjamin Franklin, who often stayed at West Wycombe, wrote to his son in 1773: 'I am in this house as much at ease as if it was my own: and the gardens are a paradise. But a pleasanter thing is the kind countenance and the facetious and very intelligent conversation of mine host, who, having . . . seen all parts of Europe and kept the best company in the world is himself the best existing.'

The saloon at Uppark is flanked by two
smaller drawing rooms which, with
their faded colouring, original festoon
curtains, George III cut-glass chandeliers
and Grand Tour pictures, can have
changed little since the death of Sir
Matthew Fetherstonhaugh in 1774. The
so-called Little Parlour (*left*) has a carved
and gilt chimneypiece in the style of the
1740s, but everything else, from the
ormolu wall-sconces to the white and
gilt pelmet boxes and the simple
giltwood pier glasses, is of about 1770, as
is the Neoclassical ceiling. The unique
japanned pagoda cabinet by William
Hallett combines Chinese lacquer panels
with ivory cameos and Florentine *pietra
dura* plaques, brought back by Sir
Matthew and his wife from their Grand
Tour in 1751.

The same mixture of Oriental and
European forms can be seen in the rare
serpentine commodes between the
windows in the Red Drawing Room
(*right*). Attributed to the French emigré
cabinet-maker Pierre Langlois, these are
veneered in Chinese lacquer and have
'mounts' of carved wood instead of the
more usual ormolu. Above them hangs
a pair of magnificent Rococo pier glasses
of about 1755.

Robert Adam's drawing room at Syon is hung with a crimson Spitalfields silk brocade, strong in colour after the comparative simplicity of the white and gold dining room. The vivid reds and blues of the Moorfields carpet, dated 1769 on the border, are picked up in the *paterae* of the ceiling, painted on paper by Angelica Kauffmann (*right*), and criticized by Adam's rival, William Chambers, as looking like 'a myriad skied dinner plates'. The wooden coffering of the ceiling is one of Adam's few borrowings from an Italian Renaissance source – Raphael's Villa Madama – and after the stricter Greek and Roman prototypes used for the preceeding rooms, this must have been an intentional change of mood, encouraging a greater degree of relaxation and informality.

None of the rooms so far encountered on our tour of the English country house was necessarily supplied with curtains, although some later saloons like that at Saltram were provided with them. In drawing rooms, however, they were considered essential from an early period: those at Ham had single white damask curtains to each window, hung on iron rods which, in the Green Drawing Room, were gilded. With the enormously increased height of Palladian rooms, based on single and double cubes, the festoon curtain was almost universally employed – though it can be seen earlier in the engravings of Daniel Marot. This type of curtain, made to pull up with four or more draw-strings so as to form folds or 'festoons' above the window, had the advantage of filling the large area of 'dead light' between the top of the window frame and the cornice. It also allowed the architectural detail of the window frames and shutters to be seen, and did not cut down the amount of daylight entering the room as heavy draw-curtains were bound to do. Modern festoons are rarely as full and architectural as those seen in contemporary paintings – or as Thomas Chippendale's astonishing carved wooden festoons, painted to look like real curtains, in the gallery at Harewood House in Yorkshire.

Another type that was popular in the middle part of the century was the 'reefed' curtain, still seen in some theatres though hardly any domestic examples have survived. This was a divided curtain with cords fixed diagonally so as to pull each half up and to the side, thus parting in the middle and leaving 'tails' to hang down, framing the window in a decorative way. The Blue Drawing Room at Chatsworth, remodelled by Carr of York for the 5th Duke of Devonshire in 1775, has carved and gilt swags of this type arranged in arched window frames and 'held' at the top by gilt vellum bows. Presumably real reefed curtains were designed to draw up behind these, just as real festoons must have been hidden by Chippendale's Harewood pelmets, but the height of the windows would have made it difficult to arrange these neatly – hence the show fronts. Carr's decoration of the Blue Drawing Room shows a precocious use of Louis Seize detail, generally to become fashionable only with Henry Holland. The charming Reynolds portraits of the Duke's wife Georgiana playing with her child, and Lady Elizabeth Foster, the third member of this famous *ménage à trois*, have always been in the room and share its atmosphere of civilized informality, combining taste and comfort in a quintessentially English way.

The White Drawing Room at Houghton, denuded of Sir Robert Walpole's pictures after their sale to Catherine the Great, was hung with Spitalfields silk in the 1790s, again based on contemporary Parisian designs, and given to the 1st Marquess of Cholmondeley by the Prince Regent. Not only are the window curtains and some of the very French-looking chairs upholstered in the same exquisite material, but the carpet was made (perhaps at Wilton) to match it in colour, and to complement its floral design. An interesting detail is the way this carpet was made up from strips, with a wide border, and with the pattern 'dropped' in each alternative width to give a more subtle effect. This technique is more usually encountered in wall-hangings like those in the drawing room at Syon.

Increasing informality and higher standards of comfort are expressed in the Regency interior as much as in Regency dress: looser, flowing robes are matched by the draped and swathed pelmets fixed above the new style of French draw-curtains, overlapping when

Opposite] The Blue Drawing Room at Chatsworth, designed by Carr of York in the 1770s for the 5th Duke of Devonshire, has a Louis Seize elegance which suits the great Sargent group of the *Acheson Sisters* now hanging there – along with family portraits of every period from Reynolds to Lucien Freud. A peculiarly English mixture of grandeur and informality, together with a balanced asymmetry in the arrangement of the furniture, have made the drawing room, filled with flowers, books, writing tables, deep sofas and armchairs, the centre of country-house life since the Regency period.

closed and made so full that they 'break' on to the ground. These pelmets were often carried over a row of three or four windows as one continuous composition, particularly in a bay window. The chairs, instead of being arranged formally round the walls and drawn out into a circle in the centre for the stilted after-dinner conservations of the mid-eighteenth century, were scattered over the room with low 'Grecian couches' and deeply-sprung bergères, music-stands and sewing boxes, and occasional tables covered with books and bibelots, bowls of flowers and watercolour cases. The classic illustration of this revolution in taste is the pair of contrasting mezzotints in Humphry Repton's *Fragments*, published in 1816, with the accompanying verse:

> *No more the Cedar Parlour's formal gloom*
> *with dulness cheers, 'tis now the Living Room;*
> *where Guests, to whim, a taste, or fancy true,*
> *scatter'd in groups, their different plans to pursue.*

Drawing rooms like that at Attingham in Shropshire still have the cluttered look so typical of the Regency period. The white and gold Neapolitan furniture here was acquired by the 3rd Lord Berwick from the effects of Caroline Murat, Queen of Naples, but it is of the standard Empire type that became as popular here as in France and Germany at a time when the international market in books, engravings and mezzotints made English fashion and decoration less insular. The concept of the 'living room', which Repton supplied at Sheringham Hall in Norfolk in place of what he called 'a useless Drawing Room', almost exactly characterizes the modern drawing room or lounge – a horrible word that does at least suggest the extremes of informality and relaxation that a servant-less society has made possible. Just as when an Edith Wharton heroine led the way into 'that wilderness of red velvet and palms they called the Winter Drawing Room', so it is hard today to see, among the beanbags and coffee tables, an echo of the formal circle and the cultured *conversazione* of the ladies' withdrawing room in an Adam country house.

Opposite] A breath of the Mediterranean in rural Shropshire: the drawing room at Attingham Park, designed by George Steuart for the 1st Lord Berwick in 1782, and largely furnished in the 1830s by the 3rd Baron with the fruits of his embassy to Naples. The daybed in the foreground and many of the white and gold chairs, upholstered in painted silk, belonged to Queen Caroline Murat whose villa he had rented. The pictures by Philipp Hackert and Angelica Kauffmann were bought slightly earlier by his brother who was in Italy in the 1790s, and their hanging – widely spaced and interspersed with great sheets of mirror – reflects the new fashion for uncrowded simplicity made popular by the Prince Regent at Carlton House.

8   Bedchambers

Sixteenth-century needlework bed-hangings, with a seventeenth-century fringe, in King Charles's Room at Cotehele. The state bed in an Elizabethan house was a status symbol that could cost as much as all the rest of the furniture put together.

To 'go up to bed' has become as natural in the twentieth century as to 'come down to breakfast'. But for the greater part of the period covered by this book – until at least 1770 – such phrases would have been meaningless in England, for life, whether in the state rooms of a country house or in the private family apartments, was often lived on one level. To have a withdrawing room without a bedchamber beyond it was almost unthinkable: hence the enfilade of eight or more doors offering a vista the whole length of the *piano nobile* in a Baroque or Palladian house, from the saloon in the centre to a drawing room, bedroom, dressing room and closet on each side.

The term 'bedchamber' itself dates back only to the mid-sixteenth century, for in the Middle Ages a 'chamber' was used for receiving guests, doing business with tenants or vassals, eating, sleeping, sitting, and a hundred other activities – curiously like the 'open-plan' living advocated centuries later by Le Corbusier. Such a chamber combined the functions of the saloon, dining room, withdrawing room and bedchamber in a fully-fledged eighteenth-century house, and we have already seen how its division and sub-division into separate compartments accompanied a search for greater privacy and comfort on the part of owners.

The emergence of the bed as the most important piece of furniture in the house, and a potent symbol of rank and wealth, developed from the desire for privacy. Long curtains were suspended from a canopy or 'sparver', often hung from hooks on the ceiling, to protect its occupants from the gaze of servants and attendants who slept on straw pallets which they unrolled on the floor of the chamber at night – as still happens in parts of the Arab world. This tent form of bed was easily movable, for it could be erected above any simple oak-framed bedstead, and suited the nomadic life of most medieval landowners. The hangings needed to be thick both for warmth and to cut down the noise made by other inhabitants of this semi-public room. Textiles were relatively one of the most expensive commodities in life until Sir Richard Arkwright's invention of mechanized spinning in the late eighteenth century. So bed curtains of this sort (which long preceded the fashion for window curtains) were from the beginning considered luxuries, which in turn conferred prestige on their owners.

The growth of sheep farming in England as a result of the land enclosures of the fifteenth and sixteenth centuries meant that wool became one of the country's most important exports to the rest of Europe and was more easily obtainable than other materials. Thus many of the earliest bed-hangings to have survived are woollen, elaborately embroidered in flame-stitch or crewel-work. At Cotehele in Cornwall, which still preserves the atmosphere of a late fifteenth-century manor house even if its furniture and tapestries were largely added over the following two centuries, there are examples of both these types. The colours are still remarkably fresh, for after about 1700 the family chose to live at their main seat Mount

Edgcumbe, fifteen miles away, and Cotehele stood shuttered and dust-sheeted like a sleeping beauty, to be re-awoken only in the Victorian period.

The Cotehele bedsteads are already of the four-post type generally in use by the mid-sixteenth century, with a solid oak frame supporting a ceiling (known as a tester) as large as the area of the bed itself. Outer and inner valances, or pelmets, hid the iron rails from which the curtains hung on rings and prevented draughts from entering at the top, while similar foot or base valances hung down from the sides of the slatted bed-frame to the floor. Considerable heat could be built up inside a bed of this type by leaving the curtains nearest the fire open, and closing the rest. Nowadays most four-post beds are kept with their curtains permanently open, but in paintings and engravings right up to Hogarth's *Marriage à la Mode* series of 1743–5 they are shown closed during the daytime when the room was used for a multitude of other activities and when the sight of sheets and pillows might have been thought immodest. In *The Levée* Hogarth shows the young Countess at her *toilette* attended by the family lawyer, a castrato singer and musicians, a fop with his hair in curlers, her hairdresser and dancing-master, a negro page unpacking purchases made at the sale-room and various other hangers-on. A vivid commentary on eighteenth-century life, the picture also demonstrates the way bedchambers had been used in a country house for at least two hundred years previously: they were particularly crowded at the time of the morning *levée*. The 'Old Masters' on the walls, representing the Rape of Ganymede, the Rape of Io, and Lot's daughters getting him drunk in order to seduce him, are perhaps more explicit in their sexual overtones than the pictures usually found in an Elizabethan bedchamber, but love and marriage are themes constantly found in the decoration of bedchambers from the earliest times.

In Bess of Hardwick's Best Bedchamber at Hardwick, the overmantel has a carved alabaster figure of Charity suckling a child with another pulling at her skirts – perhaps also a symbol of fertility – while in the Pearl Bedchamber beyond is a bas-relief by Thomas Accres of *The Marriage of Tobias*, a story that this much-married old lady was fond of applying to herself. The Brussels tapestries representing allegories of the Planets were already in this room in 1601, when the carved and gilt bed was described as having valances 'imbrodered with silver golde and pearle with sivines [i.e. raspberries] and woodbines fringed with golde silver and black silk'. Bess's arms with those of her second husband Sir William Cavendish appeared on the head-cloth, though in general coats of arms were more usually reserved for the back-cloths of canopies of state.

While some of the original embroidered bed-hangings survive at Hardwick, as at Cotehele, re-applied on to later damask or velvet, it is hard to imagine how dazzling the blue and red satin curtains of those in the Best Bedchamber must have seemed, striped with gold and silver and crowned by a double valance of cloth of gold, cloth of silver and 'sondrie coulers of velvet imbrodered fayre with divers armes with portalls and pictures'. The room also contained one 'greate chare' covered in crimson velvet embroidered with gold, and given a cushion of the same material with the addition of pearls in the embroidery, gold fringe, and tassels of silver and yellow silk. This must have been like the X-frame 'chairs of state' seen in the background of early seventeenth-century portraits by William Larkin and

Marcus Gheeraerts, always with fat cushions placed across the arms so as to look more like symbolic thrones than everyday chairs to sit in.

The use of such a chair was indeed ceremonial, for it was placed at the foot of the bed for its occupant to sit in when receiving the elaborate courtesy calls that were a part of formal entertaining right up to the eighteenth century. The system can be seen in action from a rare description of a visit to Petworth made in 1703 by the King of Spain (the future Emperor Charles VI) and Prince George of Denmark, Queen Anne's husband, at the invitation of the 'Proud Duke' of Somerset. When the Prince came to visit him, the King advanced to the bedchamber door to receive him, then sat in an armchair at the foot of his bed, inviting his guest to sit in another chair directly opposite. Etiquette demanded that when the King repaid this call, the Prince – being of lower rank – should come to the door of his apartment to welcome his guest before leading him back through a withdrawing room and ante room to his bedchamber.

In form, these chairs of state derived from the folding medieval throne or *sella curulis* used by kings and bishops, which can be traced back to the Bayeux Tapestry and to even earlier illuminated manuscripts. Hardly any original examples survive today, except for those at Knole which are thought to be royal in origin and to have been acquired as perquisites by Lionel Cranfield, Earl of Middlesex, Lord Treasurer and later Master of the Wardrobe to James I and Charles I. Perhaps the most interesting of them all is to be found in the Spangled Room at Knole, upholstered to match the Spangled Bed, so called after its magnificent crimson and white satin hangings originally sewn with thousands of small silver spangles or sequins, some of which can still be seen on close examination. When new, the bed, the armchair and its footstool, and the eight other high stools, must have shimmered as the breeze from the open windows stirred the hangings and covers.

If the furniture of the Spangled Room gives a unique glimpse of the grandeur of an early seventeenth-century state bedchamber, two other outstanding beds at Knole, complete with their sets of chairs and stools, show the still greater triumphs of carving and upholstery that were to follow in the Restoration period . Once again these came to the house as royal perquisites, but this time through Cranfield's grandson, the 6th Earl of Dorset, who was Lord Chamberlain of the Household to William III. The custom (the origin of the modern 'perks') was for such officials to take any outmoded furniture or fittings from the palaces under their jurisdiction, and indeed the contents of whole rooms after a sovereign's death. Thus, after Queen Mary's death in 1695, Lord Dorset was given a magnificent state bed ordered by James II and delivered to the Palace of Whitehall in November 1688, only a month before the King fled to France.

The bed, now in the Venetian Ambassador's Room at Knole, is complete with its two armchairs and six stools, 'richly carved with figures and gilt all over with gold', forming one of the most splendid sets of late Stuart furniture in existence. The carving on the tester – including James II's monogram and crown, supported by lions and unicorns – and on the chair frames, with their draped figures and trumpeting putti, was executed by Thomas Roberts, while the hangings, described in the Royal warrant as 'green and gold figured velvet with scarlet and white silk fringe', were almost certainly made by a Huguenot

Opposite] The Spangled Room at Knole is called after the 'spangled' hangings of the bed, sewn with tiny silver sequins on a scarlet silk background that must have rustled and glinted in the breeze. An X-frame 'chair of state', upholstered to match, still survives in the room (*above*) and both may date from before the Civil War. Chairs of this form appear in the backgrounds of portraits by Marcus Gheeraerts and William Larkin, and ultimately derive from the *sella curulis*, or folding throne, made for itinerant medieval households.

upholsterer, Jean Poitevin. In style this magnificent furniture is very obviously inspired by French prototypes, and the influence of Louis XIV's court was to make itself felt in bedchambers more than perhaps any other rooms in English country houses at this date. The influx of Huguenot craftsmen after the Revocation of the Edict of Nantes in 1685 was one reason for this, but another was the direct import of fashionable Parisian furniture.

The third state bed at Knole, and the most magnificent of all, is that in the King's Bedroom, which recent research suggests is French rather than English, and which may have been supplied by Louis XIV's own upholsterer Jean Peyrard who paid visits to England in 1672 and 1673, bringing no less than six beds for Charles II. 1673 was also the year of James II's marriage (while still Duke of York) to Mary of Modena, and the chairs and stools at Knole, carved with *amorini* holding bows and quivers, and pairs of billing doves, may have been intended to celebrate this event. The rare combination of gilding and silvering, intended to match the gold and silver brocade of the covers and bed-hangings, was found under a later layer of black paint – a reminder that bedchambers were often used for formal visits of condolence after a death when their contents would be painted black for the period of mourning and when black or purple serge would be substituted for tapestries and bed-hangings. On the death of the 1st Duke of Kingston in 1726, his granddaughter recalled that

the apartments . . . were hung with black cloth; the Duchess, closely veiled in crepe, sat upright in her State-bed under a high black canopy . . . the room had no light but for the single wax taper, and the condoling female visitors, who curtseyed in and out of it . . . approached the bed on tiptoe, and were clothed, if relations down to the hundredth cousin, in black glove mourning.

Because of the sheer weight of the gold and silver thread, the hangings of the King's Bed at Knole had already begun to decay by the early nineteenth century, when the novelist Maria Edgeworth described 'in the silver room a bed, as the show woman trumpetted forth, of gold tissue which cost 8 thousand guineas new, now in tarnished tatters not worth, with Christies best puffing, 8 thousand pence this day'. Today, after a ten-year restoration programme, this precious object has regained much of its former glory, and although the crimson and white of the ostrich plumes and the 'Cherry Coloured Satin' of the lining have long since flown (except in a few folds never exposed to daylight), it remains perhaps the finest example in Europe of a state bed of the Louis XIV period.

The silver furniture in the King's Bedroom is almost as celebrated and as rare a survival as the bed. By the early seventeenth century bedchambers were almost invariably supplied with a matching set of looking glass, table and candlestands to stand against the pier between the windows (hence the term 'pier glass' and 'pier table') – usually on the wall opposite the bed, so that those using them should be brightly lit by the windows in daytime and by candles at night. However, the development of the dressing room and closet meant that ladies' (and gentlemen's) *toilettes* were less frequently performed in the bedchamber as the century wore on, and this set of furniture (referred to by some modern historians as the 'triad' because of its three component parts) was consequently conceived more for show and less for practical purposes. Elaborate examples were made in almost every medium: lacquer and coromandel, walnut inlaid with pewter, seaweed marquetry, boulle, and even silver –

Opposite] The bed in the Venetian Ambassador's Room at Knole, made for James II and given to the 6th Earl of Dorset as a perquisite in his capacity as William III's Lord Chamberlain. Bedchambers in the Baroque period were usually equipped with a set of furniture comprising mirror, table and stands in walnut, marquetry or lacquer. The silver set in the King's Room at Knole (*above*) is an extraordinary survival, recalling the splendour of the silver furniture at Versailles, melted down to pay for Louis XIV's Flemish campaigns.

with decorative tops to the tables which can never have been meant for the laying out of a toilet set.

Apart from a set at Windsor Castle, presented to Charles II by the City of London, no other English silver 'triads' like that at Knole survive, for the very good reason that the embossed plate could be removed and melted down at any time – as happened to the famous silver furniture at Versailles in the later stages of Louis XIV's Flemish campaigns. Since 1701, when the room assumed its present appearance, the mirror has hung in true Baroque fashion against one of the Mortlake tapestries representing the story of Nebuchadnezzar, and the way the astonished figures gesture towards it in surprise adds to the effect of dramatic splendour. At night, with candles in the silver sconces all round the room reflected in the mirrors, the polished doors of the great ebony cabinet, and the glinting gold and silver thread of the bed curtains, this must have seemed an unforgettable Aladdin's cave.

Despite its richness, the King's Bed at Knole is comparatively simple in outline compared with many of the elaborate confections put together by Huguenot upholsterers at the end of the seventeenth century, influenced by the designs of Daniel Marot. The state bed at Dyrham has its original crimson and yellow velvet outer hangings which have lasted better than the sprigged satin used for the interior. Both the cornice and the base have heavy broken mouldings not so very different from a state coach of the period, but applied with material, edged with braids and fringes of incredible complexity. The high-backed chairs *en suite* with the bed at Dyrham are of a characteristic bedroom type with upholstery totally covering the frames except for the legs, unlike withdrawing room chairs where the arms and the outer framework of the back were generally uncovered wood or gilt gesso: a distinction that prevailed throughout the eighteenth century. By this date most bedchambers also contained a clock – either a walnut or lacquer longcase, or a smaller bracket clock in an ebony case perhaps with silver mounts. English clockmakers like Joseph Knibb and Thomas Tompion led the world, and examples of their work were highly prized on the Continent, reaching even Russia and Turkey.

A bed like that at Dyrham would be far and away the most expensive single item in a house. For instance, the one made by Francis Lapiere for the 1st Duke of Devonshire at Chatsworth in 1697 cost £470, while its frame (though a considerable feat of engineering) came to only £15. The canopy of this remarkable piece of furniture still survives in the long gallery at Hardwick, and shows Lapiere to have been one of the outstanding craftsmen of his day. It is of the form known as a flying or 'angel' tester, hung out from the wall so as to dispense with the need for end-posts and foot-curtains. The cresting consists of scrolling acanthus leaves, flowers and pierced cartouches worthy of Grinling Gibbons, close-covered in crimson damask with silver braids of different patterns, while below it hang great festoons and *mouchoirs* – like the neckerchiefs used in contemporary dress. It is no accident that these valances also resemble Marot's designs for window curtains. In the highly unified interiors he advocated, not only would bed and window curtains exactly match (as they do at Dyrham and Beningbrough) but the wall-hangings might also have the same gathered festoons and flounces carried all round as a pelmet – even over the doors as headings to the *portières*. The chairs, strictly regimented against the walls, would also be upholstered to

Opposite] The state bed at Dyrham Park, covered with crimson and yellow velvet and with an interior of sprigged satin, is typical of the elaborate upholstery of bedchambers made popular in England at the end of the seventeenth century by Daniel Marot, William III's *chef du dessin*. William Blathwayt, the owner of Dyrham and William's Secretary at War, had his own apartments in the Dutch royal palace of Het Loo where he would have encountered Marot and his work at first hand, just as he purchased Delft tulip vases from Adriansz Kocks, the potter particularly favoured by Queen Mary. The bed not only has a set of chairs upholstered *en suite*, but also matching valances for the window curtains, all of them probably supplied by a Huguenot upholsterer in Marot's circle such as Francis Lapiere or Jean Poitevin.

match, leaving only the chimneypiece and the overmantel outside of the upholsterer's responsibility.

With so much money at stake, care was always taken to protect these chairs with case-covers, often only removed on the grandest occasions. To prevent dust and light falling on the bed, case-curtains like those recently re-introduced at Dyrham were hung from a metal rod, which was usually gilded, projecting outwards from the tester, and these are visible in most of Marot's engravings. Alternatively, loose covers of expensive material are occasionally found, as at Erddig, and these could be removed when the room was not in use.

The French fashion for a bed alcove separated by a balustrade from the rest of the room was followed in Charles II's palaces, and may have been more widespread in country houses than now appears. A balustrade is known to have existed in the Queen's Bedchamber at Ham, and another still exists in the state bedroom at Powis Castle, probably prepared for the visit of the Duke of Beaufort who was the King's representative in Wales as Lord President of the Council in 1684. Grand 'public' bedchambers like this often had a little door near the bed which provided an escape route to a smaller and more comfortable room behind, once the formal ceremony of going to bed known as the *coucher* was over and the company had retired – and a means of emerging in time for the formal *levée* in the morning. In the state bedchamber at Boughton this is in the form of a jib-door cut through the Mortlake tapestry and virtually invisible. The alcove continued to be popular in later Palladian houses because it allowed the rest of the room to be used for other purposes during the day, as in Hogarth's *Marriage à la Mode*. But the balustrade disappeared with the increasing informality of upper-class life long before it was abandoned in the rest of Europe.

Marot's engravings of bedchambers have a fantastic character, setting them apart from the halls, saloons and withdrawing rooms that precede them, each more ornate and less architectural than its predecessor. This taste for the exotic was often expressed by the use of Oriental materials like the embroidered Chinese silk of the state bed at Erddig in North Wales, possibly obtained through a near-neighbour, Elihu Yale, Governor of Fort St George in India between 1682 and 1690. Yale (later famous as the founder of the great American university) also brought back a Chinese lacquer screen, which was listed in the state bedroom in 1726 in company with a mid-seventeenth-century boulle *bureau mazarin* which was used as a dressing table. The latter was interestingly described by a visitor to the house in 1732 as 'Henry VIII's writing desk' – a good instance of how an old-fashioned object, considered suitably bizarre for such surroundings, could easily acquire a picturesque history all its own.

There could be no better illustration of the revolution in taste brought about by William Kent than the two state beds at Houghton. The first has hangings of English needlework in the Oriental style, probably based on pattern books like Stalker and Parker's famous *Treatise on Japanning and Varnishing* published in 1688. Its tester and headboard are decorated with scrolls and cartouches in the Marot style, including the Walpole coat-of-arms with its prominent crest of a Saracen's head said to have been granted to an ancestor at the siege of Acre in 1191. As a convinced Palladian, Sir Robert must have considered this bed old-fashioned by 1731, when it was occupied by the future Emperor Francis I of Austria, and in

Opposite] The Embroidered Bedchamber at Houghton is named after the early eighteenth-century bed-hangings of so-called 'Indian Needlework', actually English but worked with bright flowers and birds in chain-stitch on a white quilted ground, imitating examples of Chinese lacquer and silks which were then being imported through the East India Company. The colours both of the bed and the Brussels tapestries which surround it seem as fresh as the day they were made, and the immense height of the canopy, rising away above the cornice into Kent's blue and gold painted cove, gives an extraordinary sensation of grandeur in a room of comparatively small proportions.

A corner of the tester of the
Embroidered Bed at Houghton,
showing Sir Robert Walpole's arms
(three cross-crosslets or, on a fesse
between two chevrons sable) encircled
by the Order of the Garter and
surmounted by the Saracen's head crest,
said, somewhat dubiously, to have been
granted to a Walpole at the siege of Acre
in 1191. The braids, fringes and
needlework with which the carving is
close-covered make this a masterpiece of
the upholsterer's art.

Part of the tester of the Green State Bed at Holkham almost certainly supplied to the Countess of Leicester by the tapestry-weaver and upholsterer Paul Saunders of Greek Street, Soho, soon after her husband's death in 1759. Many would have considered the use of a 'mixed' red and green Genoese cut velvet old-fashioned by this date, but it was perfectly suited to the highly architectural rooms devised by William Kent and Lord Leicester in the 1730s. Because the Green State Bedroom was on the circuit of state apartments generally opened for county balls and other entertainments, a settee upholstered in the same velvet generally stood under the canopy, and this only folded out to become a bed on the rare formal occasions that the room was actually occupied. Saunders also wove one of the four tapestries in the room representing the Continents to accompany three others from an earlier Brussels set.

the following year he commissioned Kent to design a new green velvet bed which was to be the culmination of his interior decoration at Houghton. No prototypes for canopied beds were to be found in the sixteenth-century treatises of Palladio and his followers, so Kent devised a strictly architectural form which would complement the harmonic proportions of the rooms, based on variations of the cube. The tester is an adaption of a full Doric entablature, with the 'mouldings' carried out in appliqué gold and silver thread or 'galloon'. This 'gold lace', as it was described in the accounts of 1732, cost Walpole nearly £1200, a staggering sum of money which did not include the green silk velvet used for the hangings and for the upholstery of the chairs.

The tapestries in the room, made at Brussels after designs by Francesco Albani, represent Venus and Vulcan, and Venus and Adonis – highly appropriate scenes for the decoration of a bedroom – and the colour green, generally associated with Venus, may have been specially chosen to continue this theme. The great double shell of the headboard may be derived from the early seventeenth-century *sgabello* chairs in the Italian style which Kent would have associated with his hero Inigo Jones, but it must, too, be a reference to the scallop shell in which Venus arose from the sea at the moment of her birth.

Ransacking the work of Inigo Jones and his contemporaries for new ideas was a favourite occupation of the Palladians, and seems even to have appealed to Robert Adam in his designs for the remarkable state bed at Kedleston which dates from 1760. Its palm-tree posts with great gilded branches and almost comic roots, carved out of cedar wood, seem to derive from an engraving for a bed-alcove designed for Charles II by John Webb, and wrongly attributed to his master in John Vardy's *Designs of Mr. Inigo Jones and Mr. William Kent*, published in 1744. Adam's immediate inspiration may, however, have been a set of earlier gilt chairs and settees and two small mirrors dating from the 1740s here and in the adjoining boudoir. The builder of Kedleston, Sir Nathaniel Curzon, presumably told Adam to retain these in the scheme for his new apartment – and the latter responded with the extraordinarily imaginative bed, pier glass and candlestands, all decorated with palm fronds and very different from the polite palmettes and anthemions of the plasterwork ceiling.

Contemporary theories about the origin of the Corinthian order, whose columns were said to derive from sprouting tree trunks, may also have given him some justification for this bold essay in the Italian Baroque manner. At the same time the Italian feeling of the room is enhanced by the blue damask of the wall-hangings with its elaborate gilt fillet, the earlier family portraits in the exuberant Van Dyck manner, and the chimneypiece of variegated marbles with a central plaque of local Derbyshire blue-john, England's only serious answer to the coloured Italian marbles of Siena and Volterra.

Adam's most celebrated bed was designed much later, in 1776, for the banker Robert Child at Osterley in Middlesex. Here there were no earlier pieces of furniture or family portraits to use, for the Childs were relatively parvenu. So the architect was free to create one of his most unified interiors, an allegory of the garden of love which continued the theme of the Boucher tapestries representing the *Les Amours des Dieux*, and the chair covers from the series known as *Les Enfants Jardiniers* in the adjoining drawing room. The walls and the outer hangings of the bed are of green velvet and the valances are embroidered with the

The interior of the Green Velvet Bed at Houghton, designed by William Kent in 1732. The gold trimmings alone cost £1,219. 3s. 11d., and the surviving bill from 'Turner, Hill & Pitter in the Strand' specifies every fringe, flower and tassel. The tapestries in the room represent the loves of Venus and Adonis, a suitable theme for a bedchamber, and it is possible that the great double shell of the headboard was intended as a reference to the birth of Venus, rising from the waves, as depicted by Botticelli. The shell motif was often used by Inigo Jones and his contemporaries, and it may also be that this was Kent's tribute to the first English disciple of Palladio – just as Adam's later state bed at Kedleston with its palm-tree posts (*opposite*) pays tribute to a design for Charles II's bedchamber at Whitehall, then considered to be by Jones but in fact by his disciple John Webb.

Overleaf] The state bedroom at Blickling Hall was given its present form by William Ivory about 1779, and the quality of the plasterwork by William Wilkins, preserving its original gilding on a parchment white ground, shows a new awareness of French Neoclassical decoration in the Louis Seize period. The placing of the bed behind a screen of columns is by contrast an old-fashioned idea, derived from late seventeenth-century alcove chambers, while the bed itself is an adaptation of a royal canopy of state of George II, given to the 2nd Earl of Buckinghamshire as Lord of the Bedchamber after the King's death in 1760.

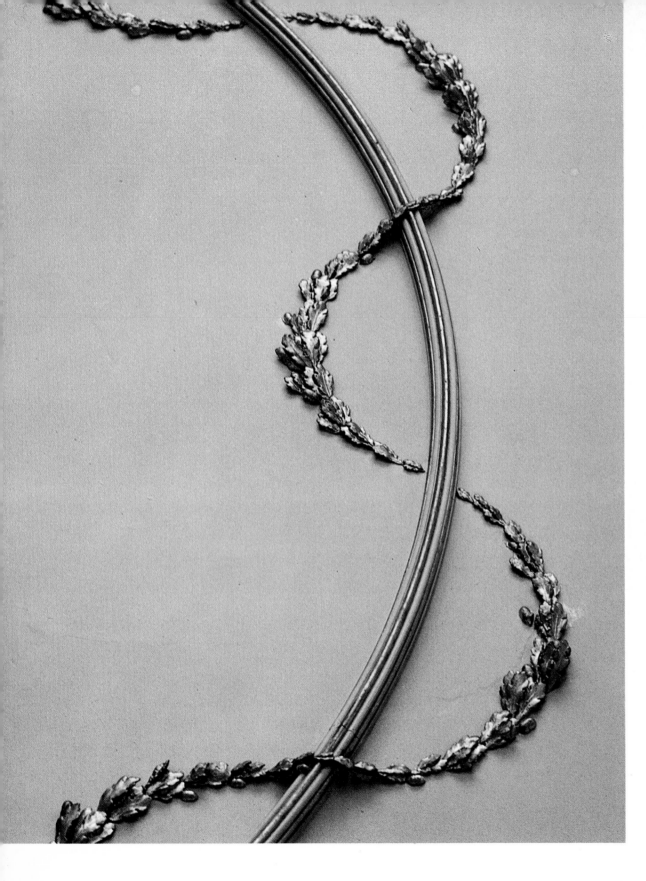

Child crest – an eagle holding an adder in its beak – alternating with a marigold, the sign of the shop in the City where the family fortunes had prospered. A circular dome surmounts the square tester, giving the bed something of the air of an emperor's chariot seen on antique medals and in classical Roman wall-paintings, but Horace Walpole found it 'too theatric and like a modern head-dress, for round the outside of the dome are festoons of artificial flowers' – which have recently been reinstated. 'What', he asked, 'would Vitruvius think of a dome decorated by a milliner?'

One interesting detail of the Osterley bedchamber is the Moorfields bed-carpet, a three-sided strip specially woven to Adam's design with rosettes echoing the embroidered wreaths of the valances. Carpets of this sort were regularly supplied with beds from the early eighteenth century, though few survive. That in the state bedroom at Blickling is an Axminster, matching the border of the large floral carpet in the centre of the room. The bed itself, with the arms of George II embroidered on the headcloth, looks decidedly old-fashioned in its Neoclassical surroundings designed by the Norwich architect William Ivory in 1779. Like several others in English country houses, it is in fact an adaptation of a canopy of state, either from a royal palace or from an ambassador's equipage issued by the Royal Wardrobe. The 2nd Earl of Buckinghamshire was Lord of the Bedchamber to George II at the time of the King's death in 1760, and it therefore seems certain that it came to Blickling as a perquisite. The screen of Ionic columns forming a bed-alcove is also old-fashioned in feeling. But the serpentine chest of drawers and dressing-table by Vile and Cobb, supplied in the 1760s, show a greater attention to comfort and convenience than the rows of chairs against the wall that still provided the standard furnishing of most state bedchambers.

The gilding of the architectural details at Blickling is of the very finest quality, and is a reminder that particular store was set by gilding in rooms designed to be seen at night, when picture and mirror frames, doorcases and ormolu mounts on furniture would pick up the dancing flames of candles in sconces and chamber sticks, and be visible by the dying embers of a log fire even after these had been extinguished.

The fashion for *chinoiserie* bedrooms, already seen at Erddig and Houghton, had not abated as the century wore on. At Nostell Priory in Yorkshire, Thomas Chippendale not only supplied the green and gold lacquer furniture in 1771, but also the Chinese hand-painted wallpaper, thirty-six sheets in all as 'the person they belong to will not sell them separate nor will he take under 15s. a sheet'. In the Chinese Bedroom at Saltram, the wall-hangings are painted on cotton rather than paper, and are also accompanied by furniture in the so-called 'Chinese Chippendale' style: padouk-wood chairs with pagoda crestings, hanging shelves for the display of Oriental porcelain, and Chinese mirror paintings in English Rococo gilt frames. The bed may well have been supplied by Chippendale himself and is close to designs in his famous pattern-book *The Gentleman and Cabinet-Maker's Director*, published in 1754, while its earlier needlework hangings were probably produced by ladies of the Parker family. The delicacy of their endless different stitches (long, short, chain, back and other varieties) is a perfect accompaniment to the small-scale ornament of the wall-hangings, and the decoration must have given the guests who stayed here pleasantly fantastic dreams. The bedchamber at Osterley was one of the last to be

Opposite] *Chinoiserie* was a favourite theme for bedrooms in the mid-eighteenth century, and its exotic fantasies may have been considered a suitable accompaniment to the world of dreams. The Chinese Bedroom at Blickling, dating from the 1760s, has a hand-painted Oriental paper without any exact repeats, but filled out at top and bottom with a wide border using the same colours in a mottled pattern – evidently because the sections it came in were not tall enough. The furniture includes a pair of Chinese ivory pagodas, and white japanned wardrobe probably from a set of furniture made by Chippendale for David Garrick's house in the Adelphi in the early 1770s. The knotted Exeter carpet, and the Norwich shawl valances of the bed embroidered with the Hobart and other family arms, have preserved their original colours to a remarkable extent.

Overleaf] The Chinese Chippendale Bedroom at Saltram has painted cotton hangings also imported from the Far East, together with two of a set of eight Chinese mirror paintings in English Rococo frames. The bed is close to a design in Chippendale's *Director* and may have been supplied by his workshop about 1760, though its exquisite embroidered hangings are slightly earlier and perhaps the work of Lady Catherine Parker and her ladies.

THE LIBRARY
COLLEGE OF FURTHER EDUCATION
NORTHAMPTON

constructed on the *piano nobile* as part of the state apartments intended primarily for show, and already in the early 1770s many earlier beds were being moved upstairs, like those at Petworth and Erddig. Because these rooms were more regularly used and were not part of the 'public route', they tended to become smaller and more intimate, and Saltram is a good example of this trend.

The vogue for Chinese and Japanese artefacts, still indiscriminately called 'Indian' because of their arrival in the trading ships of the East India Company, led to the manufacture of English printed cottons imitating hand-painted silks like that at Saltram. The results, soon Europeanized and more floral than figurative in design, were the innumerable 'chintzes' which, since the early nineteenth century, have been considered a peculiarly English phenomenon by the rest of the world and a symbol of the informal way of life adopted by the upper classes in the Regency period. The Mary Queen of Scots Apartments at Chatsworth recall that unfortunate Queen's imprisonment here in the sixteenth century, but they were entirely remodelled first by William Talman in the 1690s and then by the 6th Duke of Devonshire in the 1820s. It would be hard to find more magnificent examples of the upholsterer's art than the bed and window curtains in the Scots Bedchamber. The enormously heavy draperies seem not in the least pompous because they are made of a chintz with a white ground and naturalistic flowers of every hue, lined with a pale blue silk equally light and summery in effect. In the ceiling of the tester this lining is crushed like the inside of a jewel-casket, while the fringes are so deep that they consist of carved wooden toggles, nine or ten inches long, bound in silk thread and finished with gimp and metalled braid.

Bedroom furniture of this date, made by Gillows of Lancaster and other leading makers, included bed-steps – often essential to surmount the heavily-stuffed mattresses and feather bolsters that were customary – Grecian couches, 'curricle' chairs and fire-screens, cheval glasses, pot-cupboards and bidets. But then these rooms were intended to be used more regularly than the great state bedchambers of a previous generation, symbols of power and of ancient lineage, as strong in their effect on us today as the castellated towers and statue-lined parapets in whose shadow they lie.

Opposite] Upholstery in the early nineteenth century became almost as ornate as it had been in the late seventeenth. The designs of Gillows of Lancaster and others show immense 'continued draperies' carried over three or four windows at a time, and often matching bed-hangings such as these in the Mary Queen of Scots Apartments at Chatsworth, redecorated by the 6th Duke of Devonshire in the 1820s. The material used is a chintz whose pale colours lighten the heavy effect of the festoons, trimmed with a 'toggle' fringe of huge scale.

9 Dressing Rooms, Cabinets and Closets

To be received in the bedchamber of a great personage was an honour accorded to few. Just as 'Princes of the Blood' were allowed by right into Charles II's bedchamber, and Privy Councillors by permission, so in a country house only an owner's close relations or most trusted advisers were generally admitted. It was therefore a sign of even greater intimacy to be invited into the dressing room or cabinet beyond, the inner sanctum of the country house. By the late seventeenth century the former was likely to adjoin a lady's bedchamber, and the latter a gentleman's, while each had a separate closet where the 'close stool' (confusingly rechristened the commode in the nineteenth century) would have stood. But just as there was an agreeable lack of rules governing spelling at this period, so the names of these rooms were bewilderingly interchangeable. At Ham, the close stool was kept in a cupboard off the Queen's Ante Room (really the state dressing room); the Queen's Closet was very much a show room with the richest decoration in the house; while the Green Closet, not attached to a bedchamber at all, was really a picture cabinet.

William III's cabinets at Hampton Court and Kensington were, as at his Dutch royal palace of Het Loo, not only where he hung his finest small pictures but also where the inner circle of his ministers met to discuss matters of the greatest secrecy – giving their name to one of England's most enduring political institutions. Queen Mary's dressing rooms, which occupied exactly balancing positions in her own apartments, were equally influential in their way, for it was here that she amassed the collections of Chinese porcelain and Delft pottery, and the examples of lacquer, coromandel and japanned furniture, which were to be imitated in so many country houses over the next century.

The planning of a typical Baroque house allowed for a dressing room, a closet and sometimes also a small servants' staircase in a space no bigger (and sometimes considerably smaller) than that of the adjoining bedchamber. The dressing room or cabinet would mark the end of the enfilade of state rooms and was generally at the corner of a building, while a right-angled turn leading off this main axis would bring one to the closet. In proportion to their size, both would also be considerably lower than their neighbouring bedchambers, sometimes allowing for servants' quarters on a mezzanine above. This rational layout was of course impossible to achieve in an older house like Knole or Drayton where bedchambers lay at the end of galleries; in these cases, retiring to a dressing room or closet might necessitate a draughty journey across or down the whole length of a gallery.

Dressing rooms were in fact unknown to the Elizabethans and it is interesting that Bess of Hardwick kept her writing desk and books, her looking glass and jewel coffers, all in her bedchamber. A closet at this time was usually no more than the word implied, a poky hole often without light and, more surprisingly, without ventilation. Bess's closet, for instance, contained only her own 'close stoole covered with blewe cloth stitcht with white, with red and black silk frenge, three pewter basons, a little close stoole' (presumably for her

The King's Closet at Knole, with a close stool in the foreground which could indeed have royal origins. Like so many other contents of the house, it may have been acquired as a perquisite by the 6th Earl of Dorset who was Lord Chamberlain to William III. The rare late seventeenth-century wall-hangings, still bordered with the original woollen tasselled fringe, are of a rough-textured mohair, dyed green and stamped (or *gauffré*) to resemble watered silk. Material like this is described in early inventories but practically no other examples of it survive.

granddaughter Arabella Stuart), a coffer, a chest and two trunks. In the absence of corridors, the chamber pots or close stool pans which stood here ready for collection by an unfortunate servant would then be carried back through the state rooms. The provision of back stairs in the 'double-pile' houses of the Restoration at least meant that these could disappear unseen, and the lawyer and amateur architect Roger North thought that this innovation had done more to introduce 'politer living' than any other architectural improvement of his day.

Though small and dark, the early-seventeenth-century King's Closet at Knole is in fact a dressing room, and the windowless cupboard across the passage is where the occupants of the great silver and gold state bed would have been expected to make their ablutions. On the other hand, the close stool (now shown in the dressing room) is a particularly luxurious example, upholstered in crimson velvet and possibly a perquisite acquired by the 6th Earl of Dorset from one of the royal palaces. The green mohair wall-hangings, stamped (or *gauffré*) to resemble watered silk and bordered with an elaborate woollen bobble-fringe, probably date from the 1690s and are an extremely rare survival of a material commonly used where warmth rather than elegance was required. Eighteenth-century close stools are more frequently found in country houses, and those at Dunham Massey in Cheshire fall into four categories depending on the importance of the apartment served: deal, mahogany, walnut, and, grandest of all, veneered walnut edged with ebony and with the Earl of Warrington's coronet and monogram in marquetry on the lids. The latter type were even supplied with silver pans.

The tradition of cabinets of curiosities, like the tradition of collecting itself, was brought to England from the Continent in the early seventeenth century by influential figures like the Earl of Arundel, Inigo Jones' patron, and was initially nothing to do with the mundane business of washing and dressing. Thus one of the earliest, the Green (or 'Fine') Closet at Ham, dating from the 1630s, was formed in a room off the long gallery quite separate from any of the bedchambers in the house. The room was devoted to a massed display of the 1st Earl of Dysart's rich collection of miniatures and other small paintings, retained here by his daughter and son-in-law, the Duke and Duchess of Lauderdale, during their redecoration of the house in the 1670s, and sadly thinned out only in this century. The paintings decorating the cove and ceiling, in tempera on paper, are by Franz Cleyn, Inigo Jones's friend and contemporary, and may have started life as tapestry cartoons for the Mortlake manufactory where he was artistic director. The subject of playing boys, after the sixteenth-century Italian painter Polidoro Caldara, probably inspired the carved stands of the two Japanese cabinets with their caryatid putti, and the similar supports of the squab frames and the silver-mounted table – all listed here by 1669.

No other surviving rooms of this date so nearly approach the atmosphere of a Renaissance prince's *studiolo*, save perhaps for the Corner and Little Ante Rooms at Wilton – in reality the dressing room and closet of the state apartment. These preserve much of their original 1650s decoration by Inigo Jones and John Webb, and their ceiling paintings by (or after) Luca Giordano and Lorenzo Sabbatini. But although the 5th Earl of Pembroke who completed the house, is known to have owned some of the pictures now displayed here, the present hanging is more likely to date from the early eighteenth century when the 8th Earl

Opposite] The Green Closet off the long gallery at Ham, part of Franz Cleyn's work for the 1st Earl of Dysart in the 1630s and one of the first picture cabinets on the Italian model to be provided in an English country house. The *Playing Boys* after Polidoro Caldara, painted by Cleyn in the cove and ceiling, were to become a favourite subject at the Mortlake tapestry works only a few miles down the Thames, where Cleyn was the artistic director.

added to the collection and re-arranged it along the same lines as his contemporary, the 6th Earl of Exeter's, two 'cabinets' at Burghley.

The idea of the picture cabinet only really prospered in the eighteenth century with the increasing popularity of the Grand Tour and Lord Burlington's championship of Italian Old Masters as a natural accompaniment to Palladian architecture: in the late seventeenth century dressing rooms and closets developed along different lines. Among the interiors at Ham redecorated in the 1670s, the Duke and Duchess of Lauderdale's dressing rooms (the latter's confusingly called the White Closet) were both supplied with *scriptores* or writing desks and were used primarily as studies. The Duchess's private closet was equipped primarily for taking tea, a new and still very expensive diversion for which she had not only a 'Japan box for sweetmeats & tea' but also a Javanese tea-table, raised on a stand so that it could be used with the six japanned chairs or 'backstools', made in England in imitation of Oriental lacquer. The 'Indian furnace for tee garnish'd with silver', which had strayed next door into the White Closet in the 1679 inventory, must also have belonged here as a rule. The Duke's Closet, and the Queen's Closet upstairs in the state apartments, had yet another function, for both were supplied with couches or daybeds in 1677, replaced two years later by the famous 'sleeping chairs' which still survive with their adjustable backs held by gilded iron ratchets. The Duke's was even referred to as the 'Reposing Closet' in 1683.

There could certainly be no pleasanter setting for an afternoon nap than the Queen's Closet, one of the smallest rooms with one of the richest decorative schemes to be found in any English house. The ceiling painting representing *Ganymede and the Eagle* is attributed to Antonio Verrio; the panelling is marbled 'white and vaind', with gilded carving, including a ducal coronet and shield above the arched alcove; the floor is of marquetry, originally protected with a leather cover; the chimney-surround, hearth and windowsill are all of scagliola – one of the earliest recorded uses in England of this imitation *pietra dura*, achieved by mixing marble dusts and colour pigments into an adhesive paste; and even the chimney furniture, fire-irons and dogs are 'garnished with silver'. The room originally had alternative sets of hangings for summer and winter, the former of Chinese silk with painted figures, the latter (which still miraculously survive) of crimson and gold brocaded satin bordered with a green and gold striped silk. Instead of the anti-climax that a room of these diminutive proportions might be expected to provide, the Queen's Closet is a worthy finale to the sequence of state rooms that precede it, breathtaking not only because of its magnificent decoration, but also because it allows a rare, almost voyeuristic, glimpse into the private lives of seventeenth-century grandees. Even a fellow member of the Cabal, Charles II's inner circle of ministers to which the Duke of Lauderdale belonged, must have baulked at disturbing their Graces in such intimate surroundings.

Besides the servants' staircase, another refinement in the planning of Baroque houses was the corner chimneypiece, first introduced by Wren at Kensington Palace and Hampton Court. Since the dressing room and closet each occupied half the space of the adjoining bedchamber, the dividing wall between them was likely to abut against the back of the bedroom fireplace, always placed in the centre of the side wall facing those who entered the room on the main enfilade. By placing the chimneypieces of both small rooms diagonally

Opposite] The sleeping alcove in the Queen's Closet at Ham, the innermost (and most intimate) of the state apartments prepared for Charles II's wife, Catherine of Braganza, in the 1670s. Perhaps originally intended for a couch or daybed, the alcove was later equipped with an upholstered armchair, the angle of whose back could be adjusted by gilded iron ratchets. Here the favoured occupant of the adjoining state bedchamber might read, doze or take tea in front of a blazing fire, and receive his or her closest friends, not more than one or two at a time.

across this corner, all three fireplaces could share the same flue and at the same time more warmth would be generated by building the chimney breast out into the room. At Beningbrough in Yorkshire there are no less than four sets of panelled dressing rooms and closets, at each end of the garden front on both main floors, all with corner chimneypieces. The Bourchiers evidently shared Queen Mary II's passion for china, for all eight of these have stepped ledges of slightly different design for the display of Delft or Oriental porcelain – vases and ginger jars, beakers and bowls – above rectangular panels intended for the usual 'landskip glass'. Tiers of blue and white, *famille verte* or polychrome in such surroundings would have been a perfect accompaniment to lacquer and Japanned furniture, caned daybeds and tea-tables. Some of it may indeed have been used for drinking tea and have been replaced on these ornamental shelves after use.

The state dressing room at Chatsworth is a room of just this type, even though the corner chimneypiece was only introduced in the early part of this century on the model of those at Hampton Court. The room was described by Celia Fiennes in 1697 as being 'the Duchess's Closet . . . wainscoted with the hollow burnt japan', meaning coromandel, and some of this still survives made into chests and cabinets at a later date. Closets with coromandel panelling still survive at Drayton in Northamptonshire and Honington in Warwickshire, using sections of screens cut up and joined together with a fine disregard for the Chinese craftsman's carefully worked out compositions. Here, in the words of Stalker and Parker's *Treatise on Japanning* 'you may observe the finest hodgpodg and medley of Men and Trees turned topsie turvie'. In the dressing room at Chatsworth there were also 'peers of looking-glass' at the four corners and an oval glass above the chimneypiece. Mirrors were used in combination with porcelain (both of them exceedingly expensive at this date) in several other houses, for instance in the Duchess of Somerset's closet at Petworth, though the fashion for the mirrored room or *spiegelkabinett* never caught on in England to the same extent as it did in Germany. But the most spectacular feature of the room is the magnificent silver chandelier, close to the designs of Daniel Marot and probably made in 1694, since it incorporates an earl's coronets in the lower stages, but a duke's (granted in that year by William III) held aloft by a putto at the top.

That graceful irregularity of Oriental art, which Sir William Temple and later Horace Walpole referred to as 'Sharawaggi', was to have an important influence on the development of the Rococo style in England, and even more on English landscape gardening. But to begin with it was the sheer novelty of artefacts brought from the other end of the earth which appealed – and particularly to feminine sensibilities. The Duchess of Norfolk's closet at Drayton is one of the most remakable survivals with its unique Chinese papier-maché panels of birds and fish, trees and flowers, still in the same glazed cases with red japanned frames listed here in an inventory of 1703. More birds and flowers appear in the marquetry floor, of a quality usually reserved for the finest Dutch cabinets, and are reflected by a mirror in the ceiling. The intimacy of small rooms like this, out of bounds to servants, was a natural setting for impropriety, though few of the elaborate canopied and curtained day-beds, or the 'pleasuring glasses' occasionally found in contemporary accounts, now survive. Returning to Blenheim from one of his campaigns, the Duke of Marlborough went

Above] The cypher of the Duchess of Lauderdale, in marquetry on the floor of the Queen's Closet at Ham, and in scagliola on the chimneypiece.

Opposite] The fireplace surround, hearthstone and windowsill of the Queen's Closet at Ham are among the first recorded uses of scagliola in England.

straight to his wife's dressing room and, according to her own testimony, pleasured her still wearing his boots.

The idea of the gentleman's dressing room as a picture cabinet was meanwhile prospering after a long gestation. The state dressing room at Burghley (later rechristened the First George Room) was arranged by the 6th Earl of Exeter in the early 1700s as a setting for some of the smaller Old Masters collected on his extensive Grand Tour and at auctions thereafter. These included works by or after Veronese, Andrea del Sarto, Correggio, Poussin and Parmigianino, most of them in uniform gilt frames of the so called 'Maratta' type made for him in London. Hung three deep on the richly-grained panelling under Verrio's coved ceiling, the finest in the house, they point to an enthusiasm for Italian pictures – particularly of the Bolognese School – that was to become an obsession with future generations of English collectors. Next door in the tiny Jewel Closet is a masterpiece by Carlo Dolci, *Our Saviour Blessing the Elements*, an essay on transubstantiation that might have seemed too much for a Protestant to take. However, its minutely-depicted chalice and paten set with precious stones must have seemed appropriate in a room which contained *objets de vertu* of every kind: not only coins and cameos acquired by the Earl in Italy but many of the exquisite enamelled pendants and boxes, rock-crystal phials and miniatures in elaborate settings which belonged to his ancestor the 1st Lord Burghley, Queen Elizabeth's faithful 'Mr Secretary Cecil'.

The Cabinet Room and Octagon Room at Corsham, really a dressing room and closet flanking the state bedchamber, are, like the gallery there, quintessential examples of Grand Tour taste, with serried ranks of Old Masters hung against crimson damask. It is interesting to find that as late as the 1770s the idea of the 'triad' was still going strong, for below the great gilt pier glass designed by Adam in the Cabinet Room is a splendid marquetry commode with a pair of matching torchères supplied for this position by the cabinet-maker John Cobb. However, these torchères support a pair of white marble vases with ormolu mounts, bought two years later in 1774, rather than the candlesticks that would have been usual at an earlier date.

The detailed diagrams made by William Windham for the hanging of his pictures in the cabinet at Felbrigg are vivid examples of the care and delight many owners, having returned from the Grand Tour, took in the arrangement of their collections. Miraculously they still remain just as he placed them, only his 'Flower'd Red Paper' having been replaced by crimson worsted damask in the early nineteenth century. Unable to afford the great Rubens and Renis, the Claudes and Salvator Rosas, bought by his neighbour Thomas Coke of Holkham, Windham's major acquisition was a series of twenty-six gouaches and seven larger oil-paintings by the Italian artist, Giovanni Battista Busiri, which he purchased in Rome in 1739–40. These charming little views of classical antiquities and landscapes in the Campagna, in Rococo frames, probably supplied by the London carver René Duffour, were used in 1751 as the basis for the hang in the cabinet, which retained the character of a state dressing room, even though the main bedroom was at that time moved upstairs and replaced by a larger drawing room. The architect James Paine designed a splendid overmantel frame for the largest of the Busiris, *The Cascade at Tivoli*, with an oval mirror

Opposite] The Blue Drawing Room at Ham, in reality a dressing room for the Queen's Bedchamber which it adjoins. The Oriental porcelain, lacquer screen and japanned chairs with cane seats testify to the high fashion for *chinoiserie* in the late seventeenth century: even the close stool kept in a dark cupboard on the inside wall was japanned to fit in with this exotic theme. The 'paned' hangings, so called because they are cut into panels with contrasting borders, are a particularly rare survival.

Spoils of the Grand Tour: the Cabinet
at Felbrigg hung with William
Windham's view paintings of the
Roman Campagna, some in oil and
some in gouache, commissioned from
the Italian artist Giovanni Battista
Busiri. Windham's own diagrams of the
walls survive, showing precisely how he
wished the pictures to be displayed, and
the crimson wall-hangings – though
renewed in the early nineteenth century
– also reflect his intentions. The room
was specially designed by James Paine in
1751 as a picture 'cabinet' leading off the
drawing room, where Windham's
larger pictures were kept, and the
architect also designed the Rococo
overmantel mirror incorporating
Busiri's largest canvas, *The Cascade at
Tivoli.*

below it that looks back to the old-fashioned 'landskip glass' of the late seventeenth century. The plasterwork ceiling of the 1680s was allowed to remain, though Paine's plasterers, Joseph Rose and George Green, tactfully extended it into the ceiling above the new bay window, and added the charming garlands of flowers in the cove, with the Windham arms flanked by cornucopias above the chimneypiece.

The new bay with its three tall sashes gave William Windham extra hanging space on the west wall where the earlier windows were blocked up; it also provided a steady north light that was ideal for looking at pictures but not so strong that it would fade the gouaches. Interspersed with the Busiris are decorative flower pieces by Karel van Vogelaer (known in Italy as Carlo dei Fiori) and Poussinesque landscapes by Jan Glauber, as well as a number of Dutch marine pictures, some acquired on Windham's homeward journey through Holland in 1742 and others obtained later at auctions in London. The most important of them, Simon de Vlieger's huge *Blockade of Amoy*, hangs in the centre of the west wall, balancing the chimneypiece on the opposite wall. The pictures are not 'centred' as they would be in a modern hang, and no museum would allow canvases to be hung so high or two such different schools of painting to be mixed. Yet the result is a perfect crystallization of eighteenth-century taste, showing how the decorative qualities of pictures *en masse* were appreciated as much as, if not more than, their individual merits. The sets of pictures so popular in English houses – the Vernets and Giordanos at Uppark; the Paninis at Castle Howard; the Wrights of Derby at Radburne – were almost always bought or commissioned with a particular setting in mind, and it is this that gives the few untouched picture 'cabinets' of the period the sort of classical balance and order sensed in the music of Mozart and Haydn.

The unifying element in the morning room at Saltram is the series of five portraits by Sir Joshua Reynolds, himself a native of Devon and a lifelong friend of the Parker family. The room can have changed little since the time of Reynolds' visit with Dr Johnson in 1762, and the enchanting informality of his pictures – their host in rough shooting clothes, his beautiful second wife Theresa, and their son and daughter above the chimneypiece, one of the artist's tenderest and most sympathetic depictions of children – would give it an intimacy and warmth even without the old red silk velvet on the walls and the comparatively low ceiling decorated with Rococo plasterwork. The pictures are even more varied than at Felbrigg, major and minor works crowded together, copies hanging beside originals, portraits beside landscapes. But once again the decorative effect of the hanging, the perfect balance of horizontals and verticals, and the emphasis on pairs, all give the room a wonderful feeling of the period. For instance, the circular landscapes after Gaspard Poussin flanking the chimneypiece may not in themselves be very exciting works of art, but as shapes relieving the rectangular lines of all about them they are one of the keys to the hanging. The garniture of Wedgwood black basalt vases on the chimneypiece and the dark mahogany chairs are also a perfect foil to the red of the walls and off-white of the woodwork and ceiling.

In the course of the eighteenth century, as the ceremonial associated with the state bedchamber waned and only the crustiest of old-fashioned figures such as the 'Proud Duke' of Somerset insisted on retaining the *levée* and *coucher*, the lady's dressing room, whether it

remained on the *piano nobile* or adjoined an upstairs bedchamber, became much more important as a setting for private activities, reading, writing, sewing and generally filling the unforgiving hour before it was time to gather with the rest of the family and guests in the drawing room before dinner. Thus bedroom and dressing room sometimes actually changed places. At Nostell Priory, the larger corner room originally intended as the state bedchamber became an ante room (in reality a large dressing room), serving the much smaller alcove bedroom next door; while at Kedleston the boudoir in Adam's scheme also preceded the state bedchamber and was on a bigger scale. The word 'boudoir', introduced to England at this time, also reflects the influence of French fashion, and 'bluestockings' like Elizabeth Montagu, imitating Walpole's friend and correspondent Madame du Deffand, used such rooms for the intellectual *causeries* that had long been a feature of Parisian life. Lady Louisa Conolly's dressing room at Castletown in Ireland was 'fitted up in ye French taste, hung with white damask' in 1772, with 'portraits tyed with knots of purple and silver ribband'.

Novelty was still the key to the decoration of these interiors, and if *chinoiserie* had become somewhat hackneyed as a style, there were other equally exotic paths to tread. Adam's state dressing room at Osterley was decorated in 1775 in the 'Etruscan' manner, loosely based on the colouring and design of Greek vases like those recently published by Sir William Hamilton and imitated by Josiah Wedgwood. Horace Walpole actually described the room as 'painted all over like Wedgwood's ware with black and yellow small grotesques', but was scathing about the overall effect which he thought was like 'going out of a palace into a potter's field'. Like its seventeenth-century predecessors, the Etruscan room would have been a highly appropriate setting for drinking tea, though from Staffordshire pottery instead of K'ang Hsi porcelain. Another popular idea was to bring the garden indoors, as in Lady Strafford's closet at Wentworth Castle which in 1766, when it was seen by the Duchess of Northumberland, had 'an arch'd ceiling painted Blue with a Trellis upon it with a Honeysuckle running all over it . . . the hangings straw colour sattin painted with sprigs of natural Flowers'.

A similar conceit is the birdcage clock which hangs from the ceiling of Adam's little circular closet at one end of the long gallery at Syon; every hour its tiny mechanical occupant spreads its wings and warbles an air whose composer has long since been forgotten. The room was made in one of the sixteenth-century towers at each end of the garden front, while its rather more conventional pair was square in shape and hung with Chinese paper and looking glasses. The wealth of ornament in such a tiny space, no more than eight feet across, makes the birdcage closet one of the most exquisite of all the architect's creations – a domed *tempietto* to make the most fashionable lady turn philosopher. The plasterwork by Joseph Rose is so finely modelled that it bears the closest inspection, while the colours – pale pinks, blues and greys recently restored following the original scheme – are like some delicious dessert after the main courses of Adam's great state rooms.

By the 1780s English wallpapers, particularly those made by the Eckhardt brothers, were able to rival those of the finest French manufacturers like Réveillon, and their naturalistic floral and trellis borders, printed in many different colours, were used for rooms like the

Opposite] Engravings of the most admired Old Masters, classical sculpture, coins and medals, and celebrated monuments of antiquity, were collected by country-house owners on the Grand Tour, much as modern travellers rely on postcards. Back at home, it soon became the fashion for ladies to paper the walls of small dressing rooms or closets with these prints, and contemporary diaries and descriptions more often than not refer to them being mounted on a 'straw-colour' background, like that in the Print Room at The Vyne. The engravings here were pasted up by Mrs William Chute and her nieces about the year 1815, which is a comparatively late date for this type of decoration.

Overleaf] The circular boudoir at one end of the long gallery at Syon, with its birdcage clock hanging from the centre of the dome. One of Adam's masterpieces in miniature, this tiny room was formed in 1770 in one of the towers at the corners of the old Jacobean house, and decorated with exquisite plasterwork by the younger Joseph Rose.

boudoir at Shugborough in Staffordshire, cut out and pasted on to panels of moiré paper, giving the effect of watered silk. Elsewhere pleated or draped wall-hangings were used, and in the early nineteenth century tent rooms based on the designs of Percier and Fontaine, and ultimately inspired by the Napoleonic campaigns, had a short vogue. In all this decoration there is a search for the insubstantial, the light, occasionally even the frippery, that becomes the more pronounced as the decoration of the preceding rooms – halls, picture galleries and drawing rooms – becomes heavier and more grandiloquent.

But nowhere does the attenuation of line, allied with naturalism in the Louis Seize style, have happier results than in Lady Berwick's boudoir at Attingham. Designed by George Steuart in the 1780s, this was almost certainly decorated by the French emigré painter Louis André Delabrière (who was to work for Henry Holland at Carlton House and Southill in the following decade) and was intended to balance Lord Berwick's much more austere octagonal study on the other side of the building, in the rigid separation of male and female apartments that makes Attingham almost unique among English houses. As at Syon it is in the form of a circular domed *tempietto* with giant Corinthian columns supporting the entablature, but the decorative panels on an ivory-coloured ground have the character of French *boiseries* even though they are painted on plaster. The scrolls of acanthus entwined with ivy are as refined as the needlework Lady Berwick might be encouraged to undertake in such a room, while the different grasses and wild flowers in thin vases flanking each medallion are observed with an extraordinary attention to detail. Delabrière's use of gold leaf, along with naturalistic reds, greens and pinks, is picked up by the gilding of the columns and the ribs of the ceiling. Between the latter 'hang' a series of incense-burners in plasterwork, appropriate for a room where scent-sprays or the newly fashionable *brûles-parfum* were doubtless used.

The metropolitan sophistication of the Attingham boudoir is surprising to find in distant Shropshire at this date, as is its formality and its position on the main floor of the house, providing a final climax to the sequence of 'show rooms'. Boudoirs in the early nineteenth century were usually to be found upstairs and decorated with an eye to comfort more than ostentation. Dressing rooms became the gentleman's equivalent of the boudoir, used literally to dress (and bathe) in, while the idea of the 'cabinet' and 'closet' disappeared altogether in England, though the latter survived – as with so many other eighteenth-century English terms – in America.

Lady Berwick's boudoir at Attingham designed by George Steuart, and painted probably by the émigré French artist Louis André Delabrière, in the 1780s. Ovals, octagons and circles were considered perfect shapes for dressing rooms and closets; on a larger scale they caused problems with the hanging of pictures and the placing of furniture.

10 Libraries

Seventeenth-century stepped bookcases in the 1st Duke of Montagu's library at Boughton. The gathering of books in specially constructed oak or walnut 'presses' was a comparatively late development in the English country house.

Books were of the greatest importance to the English country gentleman in the eighteenth century. His classical education was at the root of his appreciation for the art of antiquity, just as much as his belief in political liberty. Some of the greatest English philosophers and writers – Locke and Pope, Gibbon and Burke – were *habitués* of the country house, and this familiarity with men of letters in turn encouraged scientific enquiry and intellectual pursuits, even in those who followed the hounds and shot the partridges over their own broad acres.

What is surprising is that the idea of collecting books and gathering them into a library took so long to emerge. Those few great lords who collected them in the Middle Ages were closely connected with the Court, like Duke Humphrey of Gloucester, the brother of Henry V, whose collection forms the nucleus of the Bodleian Library at Oxford, and Thomas Percy, Earl of Worcester, Richard II's Steward of the Household, whose literary tastes were to be inherited by his brother's descendants, the 5th and 9th Earls of Northumberland. But learning was on the whole the province of the Church. Few sons of noble houses were sent to Oxford or Cambridge, and courage, skill in field sports and feats of arms were far more highly prized. There is even evidence that some social stigma could be attached to intellectual pursuits, as was to happen again at the end of the nineteenth century, with a squire in the 1480s reported as saying that he would rather his son should hang than study letters, a pursuit which 'should be left to the sons of rustics'.

The small numbers of books found in most Elizabethan houses is not fully explained by their high cost and the comparative difficulty of obtaining them. In a house as extravagantly appointed as Hardwick, for instance – where the philosopher Thomas Hobbes was to spend many years as tutor to the 2nd Earl of Devonshire – the 1601 inventory lists only six books, all of them kept in Bess of Hardwick's own bedchamber. One of these six was by Calvin, another 'Salomans proverbes' and another 'a booke of meditations': in other words these were works for instruction and edification rather than pure enjoyment. Among Bess's contemporaries there were of course exceptions to this general rule, but only two, Lord Lumley and Lord Burghley, owned over a thousand books – enough to constitute a library by eighteenth-century standards.

What books there were in country houses were rarely kept on shelves in one place, nor were they displayed with the spines facing forward as is now the custom. The early seventeenth-century books at Charlecote all have their titles written on the fore-edge, across the leaves, and this is how they are also seen carved in marble on Sir Thomas Lucy's tomb in Charlecote church. The 9th Earl of Northumberland, whose scientific experiments earned him the lasting nickname of the 'Wizard Earl', was allowed to take a considerable library to the Tower of London with him when implicated in the Gunpowder Plot in 1605. Most of these books still survive at Petworth, covering every subject from architecture and

Sir Robert Walpole's library at Houghton, designed for him by William Kent about 1729, was one of the first to treat bookcases as part of the architecture of the room. The shelves, all of solid mahogany, are sunk into the inner walls and echo the shapes of the two Venetian windows opposite. They still contain many of the Prime Minister's books, bound in calf and morocco, tooled in gold, and testifying to the width of his interests – from science and natural history to music, painting and literature.

engineering to the classics and liberally annotated in his neat italic hand. But their particular interest lies in the uniform vellum, and occasionally calf, bindings embossed with the gilt crescents of the Percy arms. Examples of even earlier books bearing Sir Thomas Tresham's punning trefoil crest also survive, and these are particularly early examples of the so-called 'livery bindings' which were to become such an important feature of country-house libraries in the future.

The sudden increase in learning among the gentry in the Restoration period, associated with the founding of the Royal Society, meant that books became far more numerous and that some ordered way of storing them became necessary. The room they were usually gathered in was the gentleman's closet, and the earliest libraries like that at Ham were developed as extensions to such a closet – in this case positioned immediately above and reached by a small back stair. These rooms, like the earliest known design for a 'book closet' by Robert Smythson, were strictly utilitarian in appearance, though that at Ham has a cedarwood desk, with a fall-front and drawers above and below, built into the bookshelves. The library in Pepys' London house was fitted up in 1666 with a series of glazed oak bookcases or presses by the joiner Thomas Sympson, rather than with fitted shelves, and similar examples survive at Dyrham in Avon, probably commissioned by Pepys's friend Thomas Povey. But few other country houses adopted the idea of free-standing bookcases until the mid-eighteenth century, when Vile and Cobb's glazed cabinets for Queen Charlotte and Chippendale's for the Earl of Pembroke set a new fashion.

Robert Hooke's designs for Ragley in Warwickshire, made in the 1680s, provided for a large rectangular library balanced by a chapel either side of the 'state centre' (hall and saloon) and separating the four 'apartments'. But William Kent's library at Houghton, dating from the late 1720s, is one of the first in any private house to have real architectural pretensions, though it takes its cue from Lord Burlington's at Chiswick where the desks and mirrors, also designed by Kent, incorporated the owl crest of the Saviles, Lady Burlington's family – conveniently doubling up as the symbol of wisdom. At Houghton, the library adjoins Sir Robert Walpole's dressing room and bedroom – in other words occupying the place where one would expect to find his closet. Another old-fashioned feature is the Prime Minister's desk which, although made of West Indian mahogany, is similar in form to the inlaid walnut or boulle bureaux being made by Gerrit Jensen in the 1690s. But the lavish use of the same wood for the great bookcases on the inside walls, echoing the shapes of the Venetian windows opposite, was a wholly new concept, as was the idea of hollowing out pilasters, overdoors and panels in the frieze to contain books. Their dark brown leather bindings, tooled in gold, perfectly complement the rich colouring of the woodwork and the polished brass hinges and lockplates of the doors. The solid virtues of Whiggery were never more literally expressed.

One of Kent's earliest supporters, who helped him study in Italy, was Sir Thomas Chester of Chicheley in Buckinghamshire. In his 'secret library' on the top floor of the house, all the bolection panels including those in the dado, the fluted pilasters and their bases, open up to reveal bookshelves behind. As at Houghton, the architecture comes first and the books are ingeniously fitted into the scheme. But at Holkham in 1741 Kent achieved a breakthrough in several ways. His long library, 54 feet by 18 feet, is still part of Lord Leicester's own apartments rather than the state rooms, but running the depth of the south-west wing (which is like a self-contained private house) it was, and has always remained, the communal family or 'living room', to borrow Repton's much later phrase, rather than being merely a study. Hogarth's conversation piece of 1732 of the Cholmondeley family, portrayed with their children and dogs at ease in such a library, shows just the sort of informal life it must have experienced.

The extension of the main enfilade of state rooms into the wings also meant that Lord Leicester, standing at the entrance to his library, could look through nine sets of doors to the far end of the chapel in the south-east wing. Inigo Jones had predicted this development with his two Palladian pavilions containing a library and chapel at Stoke Bruerne in Northamptonshire, designed for one of Charles II's courtiers, Sir Francis Crane, exactly a hundred years earlier. But these were joined to the main house by open quadrant colonnades, whereas on the main cross-axis at Holkham they became component parts of an overall plan, and could forget their ignominious pedigrees as farm buildings and stables in the villas of the Veneto.

A third and still more revolutionary feature of the library at Holkham was the way that the pedimented bookshelves, echoing the chimneypiece, dictated the architectural scheme. Sunk half-way back into the wall so as not to push the doors and windows into dark recesses, they set up a rhythm accentuated by the groin-vault of the cove. A perennial problem with bookcases was what to place above them, and although portraits and busts became the norm, Kent's vault offers a still happier solution, even without the elaborate plasterwork decoration of his original proposal. Another change of heart resulted in the adaptation of the overmantel to contain an antique Roman mosaic of a lion and leopard, a suitable accompaniment to the splendid bound sets of the classics – Homer and Virgil, Horace and Cicero – which lined the shelves.

To house a great collection of books in the country rather than in London made even more sense than bringing down Old Masters and antique sculpture, for here there would be leisure to study them, to improve the mind after a day's hunting, perhaps to offer hospitality to a whole circle of literati, whose erudite conversations would offer parallels with the disputations of the Greek philosophers. Edward Harley, 2nd Earl of Oxford, the son of Queen Anne's minister and the close friend of Pope, Swift and Matthew Prior, was one of the instigators of this trend. In the summer of 1730 Pope wrote to him: 'I will fancy I am standing on the stone steps of the great door to receive you and . . . am impatient to follow you to your new-roofed library and see what fine new lodgings the Ancients are to have.' This was a reference to the huge room that James Gibbs had been commissioned to design at Harley's country house, Wimpole in Cambridgeshire, to house some of the thousands of volumes hitherto kept at his London residence. The library proper was approached by three small 'cabinets' which contained collections of coins, antique cameos and seals, manuscripts and pamphlets, all catalogued by Lord Oxford's full-time librarian, the antiquary Humphrey Wanley.

The Harleian library was conceived on too grand a scale to last; the mania for collecting

soon depleted even his enormous resources and after his death some 50,000 books and 300,000 pamphlets were sold by his widow, though the manuscripts were acquired by the nation and still form the basis of the British Museum's holdings. A handful of country-house owners, including Lord Leicester, followed Harley's example in collecting rarities. But for the most part useful and instructive books were preferred, covering the widest possible range. Lord Warrington's library at Dunham Massey in Cheshire dating from the 1730s is one of the most typical and atmospheric of the period. The walls are entirely covered with oak shelves or 'presses' mostly arranged by subject – architecture, topography, botany, genealogy (one of the noble Earl's particular obsessions), philosophy, theology, science – while in the centre stand an orrery and armillary sphere in their original glazed cases. A pair of globes, celestial and terrestrial, a telescope, reading desks and ladders to reach the upper shelves (sometimes combined to form a sort of pulpit on wheels) were among the standard equipment one would expect to find in a library by the middle of the century, and William Constable of Burton Constable in Yorkshire went even further in having a whole series of scientific instruments with his name engraved on them in brass, very like those seen in Wright of Derby's pictures of the air pump and other experiments conducted by candlelight.

As well as appreciating the classics, bibliophiles of Horace Walpole's generation were becoming aware of Britain's own literary heritage, from Piers Plowman and Chaucer to Shakespeare and Ben Jonson – associating it with the triumphs of English Gothic architecture, from Norman and Early English to Perpendicular. This revival of antiquarianism resulted in a fashion for 'Gothick' libraries even occasionally in houses which were predominantly classical. Walpole's own library at Strawberry Hill, completed in 1754, had arcaded bookcases based on an engraving of a doorway in Old St Paul's Cathedral, and a chimneypiece copying a medieval tomb in Westminster Abbey, while there were stained-glass panes in the upper lights of the window and a painted heraldic ceiling. Sir Roger Newdegate of Arbury in Warwickshire chose to be portrayed by Arthur Devis in his own Gothick library, the quintessential image of a squire who was also a talented amateur architect and archaeologist.

A visitor to Felbrigg in 1795 remarked that 'the old stile of architecture observable in the south front, has been happily kept up in the hall and in the library, which is well furnished with the most valuable authors'. The Gothick style which James Paine adopted for the remodelling of the room in the 1750s may now seem typically eighteenth-century in character, but there is little doubt that it was chosen to complement the Jacobean south range of the house, probably designed by Robert Lyminge, the architect of Hatfield and Blickling, and particularly to make sense of the deep bay windows with their stone mullions and leaded lights which would have been hard to incorporate in a classical scheme. George Church, the carver of the bookcases with their slender cluster-columns and curious little conical pinnacles, appears to have designed as well as made the great double-sided desk with its 'fretwork' pattern of trefoils and quatrefoils, at the modest cost of £21.

Many of the large folios on architecture and classical antiquities were bought by William Windham on his Grand Tour of 1737–42, while his purchase of a copy of Gauffecourt's

Opposite] The long library in the family wing at Holkham, completed before William Kent's premature death in 1748 and one of the rooms in the house that most clearly displays his genius. The groined vault, which stricter Palladians might have felt fatally Gothic in character, helps to fill the space between the bookcases and ceiling, where good pictures would have been wasted, and sets up a rhythm even without the use of pilasters. An oval painting of Apollo with his lyre appears in the original design for the overmantel, but in the event this was replaced by an antique Roman mosaic of a lion savaging a leopard, acquired by Lord Leicester on the Grand Tour.

Overleaf] The White Library at Petworth was created for the 3rd Earl of Egremont by Matthew Brettingham the younger in 1774, when the state bedchamber was moved upstairs. *Dewy Morning*, Turner's haunting picture of Petworth seen across the lake, hangs over the chimneypiece, with a wind-dial above suggesting whether or not the book-worm should risk a walk in Capability Brown's incomparable landscape.

Traité de la reliure in Geneva stimulated a practical interest in bookbinding. He owned a large outfit of binders' tools and materials, and the library at Felbrigg still contains about three hundred volumes of miscellaneous pamphlets, poems and plays, bound uniformly in quarter-calf with marbled boards and red morocco labels, which are thought to be examples of his work. His son, the statesman William Windham III, was a close friend of Dr Johnson and was given the sage's own copies of the *Iliad*, *Odyssey* and New Testament, when he attended him on his deathbed – a typical example of the incidental treasures to be found in English country-house libraries.

The central 'library table' (in fact a desk with a broad flat top and with drawers, cupboards and kneeholes each side) became an inevitable part of the furnishing of the room in Adam's houses. Those at Nostell Priory and Harewood are among Thomas Chippendale's finest documented works, while that at Osterley, inlaid on the cupboard doors with emblems representing the arts – Architecture, Sculpture, Music and Painting – is attributed to John Linnell. Both Chippendale's chairs at Nostell and Linnell's at Osterley have pierced splat-backs in the shape of lyres, the instrument associated not only with Homer, but with Erato, the muse of lyric poetry. This reference to classical mythology and literature is brought firmly up to date in both rooms by Zucchi's inset paintings: at Nostell the overmantel shows Minerva presenting the Arts to Britannia whose throne is flanked by a lion and unicorn; at Osterley panels representing Catullus and Pythagoras, Ovid and Sappho, among other heroes and heroines of the mind, culminate in the overdoor, described as 'England encouraging and rewarding the Arts and Sciences'.

The late eighteenth and early nineteenth centuries saw the apogee of the library. At Kenwood, Adam prophesied what was to come with his library-cum-sitting room designed for the bookish Lord Mansfield, and although the room occupied a wing off the main block it was clearly intended to be used not just as a private apartment for the owner and his immediate family, but as a communal meeting place for the whole house party. In the 1770s Mrs Lybbe Powys, visiting Middleton Park, Oxfordshire, found 'a most excellent library out of the drawing room, seventy feet long – in this room, besides a good collection of books there is every other kind of amusement, as billiard and other tables, and a few good pictures. As her Ladyship is, according to the fashion, a botanist, she has a pretty flower garden going out of the library.' Humphry Repton's *Fragments*, published in 1816, illustrates just such a library, full of people engaged in different occupations, and with French windows leading out into a conservatory, while in the text he explains that 'the most recent modern custom is to use the library as the general living-room; and that sort of state room formerly called the best parlour, and of late years the drawing-room, is now generally found a melancholy apartment, when entirely shut up and opened to give the visitors a formal cold reception'.

'Sitting-libraries' of this character were not quite as recent and modern as Repton suggests. At Petworth, as early as 1774, the 3rd Earl of Egremont banished his father's great Rococo state bed upstairs and converted the King of Spain's Bedchamber on the ground floor into what is now the White Library. Matthew Brettingham the younger designed the bookcases, originally extending through into the old bed-alcove, and lowered the sash-

windows so that those feeling 'frowsty' after an afternoon's study could walk straight out into Capability Brown's incomparable landscape – having first checked the wind-dial above the chimneypiece to see whether an overcoat might be necessary. Turner's watercolour of the room, made in about 1828 (now in the British Museum), shows it just as comfortable and perhaps even more crowded with furniture than it is today.

The busts of philosophers crowning the bookcases not only stress the visual importance of the uprights dividing the bookshelves, but alternate with the portraits, which in many country-house libraries depicted British literary worthies: another conscious juxtaposition of Ancient and Modern Virtue. Pope's portrait by Jonathan Richardson, and busts of Spenser, Shakespeare, Dryden and Milton, all by Peter Scheemakers, still survive in the library at Hagley, while Lord Chesterfield's set of literary portraits at Chesterfield House started with Chaucer and ended with Dr Johnson.

Architectural grandeur sometimes outweighed the desire for comfort and clutter. The library filling the whole upper floor of the west front at Sledmere in Yorkshire was designed by its owner Sir Christopher Sykes and the plasterer Joseph Rose the younger in the 1780s, apparently on the model of the giant vaulted interiors of the Roman Baths of Titus and Caracalla. The books here are incidental, and it is interesting that they are recessed so as to become simply the flat surface of the wall, with no attempt to make the cases architectural features in their own right. Malton's watercolour of the room in 1790 shows it with no furniture except for the central library table, a globe and telescope – and although other tables and chairs must have been introduced on occasion, it still looks its best as a bare, formal space with nothing to distract from the essential nobility of its proportions, and the exquisite precision of Rose's decoration.

Henry Holland's library at Woburn Abbey, in his most elegant Louis Seize style, also has bookcases wholly recessed into the wall, but the scale here is much more domestic. Lady Bessborough, who stayed in 1797, wrote: 'I never saw so delightful a room as the library here; it is very large, all the finest Editions magnificently bound. Over the bookcases some very fine pictures (portraits) most of them Titians, Rembrandts, etc. three great looking glasses, all the ornaments white and golden, and the furniture blue leather.' Library chairs were often upholstered in leather, perhaps partly to reflect the colour and texture of book-bindings, but also because libraries, like dining rooms, were still considered essentially masculine in character and permanent in decoration. The silks and velvets of the drawing room would need to be replaced as fashion changed, but leather, mellowed and improved with age, like his hunting boots and saddles, was something a squire could be proud of.

The Woburn library still contains many of the French ornaments specially bought for it, including the great ormolu clock by Pierre Philippe Thomire on the dwarf bookcase opposite the chimneypiece, probably acquired through the Parisian dealer, Dominic Daguerre, who opened a shop in London in the 1770s, and was much patronized by Holland's clients. The chandelier here and those in the adjoining rooms on either side were designed by the architect himself and show how thoroughly French fashion was to capture the English imagination, despite the horrors of the Revolution and the subsequent threats of Napoleonic invasion.

Opposite] Drawings by Piranesi, acquired in Italy by the plasterer Joseph Rose the younger, were recently discovered in a cupboard in the library at Sledmere, and this magnificent room modelled on the imperial Roman baths is thoroughly Piranesian in its scale and splendour. The books themselves, once forming one of the most famous collections in England, are relegated to the background, their cases fitted flush with the walls, while the pilasters, chimneypieces and great tripartite 'Wyatt' windows give the room a sense of colossal space. Sledmere was gutted by fire in the early part of this century, but the existence of many of Rose's original carved wooden moulds made it possible to restore his plasterwork exactly, and the only major loss was the great carpet reflecting the pattern of the ceiling, now rendered in parquet.

A scholar's retreat: Sir Richard Colt Hoare's library at Stourhead in Wiltshire, built in 1792 and furnished by Chippendale in 1804–5. It was here, at the younger Thomas Chippendale's desk, that Colt Hoare wrote his two-volume county history, one of the most influential works of English topography.

Thomas Chippendale the younger visited Paris after the Peace of Amiens in 1802–3, just at the moment the Jacob *frères* were engaged on furnishing Malmaison and the Tuileries for Bonaparte, then First Consul. His furniture made for Sir Richard Colt Hoare's library at Stourhead in 1804–5 is directly influenced by what he saw, while the Greek *klismos* form of the chairs, and the Egyptian terms on the writing table, would also have reflected Colt Hoare's own studious interest in these two countries. Both the French and English versions of Denon's *Voyage dans la Basse et la Haute Egypte* (the direct result of Bonaparte's Egyptian campaign of 1797–8) were acquired for the library at Stourhead in 1802, immediately after they were published.

Henry Holland's library at Woburn Abbey, created for the 5th Duke of Bedford in the 1790s, and one of the architect's most satisfying essays in the Louis Seize style. Humphry Repton, who remodelled the park at Woburn in the same decade, extolled the virtues of the 'sitting-library', where groups of family and guests could enjoy different pursuits in an atmosphere that was cultivated but at the same time informal. The books here, many of them on natural history and including volumes on the flora and fauna of the Bedford estates specially printed by the 6th Duke, cry out to be read, unlike the series of stodgy law reports and parliamentary proceedings that were considered essential to 'furnish' earlier libraries.

Kenneth Woodbridge has described the room as 'probably Colt Hoare's supreme achievement as a patron, as complete in conception as his grandfather's garden; and it represents the introverted way of life he found in the Italian monasteries without any of the attendant disadvantages . . . .' One of his aims was to amass here all the available books and manuscripts relating to his native Wiltshire, and it was from these that he produced his two-volume county history which still remains one of the fullest and most scholarly works of English topography. The elliptical arches to the tops of the bookcases echo the shape of the lunettes at either end, formed by the barrel-vaulted ceiling. One of these contains a version of Raphael's *Parnassus* by the Revd Samuel Woodforde, and the other part of the *School of Athens* in stained glass by Francis Eginton. High-mindedness was, in other words, the keynote of this somewhat austere widower's taste, and it can be sensed too in the carpet, which is based on a Roman tessellated pavement, echoing the bare lattice-work pattern of the ceiling where vines and ivies, one feels, would never be allowed to grow.

If there are not many jokes to be cracked in the library at Stourhead, some welcome light relief is provided in many country-house libraries by the jib-doors, covered with false book-backs, that preserve the symmetry of the plan while providing a convenient exit, perhaps to a back stair leading to the gallery as at Chatsworth. The scope these book-backs give for fearful puns is almost limitless, and the 6th Duke of Devonshire's – 'Barrow on the Commonweal', 'Boyle on Steam', and 'Burnet's Theory of the Conflagration' – have been supplemented in recent years by such modern classics as 'Consenting Adults by Abel N. Willing', 'Intuition by Ivor Hunch' and 'Dipsomania by Mustafa Swig'.

Until the early nineteenth century, the library at Chatsworth was the 1st Duke of Devonshire's long gallery, designed by William Talman and with a plasterwork ceiling by Edward Goudge, embellished with roundels by Verrio. Only the latter now survives for between 1815 and 1830 the 6th Duke wholly remodelled it, covering the walls with books, adding the gallery, and employing Crace & Co. (who also worked for Wyatville at Windsor Castle) to provide the Axminster carpet, curtains and upholstered furniture. In his own words, 'he who has to furnish a great house is embarked in a sea of trouble, and nothing but experience can teach what ought to be done – except Mr. John Crace, who, I have latterly found, can teach it still better'. The room today contains some of the rarest volumes in any English country house – Lord Burlington's architectural folios, including Inigo Jones's annotated copy of Palladio, illuminated manuscripts from the library of Bishop Dampier of Ely bought *en masse* in 1812, collections of botanical plates by Joseph Paxton who was the 6th Duke's gardener, and countless other treasures. But it is its overwhelming sense of warmth and comfort, like the library of a luxuriously appointed London club, that seems to sum up a very English attitude to culture: not as something remote and chilly to be acquired as a means to social or political advancement, but a natural and enjoyable propensity to learn about life for its own sake, and in all its variety.

The 1st Duke of Devonshire's long gallery at Chatsworth (*opposite*) was turned into a library by the 6th Duke in the early nineteenth century, to designs by Sir Jeffry Wyatville and the decorator J. C. Crace. Like a sumptuously appointed London club, it provides a perfect setting for one of the greatest collections of books still in private hands. The Dome Room (*above*), linking the ante library to Wyatville's new dining room, is one of the architect's most successful *jeux d'esprit*, with yet more bookcases framed by screens of columns and rare marble vases.

11   Chapels

'"Now", said Mrs Rushworth', as she led the party from Mansfield Park, in Jane Austen's famous novel, towards the end of an interminable tour of the ancient house of Sotherton, '"we are coming to the chapel, which properly we ought to enter from above, and look down upon; but as we are quite among friends, I will take you in this way, if you will excuse me". They entered. Fanny's imagination had prepared her for something grander than a mere, spacious oblong room, fitted up for the purpose of devotion – with nothing more striking or more solemn than the profusion of mahogany, and the crimson velvet cushions appearing over the ledge of the family gallery above. "I am disappointed," said she, in a low voice to Edmund. "This is not my idea of a chapel. There is nothing awful here, nothing melancholy, nothing grand. Here are no aisles, no arches, no inscriptions, no banners . . . ."'

The chapel was an essential part of the medieval castle, and most of those that survive in English country houses are of pre-Reformation origin, even if remodelled at a later date as that at Sotherton had been. They were used for daily household prayers and for occasional marriages and christenings, but in no way replaced the church within whose parish a great house happened to lie. It was there that the family would go to worship on Sundays in company with all their servants and tenants, and it was there that the monuments, banners and achievements were to be found, as Fanny Price was reminded by her cousin Edmund Bertram.

In the case of old houses or houses built on old sites, the medieval parish church can be situated so close that it almost takes on the character of a private chapel – particularly as the rest of the village was likely to have been moved away to the edge of the park in the eighteenth century, well out of sight and earshot. At Dyrham, it stands on a bank to one side of the west front, above the garden, and so near that the Blathwayts could enter their family pew from a linking corridor without having to step outside on a rainy day. At Kedleston, the church, with its long line of Curzon tombs stretching from the thirteenth century to the present day, has been virtually swallowed by the house, and nestles behind the kitchen wing with its chancel only a few feet away from the windows of the state bedchamber.

Churches 'on the doorstep' like these were often used, and sometimes built, purely for the occupants of the big house. One of the most moving is that at Staunton Harold in Leicestershire built by the Royalist Sir Robert Shirley in 1653 as an act of defiance against Cromwell's Presbyterian régime. In the Gothic style and expressing Archbishop Laud's High Anglican ideals – the return to 'the beauty of holiness' as expressed in Catholic ritual – it became Shirley's memorial, for he died in the Tower of London before its completion. Right up to the death of his descendant Sewallis, 10th Earl Ferrers, just before the First World War, it was the custom on Sundays for the entire household, headed by Lord and Lady Ferrers and in strict order of precedence, to cross the lawn to the church in double file, men in one column and women in the other – and the sexes remained divided inside the

Opposite] The entrance to Sir Richard Edgcumbe's fifteenth-century chapel at Cotehele in Cornwall. The simplicity of its rough-hewn whitewashed walls and barrel-vaulted ceiling is relieved by the delicate flowing tracery of the oak screen, probably carved on the estate and still pure Gothic in style. The chapel also contains the earliest clock in England still unaltered and in its original position, chiming the hours from the little bell-turret that overlooks the Retainers' Court.

church, the men sitting on the right of the nave and the women on the left. In latter years the Earl was not on speaking terms with the parson who used to be confined to the vestry between services, where his lunch would be brought to him by a procession of footmen, also carrying a close stool.

Large landowners usually owned or were able to purchase the gift of the livings on their estates (that is to say the right to nominate the vicar or rector), and these would often be held by younger sons or nephews destined from an early age to take Orders. So to a large extent the parish church was under the landowner's control; his structural alterations and additions were seldom opposed by the Bishop; and he could afford to treat it almost as private property. Some went so far as to build high box-pews or special galleries for themselves, lined with crimson velvet and equipped with fireplaces as a protection against the cold during the long sermons that were then the fashion. Except in special cases where the church was a long way off, or where the family were Roman Catholics, the chapel in the house therefore assumed a subsidiary role, seldom used for the main Sunday service or for holy communion. In the case of Catholics, there were strict laws governing chapels in private houses even though they were tacitly accepted from the mid-eighteenth century – in particular they were not to look like ecclesiastical buildings from the exterior. Thus the Gothic traceried windows at Mapledurham House and at Milton Manor House, both in Berkshire, are disguised as plain sashes on the outside, while the grandest chapel of all, designed by James Paine at Wardour Castle in Wiltshire, is embedded in the west wing (balancing the kitchen in the east wing) and lit almost entirely by high clerestory windows.

One of the earliest and most beautiful chapels is that at Haddon which incorporates something of every building period in the history of the house. Twelfth and thirteenth-century work is evident in the Norman font and the massive piers of the nave. The chancel was added in the early fifteenth century by Sir Richard Vernon, and is firmly dated by the inscription in the remarkably well preserved stained glass of the east window: '*Orate pro animabus Riccardi Vernon et Benedicte uxoris eius qui fecerunt* [pray for the souls of Richard Vernon and his wife Beatrice who made this] *anno dni 1427*'. They must also have commissioned the rare grisaille wall-decorations, including depictions of the Three Quick and the Three Dead, the lives of St Nicholas and St Anne, and a burly St Christopher carrying the infant Christ shoulder-high over a river with scrolly waves and fishes, and luxurious plants on either bank. All the woodwork, roof, pulpit, screen and pews are of 1624, the date carved on one of the roof-beams with the initials GM, probably as a memorial to Sir George Manners (son of the Vernon heiress and ancestor of the Dukes of Rutland) who died the previous year. After about 1700 Haddon was abandoned by the family in favour of Belvoir and it was only in 1912 that the 8th Duke set about its restoration, which he carried out with exemplary care and sensitivity. His wife Violet was an accomplished artist, and the marble monument she designed in memory of their son Lord Haddon, who had died at the age of nine, is also a touching tribute to their own life's work in rescuing and preserving this most magical of English castles.

The much simpler chapel at Cotehele in Cornwall is, like that at Haddon, situated in the outer courtyard with a main door for retainers and tenants at the west end and a separate

The chapel at Haddon seen from one of the enclosed family pews installed by Sir George Manners in 1624. The rest of the chancel and the east window date from 1427, as recorded in an inscription below the window commemorating the then owner of the house, Sir Richard Vernon and his wife Beatrice. Rare medieval wall-paintings cover the walls, some of them in a geometrical pattern imitating damask wall-hangings, others representing St Christopher carrying the infant Christ through a river complete with life-like fishes, or scenes from the life of St Nicholas to whom the chapel was originally dedicated.

entrance for the family near the altar at the east end. Adjoining rooms to the chapel were often provided with 'squints' or narrow slits looking down on to the altar for ladies of the household or others who wished to follow the course of the mass without joining the congregation below. At Cotehele there are no less than three, looking down from the solar or great chamber on the north, and from the priest's room and the room below it on the south. The carved oak screen dates from between 1485 and 1489 when Sir Richard Edgcumbe completed the chapel, but its most remarkable feature is undoubtedly the clock of the same date, and the earliest in England still unaltered and in its original position. Set in a shaft built in the thickness of the west wall, it is powered by two hollow iron weights and has no pendulum or clock face. But its tolling of the hours has now been heard across the thickly wooded Tamar valley for almost five hundred years.

One of the last and grandest of the pre-Reformation private chapels is that at The Vyne in Hampshire, built between 1518 and 1527 by William Lord Sandys, Lord Chamberlain to Henry VIII. The splendid canopied stalls, like those found in college chapels and cathedral choirs of the same date, have an intricate carved cornice with a running pattern that is still Gothic in conception but with Renaissance motifs introduced, including boys blowing horns, shooting deer with bows and arrows, and pulling seeds out of pomegranates – the device of Queen Katharine of Aragon. The same mixture of Gothic and Renaissance is found in the encaustic tiles in front of the stalls and before the altar, mostly attributed to Guido da Savino from Urbino, who set up a workshop in Antwerp in 1512, and in three windows above the altar, their late Perpendicular tracery filled with stained glass which, for its brilliance of colour and jewel-like clarity, has no match in England. The windows are the work of a Flemish team of glaziers and painters including David Joris and Pieter Coeck of Aalst, who probably came to London in the early 1520s in the train of the Emperor Charles V. They were originally part of a larger series made for the Chapel of the Holy Ghost at Basingstoke, founded by Lord Sandys and Bishop Fox of Winchester, and were only brought to The Vyne in the seventeenth century, though they fit the existing windows and the style of the building perfectly.

The Vyne was bought from the Sandys family by Chaloner Chute, Speaker of the House of Commons, during the Commonwealth, and it was his descendant John Chute who was a close friend of Horace Walpole and a member of the Strawberry Hill 'Committee of Taste'. 'At The Vyne is the most heavenly Chapel in the world,' Walpole wrote to Horace Mann in Florence in 1755, 'it only wants a few pictures to give it a truly catholic air . . . If you can pick us up a tolerable "Last Supper", or can have one copied tolerably and very cheap, we will say many a mass for the repose of your headaches.' In the event the Strawberry Committee's main attentions were focused on the ante chapel, which was Gothicized and given a ribbed ceiling as a suitably romantic approach, and the 'tomb chamber' added on the south side of the chapel to house Thomas Carter's splendid marble monument to Speaker Chute, a masterpiece of mid-eighteenth-century English sculpture, though in a style which consciously evokes the seventeenth. In the chapel itself the only important additions were the *trompe-l'œil* paintings of Perpendicular fan-vaulting (based on the cloisters of Gloucester Cathedral) which were painted above the choir stalls by a Greek scene-painter, Spiridione

The chapel at The Vyne, built by the pious Lord Sandys, Henry VIII's Lord Chamberlain, and one of the last to be built in England before the Reformation. The oak screen dating from the 1520s (*above*) is still purely Gothic with no hint of Renaissance forms. Thomas Carter's mid-eighteenth-century monument to Speaker Chute in the adjoining Tomb Chamber (*opposite*) is just as old-fashioned for its date, a nostalgic evocation of the age of Van Dyck.

Opposite] The fourteenth-century chapel of the Percys at Petworth, remodelled by the 'Proud Duke' of Somerset between 1685 and 1692. The altar is insignificant compared with the family pew in a gallery over the west door. Fashioned like an opera box, its 'curtains' of carved wood are held back by life-size angels (*above*), trumpeting the Duke's glory to posterity.

Roma. Only fragments of these now survive in the gallery at the west end.

Galleried chapels were the normal practice by the sixteenth century, like that at Hardwick now sadly divided by a floor at gallery level. This enabled the household and outdoor servants who dined in the great hall to fill the pews or benches below, while the Countess and members of her family sat in the gallery which adjoined her Low Great Chamber on the floor above. Rather surprisingly, given Bess of Hardwick's Calvinist sympathies, the chapel contained in 1601 no less than three representations of 'Our Lady the Virgin Mary' – one receiving the Angel Gabriel and the other two with the Magi. The painted cloth hangings representing the Acts of the Apostles and incorporating Bess's coat of arms are extremely rare survivals of what must once have been common practice, achieved at a fraction of the cost of woven material.

The more compact 'double-pile' houses of the Restoration were seldom provided with chapels and household prayers were usually conducted in the hall or saloon. But there are exceptions to this rule, notably Belton in Lincolnshire, built in the 1670s and attributed to the Dutch-born architect William Winde. Here the chapel occupies the whole of one of the projecting wings on the garden side, rising through two storeys and panelled in cedar wood – perhaps chosen partly because of its Biblical associations and partly because of its smell, not unlike the faint odour of incense. But the plasterwork ceiling by Edward Goudge is wholly secular in feeling with its naked putti sporting among acanthus scrolls. The great reredos with its broken segmental pediment and pairs of Corinthian columns, reminiscent of one of Wren's City churches, is of carved wood, though painted to look like richly veined marble and entirely convincing when seen from the family gallery.

Some of the best seventeenth-century marbling and graining to survive in an English house can be found in the chapel at Petworth, again decorated in rich Baroque colours, urns in purples and dark greens veined with gold, and softwood panels transformed by the brush into exotic olive wood or sycamore, with knots and whorls giving it a sense of variety and depth. The chapel is basically of the early fourteenth century, dating from the time when Henry, 1st Lord Percy, was given a licence to crenellate the house in 1309. But apart from the rare fifteenth-century eagle lectern, its furnishings date entirely from the years 1685 to 1692 and were commissioned by the 'Proud Duke' of Somerset after his marriage to Lady Elizabeth Percy. The southern windows contain heraldic stained glass of the sixteenth and early seventeenth centuries depicting the arms of Percy ancestors, while the blocked-up north windows are painted with the Duke's even more magnificent Seymour lineage, featuring the arms of two kings, Henry VIII and Edward VI, in pride of place.

The marvellously expressive winged cherubs' heads on the stalls, looking towards the altar and apparently caught in a 'rushing mighty wind' like that which assailed the Apostles at Pentecost, are equalled only by those on Grinling Gibbons's choir stalls at St Paul's. It is possible that they are indeed his work, though they could also be by a local carver of almost equal talent, John Selden, who also worked for the Proud Duke. The climax of the chapel is not the altar and reredos, as might be expected, but the family pew, like a gigantic opera box at the west end. It rests on a screen of Ionic columns and is framed by a wide proscenium, carved and painted to look like damask drapery. In the centre the Duke's arms and great

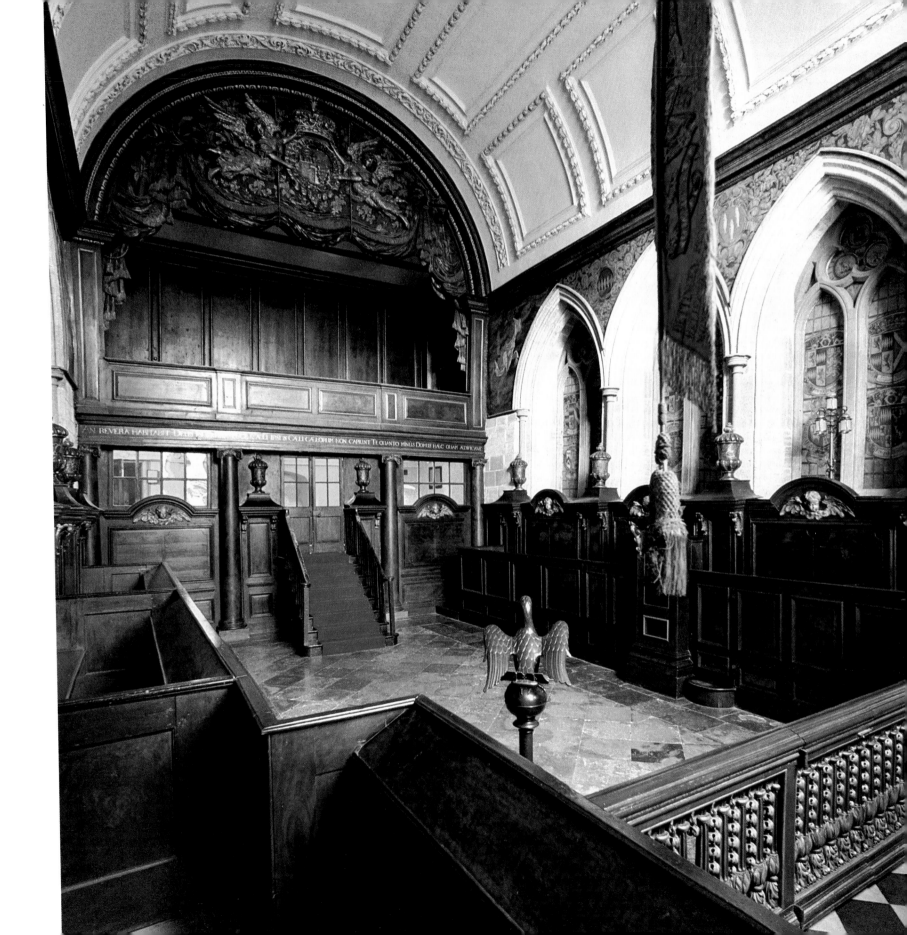

coronet are borne aloft by angels with prominent wings (the Seymour crest), while another pair of painted angels trumpet his fame to posterity from the side walls. Perhaps nowhere in England is there so advanced an expression of the Baroque and indeed its prototypes are rather to be found at Versailles or in the Roman churches of Bernini.

Not all English dukes had such high opinions of themselves, and it is interesting that the 1st Duke of Devonshire's exactly contemporary chapel at Chatsworth has a comparatively plain, panelled family gallery looking towards an altarpiece of quite extraordinary richness. But again the inspiration is primarily French, with a *Doubting Thomas* by Verrio that is close in style to Le Brun, framed in a reredos that could be by Jules Hardouin-Mansart, while the other decorative paintings of the *Life of Christ* by Louis Laguerre and his assistant Ricard (or Riccar) are in the academic style so rigorously instilled in the *ateliers* of the Louvre. Another parallel with Petworth lies in the Duke's discovery of a native carver of genius, Samuel Watson, who, like Selden, appears to have learnt from his association with Grinling Gibbons and to have excelled as much in stone as in wood. The altarpiece is mostly his work, carved out of local Derbyshire alabaster, though it was designed by the sculptor Caius Gabriel Cibber who also contributed the life-size figures of Justice and Mercy flanking the pediment. The four black marble columns also came from the neighbourhood and were hewn from a single block quarried on Sheldon Moor, only a few miles away from Chatsworth.

The way in which a private chapel was considered a desirable adjunct to a parish church, rather than an alternative to it, is clear at Wimpole in Cambridgeshire. Here, only a few yards away from the house, lay the old medieval church of St Andrew with its pantheon of monuments in the fourteenth-century Chicheley Chapel, which Edward Harley, 2nd Earl of Oxford restored, and obviously cared for. This did not prevent him adding a magnificent chapel to the house, designed by James Gibbs and built in the early 1720s on the east side of the entrance front. The need to balance the west wing, built in the previous decade, may be part of the reason for his decision, but there was also a conscious feeling of rivalry with the Duke of Chandos's famous chapel at Cannons in Middlesex, created in the previous decade, again to designs by Gibbs. Like Chandos, who was Handel's great patron, Harley kept an orchestra and *Kapellmeister*, and the chapel at Wimpole was probably conceived as a suitable setting for their performances: the manuscript of an anthem for its 'Solemnity and Consecration' composed by Harley's Master of Music Dr Thomas Tudway still survives, though with a note added stating that 'the chapel at Wimpole was never consecrated'.

The glory of the chapel today is the superb painted interior by Thornhill, referred to in a letter from Matthew Prior to Lord Oxford of March 1721; 'Sir James, I presume has rather been speculating in the chapel he is to paint, than praying in the neighbouring church...' By this date Thornhill's illusionistic style and sombre colouring, familiar from the dome of St Paul's, were not as fashionable as they had been, and Lord Oxford's commission may partly have been an act of charity to a friend beginning to fall on hard times. At the same time the artist was at the very height of his powers and the *Adoration of the Magi* on the east wall has rightly been called 'the most notably Baroque rendering of a religious subject by an English painter'.

Opposite] The 1st Duke of Devonshire's chapel at Chatsworth, completed in 1693 and hardly touched since then. The reredos of local alabaster was carved by a native Derbyshire craftsman of genius, Samuel Watson, apart from the two female figures representing Justice and Mercy (*below*), by the Danish-born sculptor, Caius Gabriel Cibber.

Left] Laguerre's vision of heaven on the ceiling of the chapel at Chatsworth. His reredos painting of the *Incredulity of St Thomas*, in the academic manner of Poussin and Le Brun, seems in deliberate contrast to this wild Baroque fantasy.

Right] Nicholas Hawksmoor's chapel at Blenheim, with the Duke of Marlborough's tomb designed by Kent and executed by Rysbrack.

Overleaf] Hawksmoor's mausoleum at Castle Howard: one of the supreme expressions of the English Baroque. In Walpole's words, 'it would tempt one to be buried alive'.

The chapel at Blenheim was one of the finishing touches to the Palace, completed long after Vanbrugh's departure and the Duke of Marlborough's death. The shell of the building was designed by Hawksmoor, but for the Duke's monument, far grander and more conspicuous than the altar, the Duchess approached William Kent and the sculptor John Michael Rysbrack. In May 1732, she wrote to a friend:

The Chapel is finish'd and more than half the Tomb there ready to set up all in Marble Decorations of Figures, Trophies, Medals with their inscriptions and in short everything that could do the Duke of Marlborough Honour and Justice. This is all uppon the wall of one side of the Chappel. The rest of it is finish'd decently, substantially and very plain. And considering how many Wonderful Figures and Whirligigs I have seen Architects finish a Chappel withal, that are of no manner of Use but to laugh at, I must confess I cannot help thinking that what I have designed for this Chappel may as reasonably be call'd finishing of it, as the Pews and Pulpitt.

The last rays of the setting sun pick out one of Hawksmoor's giant fluted columns in the mausoleum at Castle Howard.

On the monument itself Sarah is shown with the Duke and their two sons, who both died young, but entirely omitting their four daughters through whom the title and inheritance were to pass. The bas-relief on the base shows the monument of Marshal Tallard's surrender after the Battle of Blenheim, and the black marble sarcophagus is shown crushing the dragon of Envy – a reference to those who engineered Sarah's fall from favour with Queen Anne, rather than to any very real opposition to her husband. Household prayers were held at 9.30 every morning in the chapel until the First World War, and Consuelo Vanderbilt, who married the 9th Duke, recalled that 'at the toll of the bell, housemaids would drop their dusters, footmen their trays, housemen their pails, carpenters their ladders, electricians their tools, kitchenmaids their pans, laundrymaids their linen, and all rush to reach the Chapel in time'.

Far fewer chapels were built in the great Palladian and Neoclassical houses, partly perhaps because the assurance of a Protestant line of succession made it less necessary for the Whig magnates to advertise their anti-Catholicism. The Italian altarpieces bought on the Grand Tour were thus destined to hang above chimneypieces rather than altars where their 'Popish' subject-matter could in any case be more easily excused under the guise of 'high art'. There are of course exceptions, including the alabaster-lined chapel at Holkham with its Renis and Marattas reflecting Thomas Coke's overwhelming love of Italian art and architecture. But in general far more attention was paid to tombs and mausolea in parish churches than to places for daily worship inside the country house. The idea of the mausoleum in particular gave scope for at least two great architectural masterpieces: James Wyatt's at Brocklesby in Lincolnshire and Nicholas Hawksmoor's at Castle Howard. Both are circular, having more in common with the classical temple than the Christian tradition of nave, chancel and altar; and both are conceived primarily as 'eye-catchers' in the landscape. 'Nobody had informed me', wrote Horace Walpole in a famous description of Castle Howard, 'that at one view I should see a palace, a town, a fortified city, temples on high places, woods worthy of being each a metropolis of the Druids, the noblest lawn in the world fenced by half the horizon, and a mausoleum that would tempt one to be buried alive …' Here, in his calm acceptance of religion and abhorrence of fanaticism and superstition, the eighteenth-century landowner once more returned in spirit to the classical world of Greece and Rome.

GLOSSARY

AMORINO   Small cupid or cherub used as a carved or painted decoration.

ANTHEMION   Stylized honeysuckle flower decoration which was much used as a decorative motif in Greece and Rome and throughout Europe and America during the Neoclassical period.

ASTYLAR   Without the use of columns or pillars or similar vertical features.

ATTIC FLOOR   Small top storey. In classical architecture, a storey above the main façade of the entablature.

AURICULAR   Type of sinuous ornament popular for frames and cartouches in the early seventeenth century, so called after its resemblance to the human ear.

BED-CARPET   Three strips of carpet joined together to form a border round the sides of a state bed.

BERGÈRE   Comfortable armchair, usually low and quite large, enclosed by an entirely upholstered, frequently curving back, and with upholstered arms from the armrests down to the base of the seat; the seat itself is fitted with a thick down cushion.

BIBLELOT   Small art object such as painting, sculpture, snuffbox, etc. created for personal use or decoration.

BLUE-JOHN   Stone, a variety of fluorite, which is also known as Derbyshire spar from the unique deposits at Castleton. It is usually amethyst purple in colour with striations of lilac, cream and almost white and was especially admired in England during the second half of the eighteenth century when it was used for urns.

BOISERIE   French term for the panelling of walls in carved wood, generally painted or gilded, and for doors panelled en suite.

BOLECTION MOULDINGS   Series of rounded mouldings which project far beyond the panel or wall to which they are applied. A bolection panel projects from the wall surface, as opposed to a 'sunk' panel.

BRÈCHE VIOLET   Type of Italian or French marble, purple or violet in colour.

BRÛLE-PARFUM   Perfume or incense burner, often in the shape of an urn with a pierced lid.

CHANNELLING   Incised grooving resembling a furrow of semicircular or semi-oval section.

CHINOISERIE   Any building, furniture or decoration carried out in the Chinese taste. The fashion grew during the seventeenth century, stimulated by the increasing trade with China, and was at its height during the Rococo period. It affected nearly all the decorative arts, including furniture, painting and engraving, wallpaper, textiles, ceramics and silver.

CLERESTORY   Windows near the ceiling in a high room or hall which received light from above the roofs of adjoining buildings. Upper storey of the nave walls of a church pierced by windows.

CLOSE STOOL   A stool having a seat with a hole, beneath which a chamber pot is placed.

CLOTH-OF-ESTATE   Form of ornament based on cloth thrown over a balcony for the appearance of a sovereign on a state occasion, usually shaped as three semicircular pendants, that in the centre longer than those at the sides, and all three hung with tassels.

COVE   A quarter-circle, concave, downward curve from the ceiling to the woodwork of a wall, or from the wall down the floor. It is also a large concave moulding often used in a cornice or under the eaves of a roof.

COUR D'HONNEUR   Forecourt of a castle, or palace or the like.

COUCHER   The name given to the formal ceremony performed on a king or nobleman's retirement to bed at night, as opposed to the levée held in the morning.

CREWEL-WORK   Decorative embroidery done with worsted yarn on cotton or linen, using simple stitches worked in floral or pastoral designs.

DADO PANELLING   Panelling between the skirting board or floor level and the dado railing, the moulding running roughly at waist height all round a room.

DORTER   Dormitory, especially in a monastery.

EBÉNISTE   French, originally for ebony worker. The ebénistes' work is approximately equivalent to that of English cabinet makers, and is generally veneered or decorated with wood marquetry, parquetry or some other form of inlay.

ENFILADE   An axial arrangement of doorways connecting a suite of rooms so that a vista is obtained down the whole length of the suite.

EXEDRA   Room or covered area open on one side; the apsidal end of a room.

FAMILLE VERTE   Chinese porcelain made in the reign of the Emperor K'ang Hsi (1162–1722) and decorated with a brilliant copper-green, manganese purple, antimony-yellow, overglaze enamel blue and iron-red.

FARTHINGALE CHAIR   Wide-seated chair without arms, made to accommodate the voluminous skirts (farthingales) of Elizabethan women.

FASCES   Roman symbol of power: a bundle of rods enclosing an axe. It was often used as a decorative motif in the Neoclassical period.

FESSE   Horizontal stripe across the middle of a shield.

FRET or FRETWORK   Pierced decoration. It generally takes the form of a repeated motif on a gallery round a table-top, or on chair legs or stretchers.

GAZEBO   Turret on the roof of a lattice-constructed garden house, but the name is usually applied to the whole structure. An ornamental, open summerhouse.

GESSO   Plaster of Paris (gypsum) prepared for use in modelling or as a ground for gilding and painting.

GIRANDOLE   Derived from the Italian, this word came into usage in the seventeenth century to describe a wall-light, though in France it grew to mean rather a chandelier or cluster of diamonds. By the mid-eighteenth century in England, however, it was generally thought of as the combination of carved wood and mirror plate, then fashionable for the Rococo wall-light. The word continued to be used in describing the more restrained mirrors with candle-branches of the Neoclassical period in England.

GRISAILLE   Painting in several shades of grey or stone-colour. It was popular as a *trompe l'œil* painting technique for overmantels and overdoors, especially in the seventeenth century.

JAPAN or JAPANNING   The European imitation of Chinese lacquer. Japanning has been practised since the early seventeenth century. It also stands for most painted decoration on eighteenth-century furniture, even when this is not in the Oriental but in the European or Classical style.

JIB-DOOR   A flush door which is painted or papered over to make it as inconspicuous as possible.

KEYSTONE   Middle stone in an arch or a rib-vault.

LINENFOLD   Form of decoration of, usually, oak panelling in which there is a resemblance to linen laid in vertical folds.

LONG-CASE CLOCK   Sometimes called a grandfather clock. The pendulum and weights of this type of clock hang down, anything between three and five feet below the mechanism, thus accounting for their tall and narrow casing.

'MARATTA' FRAME   Standard type of concave-moulded picture frame, called after the Italian artist Carlo Maratta (1625–1713) and commonly used in England in the early eighteenth century.

MULLION   Slender vertical or horizontal bar between windows or glass panels.

MODILLION   Projecting decorated bracket used in a series to support the Corinthian cornice; sometimes also called a console.

NARTHEX   Enclosed vestibule or covered porch at the main entrance to a church.

OBJETS DE VERTU   General term for small art objects particularly made of semi-precious and hard stones, ivory and enamel.

OCULUS   A circular opening such as might appear in the opening in the crown of a dome.

OEIL DE BOEUF   French for 'bull's eye'. Round or oval window.

ORIEL WINDOW   A large projecting window supported by a corbelled brick or stone construction.

ORMOLU   A method of fusing a layer of gold-leaf onto brass or bronze, otherwise known as gilt bronze, as made for wall-lights, candlesticks or mounts for furniture or porcelain, from the early eighteenth century onwards.

ORRERY   Mechanical model of the planetary system.

PARGETTING   In timberwork buildings, plasterwork with patterns and ornaments either moulded in relief or incised on it.

PATERA   Small motif of classical origin, carved in round or oval form, which was then applied to furniture or architecture. It was sometimes depicted in paint, particularly on Neoclassical furniture of the late eighteenth century.

PARQUET DE VERSAILLES   Decorative geometrical pattern used for the laying of floorboards, particularly on staircase landings, apparently first used at Versailles.

PARTERRE   French term for a flat and planned garden. A garden landscaped in a formal set pattern.

PATTE D'OIE   Literally, goose-foot; the form of three radiating avenues, aligned on a single central point, found in the garden designs of Le Nôtre and his followers.

PERRON   External stair leading to a doorway, usually of a double curved plan.

PERISTYLE   Range of columns all round a building, e.g. a temple, or interior courtyard.

PIANO NOBILE   Principal floor, usually with a ground floor or basement underneath and a lesser storey overhead.

PIER   General architectural term for a solid support of masonry, used to describe the solid wall between windows in the interiors of houses. Furniture designed for this position is generally referred to by this term, hence pier glass, pier table.

PIETRA DURA   Mosaic of semi-precious hard stones set into a marble ground.

PORTIÈRE   Curtain or drapery over an arch or doorway, or used in place of a door.

PORTO VENERE   Type of Italian marble, with purple, black and white striation.

PUTTI   Cherubs, commonly used as a decorative motif since Classical times.

QUATREFOIL   Gothic motif, derived from medieval window tracery or wood carving, in the form of a four-lobed medallion or flowerhead.

RÉGENCE STYLE   Name given to the transitional period of design between the Baroque and the Rococo in France, roughly coinciding with the Regency of the Duc d'Orléans, during Louis XV's minority (1715–23).

REPOUSSÉ   Process by which a design is beaten into silver, copper or brass from the inside or underneath, and finished on the outer surface by chasing, i.e. by the use of chisels and engraving tools.

REVEAL   Inward plane of a jamb which lies between the edge of an external wall and the frame of a door or window that is set in it.

RUSTICATION   Grooved joints in stonework, sometimes combined with roughened surface. Hence the 'rustic', so-called because of its rusticated stonework on the exterior, the basement or floor below the *piano nobile* or principal floor.

SCAGLIOLA   Composition of ground pieces of marble, plaster of Paris, and glue used to imitate both plain and inlaid marble. The material was fashionable for interior decoration, especially table tops, in the eighteenth century.

SGABELLO   Standard term for an Italian backstool of the Renaissance period, of a form which continued to be made until the end of the seventeenth century, the seat resting on two carved or shaped supports, canted inwards, and the back carved like a cartouche.

SGRAFFITO   Decorative technique practised in sixteenth-century Italy in which tinted plaster was covered with white plaster or *vice versa* and the top layer was cut into, or scratched, in a decorative pattern to reveal the colour below. Applied to pottery, it means ware which has been washed over with a differently coloured slip to the body through which the decoration has been incised.

SOLAR   Upper living room of a medieval house accessible from the high-table end of the hall.

SPARVER   Canopy or tester over a bed.

SPERE   Originally one of the timber uprights supporting the roof of a great hall; later used to describe the screen created between the two speres at the lower end of an open medieval hall.

SPIEGELKABINETT   German word for a small room entirely lined with mirror panels, often combined with a massed display of porcelain.

SQUAB   A very low, square or rectangular carved stool frame, usually caned, on which were placed two large, squashy cushions.

STRAPWORK   Carved surface ornaments or panels taking interlacing straplike bands as motifs. Elizabethan and Jacobean carved-wood decorated panels with ribbon-like bands in repeating and interlacing designs.

STRINGING   A narrow band or strip of contrasting veneer used as a decorative border.

STUCCADORES   From the Italian *stuccatori* for plasterers. The Italian plasterers who came to England (mostly from the Ticino) in the eighteenth century were known by this name.

'SUNDERLAND' FRAME   Picture frame in the auricular style (q.v.), said to have been a form invented by the 2nd Earl of Sunderland (1641–1702).

SUPPORTER   Representation of living creature holding up or standing beside an escutcheon or shield with armorial bearings.

TABLE-CARPET   Carpet used as a table-cover. Oriental carpets were first used in Europe as bed or table-covers, and not until the end of the fifteenth century were they used as floor-coverings.

TEMPIETTO   Small temple-like structure.

TORCHÈRE   General term for a candlestand, often made in pairs or sets of four. Applied to the tall turned stands with tray tops of the seventeenth century, and the curved Italianate Palladian versions, the Rococo fantasies and Neoclassical tripods of the eighteenth century – all intended to support candelabra or candlesticks.

TRANSOM   A horizontal bar in a window which, with the mullions, separates the panes of glass.

TURKEY CARPET   Carpet made in turkey-work, a kind of needlework that came into fashion in the late sixteenth century. The carpet was made by pulling heavy wool through canvas or coarse linen, knotting it and cutting the ends to form pile, thus simulating the pile rugs being imported from the Near East.

VAUXHALL MIRROR PLATE   Mirror made at the famous mirror and glass factory established by the Duke of Buckingham at Vauxhall, near London, in 1670.

VERDE ANTICO   Green marble from Brescia, occurring in many shades, embedded with black and greenish fragments.

England and Wales

Houses in roman type are illustrated in the book
Houses in italic are mentioned in the text and open to the public

NEWCASTLE ■

Castle
Howard

Newby Hall

Beningbrough
YORK ■

Harewood House
Sledmere
House

LEEDS ■

Nostell Priory

MANCHESTER ■
Lyme Park

Dunham Massey
Hardwick Hall
Chatsworth

Penrhyn Castle   Little Moreton Hall   Haddon Hall

Erddig

■ NOTTINGHAM   Holkham Hall

Sudbury Hall   Kedleston Hall   Blickling Hall   *Felbrigg Hall*

Shugborough

Houghton Hall

Powis Castle   Attingham Park

NORWICH ■

Burghley House   *Oxburgh Hall*

BIRMINGHAM ■   *Arbury Hall*   Deene Park

Boughton House

Hagley Hall   *Charlecote
Park*

Althorp

Ragley Hall   ■ CAMBRIDGE

*Chicheley   *Wimpole Hall*
Hall*

Honington Hall   *Claydon
House*   *Audley End House*

Chastleton House   Woburn Abbey

Blenheim Palace   Rousham House   *Hatfield House*

OXFORD ■   West
Wycombe Park   *Kenwood*

Milton Manor House   *Osterley*   *Chiswick House*

Cardiff Castle   Dyrham Park   *Mapledurham
House*   Syon House   ■ LONDON

BRISTOL ■   Ham House

Corsham Court   *Lacock Abbey*   The Vyne   *Hampton
Court
Palace*   Knole

Longleat House   *Clandon
Park*

Stourhead   Wilton House

Petworth   Bodiam Castle

Montacute House   *Cranborne
Manor*   Uppark

■ EXETER

Powderham Castle

Cotehele

Lanhydrock   ■ PLYMOUTH
Saltram House

GAZETTEER AND GROUND PLANS

ATTINGHAM PARK, SHROPSHIRE
The major surviving work by the Scottish architect George Steuart, Attingham was built for the 1st Lord Berwick from 1783 round the remains of a Queen Anne house. In 1797 Humphry Repton landscaped the park, and in the early nineteenth century John Nash remodelled the interior, adding a top-lit picture gallery to house the 2nd Lord Berwick's Italian pictures. They were largely sold in the 1820s but the collection brought back from Naples by the 3rd Baron compensated to a large degree for these losses. Attingham came to the National Trust after the death of the 8th Baron in 1947.

BLENHEIM PALACE, OXFORDSHIRE
The gift of Queen Anne to the 1st Duke of Marlborough to commemorate his victory at Blenheim in 1704, the palace was built to the designs of Sir John Vanbrugh, the architect of Castle Howard, and his assistant Nicholas Hawksmoor, and completed in 1722. The scale is of a European grandeur, with regiments of columns and pilasters flanking the portico, and military trophies carved in stone by Grinling Gibbons crowning the skyline. The interior is decorated with mural paintings by Louis Laguerre and Sir James Thornhill and Flemish tapestries recording Marlborough's victories, while in the 1760s Capability Brown greatly extended and improved the park. Blenheim is now the home of the 11th Duke and his family.

BLICKLING, NORFOLK
The creation of Sir Henry Hobart, a successful lawyer, Blickling is from the outside one of the least altered and most romantic of all Jacobean houses. Built between 1619 and 1625 in red brick with stone dressings, it has many affinities with Hatfield which was designed by the same master-mason, Robert Lyminge, during the previous decade, drawing on Netherlandish architectural pattern-books. Internally much remodelling in the Neoclassical taste was carried out in the 1770s by the Ivory family of Norwich, although all the best Jacobean features remain. Blickling came to the National

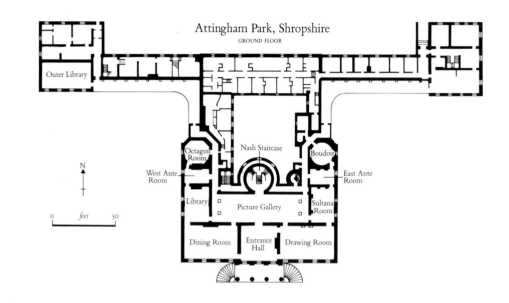

Attingham Park, Shropshire
GROUND FLOOR

Outer Library

Octagon Room · Nash Staircase · Boudoir
West Ante Room · East Ante Room
Library · Picture Gallery · Sultana Room
Dining Room · Entrance Hall · Drawing Room

N

0 feet 50

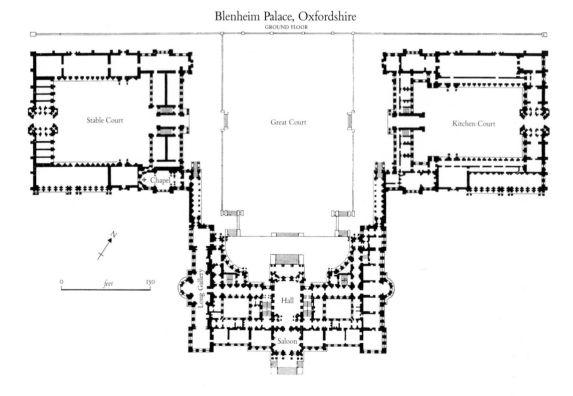

Blenheim Palace, Oxfordshire
GROUND FLOOR

Stable Court · Great Court · Kitchen Court
Chapel
Long Gallery · Hall · Saloon

N

0 feet 150

Trust after the death of the 11th Marquess of Lothian in 1940 – one of the first large houses to be acquired by the National Trust.

BODIAM CASTLE, EAST SUSSEX

Bodiam Castle was built in 1386–8 by Sir Edward Dalyngrigge, who had in the previous year received orders from Richard II to 'strengthen and crenellate' his manor house, the site of which lies farther from the River Rother. The location chosen for the new castle was a logical one, for the Rother was then navigable as far as Bodiam, the obvious place for a fortress to stem the devastating raids which the south coast of England was then suffering from the French. By the time that the castle was completed, however, England had regained control of the Channel. The interior of the castle has been ruined since the Civil War.

In 1916 the Marquess Curzon of Kedleston bought the site, carefully excavated the ruins and arrested further damage, bequeathing Bodiam on his death in 1925 to the National Trust.

Bodiam Castle, East Sussex

BOUGHTON HOUSE, NORTHAMPTONSHIRE

Transformed from a medieval monastic building into the likeness of a French château for Ralph, 1st Duke of Montagu, in 1687–99, perhaps after a design by Daniel Marot. As ambassador to the court of Louis XIV, Montagu was responsible for bringing many French artists and craftsmen back to England after the Revocation of the Edict of Nantes. Only occasionally visited by the family after the 1750s, the house survives today almost entirely as it must have appeared around 1700, the private apartments and state rooms still furnished with the finest pieces of Huguenot furniture, silver and textiles, and supplemented by the later collections of the Dukes of Buccleuch and Queensberry, to whom it still belongs.

CASTLE HOWARD, YORKSHIRE

The 3rd Earl of Carlisle (1669–1738) built Castle Howard near the site of the medieval castle of Henderskelfe to the designs of Sir John Vanbrugh. Work began in 1700 and proceeded slowly until the architect's death in 1726, and the west wing was only later completed by the Palladian architect Sir Thomas Robinson. Castle Howard is one of the greatest of English Baroque houses, and its garden buildings, including Vanbrugh's Temple of the Winds and Hawksmoor's Mausoleum, are also among the finest in the country. Still the seat of the Howard family, the house contains a great collection of Old Master pictures and antique sculpture, largely formed by the 4th and 5th Earls of Carlisle on the Grand Tour.

CHATSWORTH, DERBYSHIRE

Chatsworth has been a seat of the Cavendish family, Earls and Dukes of Devonshire, since the mid-sixteenth century when Bess of Hardwick and her second husband, Sir William Cavendish, began building a large house there. No great alterations were made until 1686 when the 4th Earl of Devonshire (later the 1st Duke) began to demolish the south front. Eventually he rebuilt all four fronts, largely to the designs of William Talman. As well as giving the building its present appearance, the 1st Duke formed the nucleus of the collections, which with the family estates were greatly enlarged by the marriage of the 4th Duke (1720–64) to Lady

Charlotte Boyle, daughter of the 3rd Earl of Burlington. Further large additions were made by Sir Jeffry Wyatville for the 6th Duke in the 1830s. Wall and ceiling paintings by Louis Laguerre and wood carvings by Grinling Gibbons and Watson make a splendid setting for Old Master paintings and drawings, books, silver, antique and Neoclassical sculpture, forming a collection of European importance.

COTEHELE, CORNWALL

A rambling courtyard house adhering to the medieval tradition on the eve of the northern Renaissance, Cotehele was given its present form by Sir Richard Edgcumbe in the 1480s, though he was enlarging and adding to the earlier house of his ancestor William de Cotehele. Subsequent alterations both on the exterior and interior continued until 1627, but the character of the medieval manor house, and its magnificent early sixteenth-century great hall, remained little disturbed after the family established their main seat at Mount Edgcumbe on Plymouth Sound. Cotehele was given to the National Trust in 1947.

DEENE PARK, NORTHAMPTONSHIRE

The home of the Brudenell family since 1514, Deene is a sixteenth- and seventeenth-century transformation of a medieval manor house, with some early nineteenth-century additions. It was the home of the Earl of Cardigan who led the charge of the Light Brigade in the Crimean War.

DYRHAM PARK, GLOUCESTERSHIRE

Dyrham was built by William Blathwayt (?1649–1717), Secretary of State to William III. Having spent several years at The Hague, Blathwayt developed a taste for Dutch painting and architecture which is reflected throughout the house. Starting with the west front in 1691, designed by the French architect Samuel Hauduroy, the building progressed until 1698 when Blathwayt called upon William Talman to provide the more impressive east façade. The collection of seventeenth-century Dutch paintings and ceramics include *trompe l'œil* perspectives by Samuel Hoogstraeten and Delft tulip vases from the workshop of Adriansz Kocks. The house and its contents were acquired by the National Trust in 1956.

FELBRIGG HALL, NORFOLK

An earlier manor house at Felbrigg was remodelled between 1621 and 1624 by the master mason Robert Lyminge, the architect of Blickling and Hatfield, for Thomas Windham. His descendants lived there until 1969 when it was bequeathed by Wyndham Ketton-Cremer to the National Trust. The Jacobean building was enlarged in the 1680s by William Samwell, and much of the interior remodelled for William Windham II between 1749 and 1756 by the architect James Paine, employing the plasterer Joseph Rose the elder. The rooms are still hung with pictures Windham acquired on the Grand Tour.

HADDON HALL, DERBYSHIRE

Set in the foothills of the Peak District, Haddon is one of the most romantic of English fortified houses, a rambling mass of towers and courtyards, mullion windows and lichened walls. Parts of it date back to the Norman period, though additions were made in every century up the to the time of Sir John Manners, who eloped with the heiress of Haddon, Dorothy Vernon, in about 1563. His descendants, who became Dukes of Rutland, preferred to live at Belvoir Castle, and Haddon was thus hardly changed until its sensitive restoration by the 9th Duke in the early part of this century.

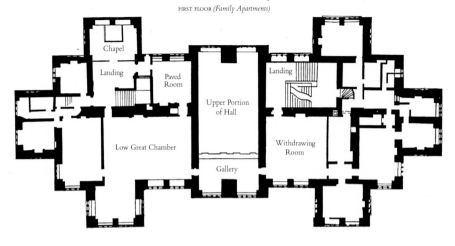

Hardwick Hall, Derbyshire
FIRST FLOOR (*Family Apartments*)

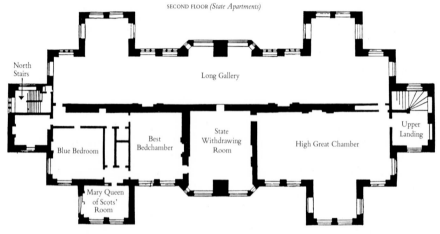

SECOND FLOOR (*State Apartments*)

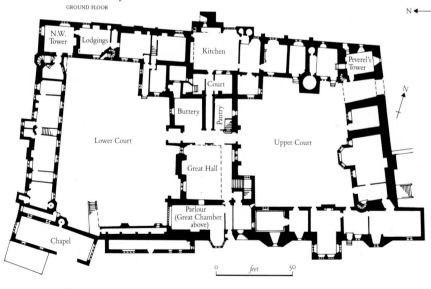

Haddon Hall, Derbyshire
GROUND FLOOR

HAM HOUSE, SURREY

A red brick Jacobean house built by the 1st Earl of Dysart on the banks of the river Thames, Ham was transformed in the 1670s by his daughter and son-in-law the Duke and Duchess of Lauderdale. The house was enlarged, extravagantly decorated and filled with lacquered and gilt furniture, and rich damask and velvet wall-hangings, many of which still survive, forming the best preserved interiors of their date in the country. The home of the Tollemache family, descendants of the Duchess's first husband, Ham was given to the National Trust after the Second World War, and is administered by the Victoria and Albert Museum.

HARDWICK HALL, DERBYSHIRE

The most splendid and least altered of all Elizabethan houses, Hardwick was built between 1591 and 1597 by one of the most colourful characters of her age, Elizabeth, Countess of Shrewsbury, known as Bess of Hardwick. As the result of the last in a series of increasingly profitable marriages, the Countess decided from 1584 to enlarge her family's old manor house at Hardwick. Before this work was complete, in 1590, her husband the Earl of Shrewsbury died leaving another vast fortune, which Bess used to build the new house, designed by Robert Smythson, that survives not a hundred yards from the ruins of the Old Hall. Hardwick preserves its original appearance to a unique extent, as the Earls and Dukes of Devonshire, Bess's descendants, chose from her death in 1608 to make Chatsworth their principal seat. Preserved in the house are an unrivalled group of sixteenth-century tapestries and embroideries, and many of the other contents listed there in Bess's day. Hardwick passed to the National Trust in 1959.

HOLKHAM HALL, NORFOLK

The extraordinary achievement of Thomas Coke (1697–1759), created 1st Earl of Leicester in 1744. Begun in 1734 on a bleak stretch of the north Norfolk coast, the house was built to the designs of Lord Leicester himself in conjunction with Lord Burlington and William Kent, interpreting the Palladian villa on a monumental scale. At the same time a landscape park of great beauty was created round it. The interior of the house employed great quantities of marble and plasterwork in emulation of antique designs, and housed the collections of Italian pictures and antique sculpture acquired on the Grand Tour by Lord Leicester and the younger Matthew Brettingham, his agent. Holkham is now the home of the present Lord Leicester's son, Viscount Coke.

KEDLESTON HALL, DERBYSHIRE

Begun in 1758 for Sir Nathaniel Curzon, later 1st Baron Scarsdale, Kedleston is the masterpiece of Robert Adam and the summit of the eighteenth-century Neoclassical revival in architecture. Adam returned from Rome in 1759 and took over the role of architect from James Paine, who in turn had succeeded the elder Matthew Brettingham. The design is

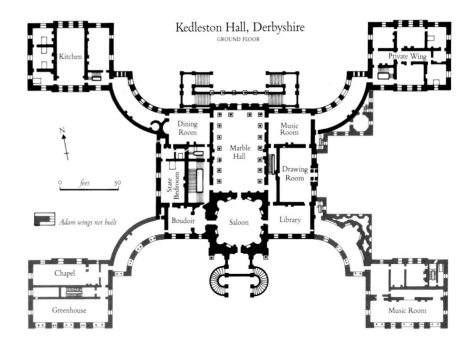

Kedleston Hall, Derbyshire
GROUND FLOOR

based on antique Roman forms, the Marble Hall modelled as an atrium, employing alabaster from the family's own quarries in Derbyshire for the columns, after those of the Temple of Castor and Pollux in Rome. The circular saloon with a coffered ceiling was inspired by the Pantheon. From 1765 the interior was finished by the leading craftsmen of the day, including the plasterer Joseph Rose and the cabinet maker John Linnell. Kedleston is now the home of the 3rd Viscount Scarsdale and his family.

KNOLE, KENT

One of the largest houses in England, Knole was built by Thomas Bourchier, Archbishop of Canterbury, between 1456 and his death in 1486, when he bequeathed it to the See of Canterbury. During the time of Archbishop Cranmer the house was appropriated by Henry VIII, who greatly enlarged it. In 1566 Queen Elizabeth presented it to her cousin Thomas Sackville, later 1st Earl of Dorset, who remodelled the building between 1603 and 1608, and whose descendants have lived there ever since. Through the 6th Earl of Dorset's position as Lord Chamberlain to William III, Knole is largely furnished with items of

furniture from the Royal palaces, which he received as perquisites. In the twentieth century it was the childhood home of the writer Vita Sackville-West and the model for the house in her friend Virginia Woolf's *Orlando*. Knole became a property of the National Trust in 1946.

LITTLE MORETON HALL, CHESHIRE

Perhaps the best-known and most remarkable example of half-timbered building in England, Little Moreton Hall was begun by Ralph Moreton around 1480, a typical Tudor structure in H-form with a great hall at the centre. The second stage of building, in the late 1550s, was carried out by a carpenter named Richard Dale, whose name, together with that of his patron William Moreton II, appears inscribed on one of the exterior timbers, while the south wing with the long gallery on the top floor dates from the 1570s. The interior displays some highly accomplished craftsmanship in wood and decorative plaster, and the mullion-and-transom windows are filled with leaded lights in a great variety of quarry shapes. Since 1938 Little Moreton Hall has been in the care of the National Trust.

THE LIBRARY
COLLEGE ... ER EDUCATION

OXBURGH HALL, NORFOLK

Begun in 1482 by Sir Edmund Bedingfeld and still the home of members of his family, Oxburgh presents the appearance of a remarkably well-preserved Tudor brick-built house, still fortified and moated. In fact, successive owners in the eighteenth and nineteenth centuries carried out extensive restoration work, latterly under the direction of J.C.Buckler and A.W.Pugin, whose work of the 1820s and 1830s in the Tudor style did nothing to detract from the fifteenth-century building. The massive gatehouse, which is almost wholly unaltered, shows similarities with those of the Tudor colleges at Cambridge. Oxburgh has belonged to the National Trust since 1952.

PETWORTH HOUSE, WEST SUSSEX

Although there has been a house on the site of Petworth since at least 1309, it owes its appearance today to Charles Seymour, 6th Duke of Somerset, nicknamed the 'Proud Duke'. It was he who in 1688 set about rebuilding the ancient house of the Percy family, which had been acquired through his marriage to the daughter and heiress of the 11th and last Earl of Northumberland in 1682. Of the earlier building, only the chapel and cellars survive. In 1750 the estate passed by marriage to the Wyndham family, and in the following year Charles Wyndham, 2nd Earl of Egremont, employed the young Capability Brown to landscape the park. His son, the 3rd Earl, was distinguished both as an agriculturalist and patron of the arts, and the great collections of pictures and sculpture for which Petworth is renowned were augmented by works of contemporary British artists, many of whom were friends of Lord Egremont and frequent visitors to his house. The house and park were given to the National Trust in 1947 by the 3rd Lord Leconfield.

ROUSHAM HOUSE, OXFORDSHIRE

Rousham was built by Sir Robert Dormer in 1635, on rising ground above the river Cherwell, and was a Royalist garrison in the Civil War. In the 1730s, General Dormer commissioned William Kent to redecorate the house, adding two pavilions, and to plan a landscape garden, which was one of the first in England to follow natural 'picturesque' lines, with serpentine paths and streams, cascades and garden buildings, statues and vistas disposed informally in woodland settings. Rousham is still the home of the Cottrell-Dormer family.

SALTRAM HOUSE, DEVON

The Tudor mansion at Saltram, built on a site overlooking Plymouth Sound, was remodelled in the 1740s by John Parker and his wife Lady Catherine Poulett. Later in the century their son John, 1st Lord Boringdon, commissioned Robert Adam to decorate the saloon and the drawing room, and these remain among the finest surviving Neoclassical interiors in England, preserving their original seat furniture by Thomas Chippendale and Axminster carpets executed to Adam's designs. The house has been in the care of the National Trust since 1957.

SLEDMERE HOUSE, HUMBERSIDE

The cultivation and planting of the Yorkshire Wolds in the eighteenth century was largely the achievement of Sir Christopher Sykes, 2nd Baronet, the builder of Sledmere. His new seat built in the 1780s in the Neoclassical style, and incorporating part of a smaller house built by his uncle, has since been the home of generations of sporting baronets. Sir Christopher probably acted as his own architect, but the interior was decorated throughout with plasterwork to the designs of Joseph Rose the younger. The house was meticulously reconstructed after a disastrous fire in 1911, and still contains most of its original contents which were fortunately saved from destruction. Sledmere is now the home of Sir Tatton Sykes, 8th Baronet.

STOURHEAD, WILTSHIRE

The house, which now belongs to the National Trust, was built in the first quarter of the eighteenth century for Henry Hoare I to the designs of the Palladian architect Colen Campbell, and finished by Henry Hoare II who formed the nucleus of the collection of pictures and sculpture. Italianate landscapes within the house by Poussin, Dughet, Vernet and Zuccarelli are evidence of the taste that led him to lay out the pleasure grounds, which are among the best preserved eighteenth-century 'poetic' landscapes in England.

SUDBURY HALL, DERBYSHIRE

Architecturally Sudbury represents the style of Charles II's reign at its most individual. The exterior, completed in 1671, is of red brick with a contrasting diaper pattern and stone features such as the monumental centrepieces to both fronts. As with many such Restoration houses there does not seem to have been an architect in the modern sense, and the house is thought to have been designed by its owner George Vernon. The interior displays craftsmanship in plaster, wall-painting and carved wood of the highest quality deployed to create some of the most extravagant surviving decorative schemes of the Carolean period. Sudbury is now a property of the National Trust.

SYON HOUSE, MIDDLESEX

Originally a convent of Brigittine nuns suppressed in 1539 by Henry VIII, the property was acquired in the early seventeenth century by Henry Percy, 9th Earl of Northumberland, and has belonged to his descendants ever since. In 1762 the 1st Duke of Northumberland commissioned Robert Adam to remodel all the rooms on the main floor while leaving the exterior largely untouched. Adam had only recently returned from Rome and his work at Syon, of startling originality and richness, is an extraordinary evocation of the antique classical world and one of his finest achievements.

UPPARK, WEST SUSSEX

Uppark, high on the Sussex Downs within sight of the English Channel, was built about 1690, probably to designs by William Talman, for the 1st Earl of Tankerville and is a late example of the Dutch-influenced 'double-pile' house popular in England in the Restoration period. The estate was purchased in 1747 by Sir Matthew Fetherstonhaugh, who remodelled the interior, probably to the designs of James Paine, and filled it with English Rococo furniture and Italian pictures bought on the Grand Tour. Further alterations were later carried out by Humphry Repton and his son John Adey Repton for the Prince Regent's friend, Sir Harry Fetherstonhaugh. Uppark now belongs to the National Trust.

THE VYNE, HAMPSHIRE

The Vyne was built by Lord Sandys, Henry VIII's Lord Chamberlain, in the 1520s, and both the Chapel with its Renaissance glass and the long gallery with its elaborate linenfold panelling are of this period. Extensive alterations were made in 1654 when John Webb added the first classical portico to be built on an English country house, and again a hundred years later when its owner John Chute, a friend of Horace Walpole, designed the remarkable Italianate staircase and other rooms in the Gothick style of Strawberry Hill. The Vyne was bequeathed to the National Trust in 1956 by Sir Charles Chute, Bt.

WEST WYCOMBE PARK, BUCKINHAMSHIRE

The Dashwood family first acquired the estate of West Wycombe, set among the beech woods of the Chilterns, in 1698. The present house was built by the 2nd Baronet, Sir Francis, who made a series of Grand Tours, establishing on his return the Society of Dilettanti and the less reputable Hell-Fire Club, largely consisting of members of the Prince of Wales's opposition party. But his principal achievements were the rebuilding of the house and the laying out of the park at West Wycombe from 1739 until his death in 1781. Full of references to antiquity and of a highly original design, the interior depends for much of its effect on the figurative ceilings and *trompe-l'œil* wall decorations by the Borgnis family, while the park remains one of the most complete 'picturesque' landscapes in England. West Wycombe now belongs to the National Trust but remains the home of the present Sir Francis Dashwood.

WILTON HOUSE, WILTSHIRE

Wilton, built on the banks of the river Avon, occupies the site of an abbey, granted by Henry VIII to William Herbert in 1542. Parts of his Tudor house still survive, though it was largely rebuilt by Inigo Jones and Isaac de Caux, and the former's assistant John Webb, in the early seventeenth century. The south range containing the famous Double Cube Room was one of the earliest Palladian buildings in England and was of immense importance for the future of English architecture. Both Sir William Chambers and James Wyatt later made alterations to the house, which is the home of the present Earl of Pembroke. The collection includes important Old Master paintings and classical sculpture collected by the 9th Earl (1688–1749), as well as a famous series of family portraits by Van Dyck commissioned by an earlier generation.

WOBURN ABBEY, BEDFORDSHIRE

Originally a Cistercian monastery established in the twelfth century and dissolved in the 1530s, Woburn was given by Edward VI to his Lord Privy Seal, John Russell, created Earl of Bedford in 1549. The Russells only established Woburn as their principal seat just under a century later when the 4th Earl employed Isaac de Caux to design additions to the earlier building. The present house was built by the 4th Duke (who also established the family collections) to the designs of the Palladian architect Henry Flitcroft, beginning in the late 1740s. From 1788–90 the interior was largely remodelled and decorated for the 5th Duke under the direction of Henry Holland, and in the early years of the nineteenth century Humphry Repton laid out the park. Woburn is now the home of the present Duke's son, the Marquess of Tavistock, and his family.

INDEX

Numbers in *italic* refer to illustrations